How to Rock Climb!

A FALCON GUIDE®

HOW TO CLIMB™ SERIES

How to Rock Climb!

Fourth Edition

John Long

FALCON GUIDE®

GUILFORD, CONNECTICUT
HELENA, MONTANA
AN IMPRINT OF THE GLOBE PEQUOT PRESS

A FALCON GUIDE®

Copyright © 2004 by John Long
Published by Morris Book Publishing, LLC
The previous edition of this book was published by Falcon Publishing, Inc. in 1998.

Text design by Mary Ballachino
Illustrations by Mike Clelland

Library of Congress Cataloging-in-Publication Data

Long, John, 1953–
     How to rock climb! / John Long.—4th ed.
          p. cm. – (How to climb series)
     Includes index.
     ISBN-13: 978-0-7627-2471-0
     ISBN-10: 0-7627-2471-4
1. Rock climbing. I. Title. II. Series.
GV200.2 .L66 2002
796.52'23—dc21   2002029907

Manufactured in the United States of America
Fourth Edition/Fourth Printing

Ian Green boulders on The Slanted Demon *(V3) at The Ragged Edge, Pikes Peak, Colorado.* Stewart M. Green photo

Contents

Ian Green hangs out on Deeper Shade of Soul *(5.13b) at Shelf Road in Colorado.*
Stewart M. Green photo

Foreword

When I started climbing thirty years ago, my friends and I learned our craft by trial and error, mostly from other climbers barely more experienced than we were. We made lots of mistakes, but were afraid enough (and conservative enough) to ensure our survival through these critical beginning years. And so we muddled along, gradually working up through the grades as our skills evolved, and having many wonderful epics (at least in retrospect) along the way.

The books we turned to were many: *Annapurna, The White Spider, Nanga Parbat Pilgrimage,* and the other great mountaineering classics inspired, but didn't say much about how our heroes learned the tricks of the trade. And one of the few instructional texts then available, *Mountaineering, Freedom of the Hills,* which offering a great overview of classic mountain craft, was weak in its treatment of the arena that most inflamed our young hearts: technical rock climbing.

Then along came *Basic Rockcraft* and *Advanced Rockcraft.* Written by Royal Robbins, one of the top practitioners of the day, these two slim volumes of wit and wisdom served to both inspire and instruct a whole generation of American rock climbers.

Now, more than twenty-five years later, much has changed in the sport. New gear, a greater diversity in style, and a rapidly expanding population of technical rock climbers has dated much of the information in the Rockcraft Series. Yet there has been precious little to take its place, at least until now.

John Long is one of that generation of climbers inspired by Robbins's books, and many of today's climbers will find similar inspiration here. Long's broad experience as a pioneering free climber is evident on every page of *How to Rock Climb!* as, in clear, concise, and entertaining prose, he brings to life the vitality and intricacy of modern technical rock climbing in all its diverse forms.

And while this book may prevent a few epics of the sort I had while learning the ropes, it will help instill a sense of personal responsibility in the reader as well. After all, that's still a big part of what climbing is all about.

MICHAEL KENNEDY
Climbing Magazine

Acknowledgments

Thanks to Dave Bengston, former head guide for the Yosemite Climbing School; Jeff Bates, gym and sport climbing maestro; Bob Gaines, director of Vertical Adventures; Hugo Montenegro of the Meridian Mountaineers; and all the many other climbers and instructors who reviewed the text and whose comments and suggestions were invaluable for this fourth edition. Thanks also to all the photographers whose outstanding work brings life and excitement to what is basically a technical text.

Introduction

When I first wrote the original *How To Rock Climb!* text, I couldn't have imagined that a dozen years later I'd be revising it for the fourth time. While climbing fundamentals have remained basically the same for fifty years, every season brings small adjustments in procedure, equipment, and style that combine to create shifts in our general strategy. Basically, the art of climbing (especially the equipment) is ever evolving, becoming a little more refined and a little more user friendly as the sport gains popularity, and as competition among gear manufacturers spawns innovative and more efficient ways of doing long-standing procedures. In the boom of the 1980s, technology and techniques evolved so quickly that even insiders had difficulty staying up to speed. Then came the sport climbing revolution and, with it, even more startling advances in gear, technique, and training. Now that sport climbing has become the most popular medium for present-day climbers, radical changes in attitudes, equipment, and prevailing style have so altered the sport that climbers and trends from just a generation ago seem like relics from King Tut's tomb.

But perhaps the biggest single change has been in the manner by which a beginning climber learns the ropes. While new tactics and teaching methods have hastened a novice's voyage from beginning to intermediate terrain—in large part due to rock shoe technology, indoor climbing gyms, and the plethora of well-protected sport climbs—the "fast-track" curriculum has oftentimes sired physically capable climbers who have a questionable grasp of overall technique and safety fundamentals. A recent magazine article stated that presently we have a whole generation of one-dimensional climbers who shine on very narrow terrain (such as steep, bolt-protected face climbs in the 50- to 80-foot range), but are lost on anything else. Put another way, you can go to most any sport climbing area and find world-class performers (on that venue) who would have no chance of success or who would risk an epic if they went to Yosemite and jumped on what were considered intermediate trad routes three decades ago. Imagine an artist who can only draw unicorns or a guitar player whose only tune is Johnny B. Goode. Even if both were superb at their chosen specialty, too much of the same thing breeds boredom and precludes learning other skills that could expand their range and experience. Hence we end up with "one trick ponies" who usually burn out or lose interest in a few seasons. The way out of this syndrome is to gain experience with traditional, overall techniques, a skill and orientation that almost became a lost art during the 1990s. In talking with many climbers from this "new breed," I was amazed to learn that most had throttled back their ambitions not so much by choice but because the current climbing community tends to favor sport climbing over more extensive involvement, and because most of these climbers' peers have so little experience with anything else but what they are always doing—sport climbing. One of the principal aims of this fourth edition is to fill the theoretical gaps for those looking to extend their curriculum into wider expressions of this tremendously varied sport.

Although the climbing world continues to change, no matter the venue, our investment in safety and efficiency remains the same. Like the three previous editions, this manual remains a nuts and bolts, ground-up how-to book that assumes you know nothing whatsoever about rock climbing. Climbing lingo can be as confounding and daffy as "surfspeak," and I've tried to break everything down into plain English.

The cautious, athletic milieu of sport climbing has overshadowed, rather than replaced, traditional "adventure" climbing. Many climbers are still out there climbing traditional, classic routes—extreme cracks, desert towers, big walls, alpine routes, frozen waterfalls, and mixed rock and ice lines. As long as the spirit of adventure stirs in a few climbers, there will still be those pitting their own basic stuff against the wildest real estate nature can offer. They are the few not to be denied the orbit of fear and risk that has vitalized the climbing game since mountaineers scraped their way onto the first summit. For the vast majority of climbers, however, the principal desire is to have fun and to challenge themselves without compromising safety, for no sport is less forgiving if you do. More than anything, safety and fun are the focus of this book.

How to Rock Climb! is based on the "Yosemite system"—methods born out of the revolutionary climbs of the 1950s and 1960s in Yosemite Valley—amply supplemented with modern-day sport climbing techniques presently used the world over. The Yosemite system is, in practice, much more of a philosophy, stressing safety and simplicity. As with any complicated enterprise, the more basic you keep things and the more you standardize generic functions, the more manageable they are.

Along with climbing's amazing popularity has come reams of misinformation. Much of it concerns "essential" gear and elaborate ways of doing simple procedures. It's one thing to invent an easier and safer (therefore better) way to belay, say, as most of the newer devices have achieved. It's quite another thing to needlessly use a piece of trick gear with a user's manual an inch thick and full of skull and crossbones graphics. Remember that many of the most technical big walls in the world were first ascended using pitons almost exclusively, with climbers belaying round the hip and climbing in what now would rate as approach shoes, and you realize how needless much of the new "essential" gear really is. Specialized gear is great for specific situations, but keeping it simple allows you to pay attention to the actual climbing—which is the point, after all. The fundamental gear will always be boots, chalk bag, and harness. Everything else is secondary.

A wasp on a flagpole, Jacob Valdez shimmies up the thrilling Triconi Nail *(5.8),* The Needles, *South Dakota.* Bill Hatcher photo

Just the same, there is much involved, and I have tried to frame the entire process with enough depth that the beginner—and even the advanced climber—can take something from the reading and safely discover how it applies to their own climbing. Studying this book, or one like it, is the standard first step for all beginners. Next is to take a climbing class (preferably a series of classes), a thing no book can, or should, attempt to replace. Virtually everyone starts off this way, or is nursed or hauled up a host of climbs by a knowledgeable friend, which amounts to the same thing. The rare individual who learns the ropes completely on his own will later realize his learning curve was little more than a flat line for the first few months or years. It's easier, and far safer, to get the basics worked out from day one.

Risk your ass if you want to, but statistically, rock climbing is the least dangerous of all the so-called thrill sports because it employs over a century's worth of refined technique and solid technology. The basic system of technical rock climbing—how a rope and specialized techniques and equipment safeguard a climber—is so simple that anyone can manage the basics in a few weekends (though mastery of all aspects is a lifelong process). There is no mystery, and you need not be even a decent climber to have a working knowledge of rope management. The art of climbing rock is another affair, but even this tends to be more of a learned skill, requiring less natural ability than other sports. I've been astonished more than once by climbers who couldn't begin to dribble a basketball but were bona fide wizards on the rock. Lastly, climbing relies more on technique and balance than brute strength (except the most extreme, gymnastic routes), so there is no reason an enthusiastic climber cannot carry on at a top level until old age, as many do.

We can discuss equipment in definitive terms. Equipment is tangible, and its function, at least in theory, is pretty clear-cut, though involved. The most important element in safe climbing is not equipment, however, but familiarity with the vertical environment combined with good judgment. Any way you shake it, climbing prowess is your principal protection, as it precludes the necessity of relying on the gear to save you. The leader who relies on the equipment to safeguard his mistakes is far more likely to make them; and even when the backup system is perfectly arranged, you can still get hurt, even on an extremely "safe" sport climb. (The word "safe" should never be applied to rock climbing.) In parachuting, even a jump master carries a reserve chute. As a climber, your main chute is your climbing ability; your backup is the equipment. This said, the number of accidents due to defective gear is very small, and even then it is often hard to establish that the gear was at fault. It's the climber who is safe or dicey, not the gear.

While equipment and its function within the whole system of climbing is fairly straightforward, the art of climbing rock is not. A lot of intangibles—judgment, instinct, and physical awareness, to list a few—factor heavily in the process, making explanations slippery affairs. The best I can hope for is to explain clearly and in some detail how things are done in a generic sense, leaving you to learn the how of it all through specific application. I've gone into exhaustive detail concerning climbing techniques, and in this respect, the book is "front loaded." A novice might find the explanations confusing on the first pass, but the more climbing he or she does, the more sense the book will make.

With any how-to book of this nature, there will remain the question of what is too much and what is too little. It is impossible to satisfy everyone on all counts, particularly since you could write ten volumes on rigging alone and still have ten volumes of material to discuss. My emphasis has been to stick with the most fundamental and practical concerns, and to serve up those things I desperately needed to know when I was just starting out. I hope to convey the fact that only so much can be learned from any book, that time spent on the rock is the best teacher of all, and that if the fine points need a little more dialing in, a professional guide is the surest means to a safe and thorough understanding. It has been said that writing about wine is like dancing about architecture. If you want to know about wine, you've got to pull the cork and drink up; if you want to know about climbing, you'll eventually have to tie in and cast off.

That climbing transcends mere sport is a conviction held by most anyone with a pair of rock boots, and everyone who has climbed a monolith like Yosemite's El Capitan. The airy exposed routes, the spectacle of ascent, the physical and mental demands—they all give a rush to your blood that continues running rich, regardless of experience. In a flash, mundane life is forgotten: Your world is focused down to a scant toe hold or saving "jug." Failure is a bitter pill, but as Montague noted, nowhere on earth is the taste of success so sweet as on the summit of some sheer granite spire that nearly drove you down in despair from the Herculean labor to achieve it. Basically, it is no more natural for man to dangle on a cliffside than it is for him to loft around the cosmos in a space shuttle. But when both astronauts and climbers gape at their world so very far underfoot, they understand how men have come to dream Gardens of Eden and Ages of Gold. And the dream never fades, the blood never cools, even in the face of chilling bivouacs and knuckle-shredding cracks. Climbing is not an easy sport, and it has a lion's share of toil. But to thousands, even millions worldwide, the rewards are worth the struggle.

CHAPTER 1

The Climbing Game

Early man was a climber. He climbed to escape predators and enemies, and to forage for food. Eons later, in the mid-1700s, man began climbing again, out of desire, not necessity. Spread throughout the European Alps, villages big and small were nestled between spectacular alpine peaks, and for a host of reasons, certain men aspired to climb the grandest peaks on the continent. The summit was the ultimate goal of these first mountaineers, and glaciers and snow slopes provided the most natural passage to the top. Following the first recorded alpine ascent, that of Mt. Aiguille, the rush was on and major peaks were climbed in succession. After the easier routes had been climbed, subsequent mountaineers found that some rock climbing skills were necessary to open up new mountains, and they discovered the lower cliffs and crags provided a perfect training ground to this end. To give some modicum of safety to the falling climber, ropes and rudimentary belaying techniques were introduced around the turn of the twentieth century. Climbing was effectively confined to the European continent and, to a lesser degree, England. It was in Austria, around 1910, that rappelling was invented, along with heavy steel carabiners (snap links) and pitons, the latter to provide the aid and protection required on the more difficult, modern climbs. With the new equipment and techniques and the confidence they spawned, Austrian and German climbers established climbs far more difficult than previously thought possible.

Though isolated rock summits were occasionally bagged, the endeavor was considered of "lesser" worth than achieving the big summits of the Alps. In retrospect, some of the "training climbs" on these "practice" cliffs were remarkably difficult considering the gear. The leaders had little more than hemp ropes (which routinely broke), hemp-soled shoes, and boldness to see them through. As late as the 1980s, in parts of Eastern Europe, particularly around Dresden, "summitless" crags were eschewed in favor of the spires that abound there; likewise, the method and style of ascent remained almost unchanged for fifty years.

Meanwhile, in pre-World War I England, rock climbing on the many backyard outcrops was being explored, albeit less aggressively than in Germany. The English discouraged the use of pitons, however, partly for ethical reasons, partly owing to the fragile nature of the "gritstone." Anyway, in the absence of big mountains, the English developed crag climbing as a sport in its own right. In the Americas, the

Flat-footed in the Flatirons (outside Boulder, Colorado), turn-of-the-century "alpinists" grapple up the hemp rope.

sport's development followed the European lead, though with something of a time delay—roped climbing didn't arrive until in the late 1920s.

The 1930s heralded the golden age of alpine climbing, though the emphasis was still on climbing the major ridges and faces of the higher peaks. During this pre-war period, rock climbing standards rose steadily throughout the world. Although most of the glory was still found in achieving mountainous summits—peaks in the Alps, North America, and Asia were conquered in succession—in many areas it was rock climbing standards that saw the most dramatic development.

World War II saw little climbing activity, but the war prompted technological developments that greatly impacted post-war climbing. Before, pitons and carabiners were expensive and rare, and ropes were still fashioned from natural fibers, bulky and prone to snap during long falls. "The leader must not fall" was the incontrovertible dictum that all climbers observed if they wanted anything but a short career. World War II changed all this with the plentiful supply of surplus army pitons, lightweight aluminum carabiners, and, most importantly, strong and light nylon ropes.

For the next twenty years, standards rose steadily in both England and the United States. English climbers maintained their anti-piton stance and de- veloped anchoring techniques that used runners over natural rock spikes, plus the wedging of pebbles—and eventually machine nuts slung with slings—as chockstones in cracks. Not surprisingly, the English also pushed standards of boldness. They had little choice, for their protection was often dicey at best. European standards were consolidated, but actual rock climbing standards advanced little (except some exploring of large boulders at Fountainbleu, outside Paris, because of the continued emphasis on attaining alpine summits). European manufacturers did, however, develop new nylon ropes that were stronger and much easier to handle.

By the early 1960s, specialized rock climbing shoes appeared that didn't look too different from the all-around shoes available today. The Varappe, essentially a high-top shoe with a smooth rubber sole, and improved piton design spurred higher standards. In the Americas and in England, rock climbing was pretty firmly established as a specialized sport, and routes that led, say, merely to a cliff feature or to rappel points in the middle of blank cliffs were commonly done and respected. Sparingly in America, but increasingly in England, climbers formulated strong aesthetic distinctions between pulling on pitons and artificial aids in order to ascend and using such anchors solely to protect themselves in case of a fall. This latter practice became known as free

A thousand feet up and ten feet out on a ring-angle peg, the late, great Willi Unsoeld (first American ascent of Mt. Everest) teeters up the "knobby wall" during the first ascent of El Capitan's East Buttress in 1953. This climb set the standard for the long, classic free climbs which remain the international draw of Yosemite Valley, California.
Allen Steck photo

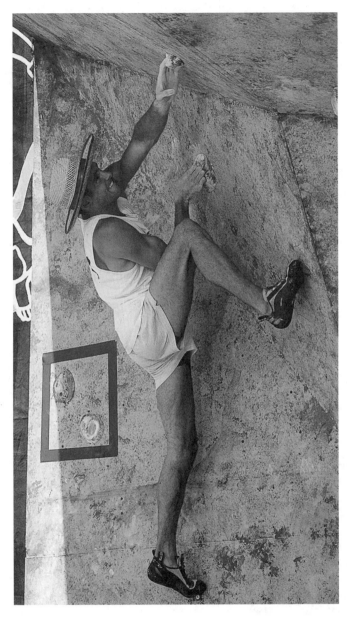

Daniel Dulac of France climbs an artificial bouldering wall at the 1999 X-Games in San Francisco.
Stewart M. Green photo

climbing. Styles and techniques remained largely provincial until the mid-1960s, however, because few climbers traveled widely to sample various climbing areas.

This changed dramatically by 1970, due in large part to the innovative development of rock climbing techniques born in California's Yosemite Valley (dur-

ing the late 1950s and through the 1960s) that allowed the ascent of the spectacular cliffs there. To learn the piton aid techniques that enabled these ascents—and in splendid weather at that—climbers from around the world traveled to Yosemite. While they learned the American techniques, they also left a heritage all their own. By the early 1970s,

American and English climbers completely dominated the development of the sport, and methods and equipment for climbing rock were becoming homogenized. Americans pitched the clunkier boots they had generally favored and adopted sensitive French and English smooth-soled shoes; in addition, the destructive and strenuous American pitoning techniques used in scaling the big cliffs were found to be less effective for free climbing than the gentler English nutting techniques. Moreover, innovative Americans started redesigning and commercially producing light and effective protection devices: first, aluminum nuts, then spring-loaded camming devices (SLCDs). Simultaneously, rope manufacturers continued fine-tuning and improving the proper balance between strength, energy-absorbing stretch, and durability, which led to a much more relaxed attitude toward falling.

By 1980, many climbers were traveling the world over to explore different areas, and climbers from many countries were involved in pushing standards. While the best climbers now trained exclusively for climbing, and the techniques and equipment were common to all, a new, pure gymnastic approach was applied to the style of ascent, particularly by the French. Inspired by the technical difficulty of the free routes in Yosemite Valley, they returned to France to begin a quest for pure difficulty, linking long stretches of bouldering moves with convenient protection afforded by bolts. With easy protection they could concentrate on difficult, gymnastic movement in relative safety, and thus "sport climbing" was born. Today's best sport climbers sometimes "climb" the hardest routes by first descending the cliff to prearrange their protection, inspect the route for available holds, and clean away any loose holds and offensive effluvium. The subsequent ascent may take days, weeks, or even months of repeated falls, all to the goal of climbing the route—now an extremely complicated gymnastic routine—straight through without falls. This approach has further led to the development of a formal competitive circuit, where climbers compete against the clock and each other on man-made and often indoor artificial climbing walls.

European-style sport climbing began in the United States about twenty years ago; it was accepted grudgingly at first, but is now the preferred form of climbing for many because of its secure and convenient nature. As we break into the next millennium, sport climbing has drawn center stage with most of the climbing community, and the media as well. While sport climbing has nearly become a sport unto itself, this movement is in fact just one more mode of ascent derived from the original contest of trying to gain the top of alpine peaks.

About a dozen years ago, sport climbing began branching out, with a few top sport climbers applying their extreme free climbing skills to big rock walls and high-altitude alpine climbs. Over the last few years, this trend has accelerated. As predicted by Yvon Chouinard in the 1960s, the techniques and skills developed in Yosemite found their way to the most dramatic mountain ranges of the world. Huge alpine walls in Patagonia, Alaska, the Himalayas, and other wild places were ascended using the "Yosemite system," further pushing the envelope of climbing and the influence of Yosemite.

To the average climber, however, climbing remains an exciting means to explore the natural world and enjoy the choreography of ascent.

Rating the Difficulty

Because the vast majority of your climbing will follow established routes already rated for difficulty and recorded in a guidebook, it is the following class system you will, with time, need to understand. It is your only yardstick as to how difficult a given climb is, and for this reason, it is both simple and comprehensive. The American rating system that follows is one of many in use around the world (see chart).

Class
1. **Walking.**
2. **Hiking.** Mostly on established trails, or perhaps slogging along a streambed.
3. **Scrambling.** Angle is steep enough where hands are used for balance. A handline is rarely used, even for inexperienced climbers.
4. **Climbing risky enough that a fall could be fatal.** Pulling with your arms required. A rope,

Amos and Coco #1:
The Attraction of Opposites

Amos McCoy, a young and gregarious firefighter in the physical mold of professional wrestler Mankind, was kicking around the local outdoor equipment shop and saw a flyer for a beginning rock climbing seminar. The photo featured a woman in a jet-black spandex ensemble she could have crammed inside a walnut shell; her finely toned body looked like so much poetry as she spidered up a luscious wall of bulbous knobs. Amos's spirit quickened, his elbows itched, and he signed up on the spot: $99 for two days of instruction.

The class first met the following Wednesday night at the local rock gym, Rock Around The Clock. Inside the gym a crowd of every conceivable age and race were swinging around plastic holds spangled over a square hectare of gunite wall space. A man, a woman, and a nine-year-old girl were flowing out the underside of the roof, dangling from their very fingertips! The atmosphere of fun and stern effort required to mount these walls impressed Amos, as did the students in his class, drawn from all walks of life and physical ability. Their attention hung on every word of the instructor, Jules Pinkus, a distinguished mountaineer who knew his ropes as Rubinstein knew the ivories. The baffling system of rope work Amos saw the climbers employing on the plastic walls made perfect sense as Jules walked the class though the fundamentals. After getting squared away with the basic gear and belaying techniques, the class got a chance to climb.

Presently, Amos found himself tending the rope of Coco Malone, an herbalist and kundalini yoga instructor who had joined the class to strengthen her upper body and learn a new and dashing outdoor activity. For her first climb, Coco scaled a low-angled slab, floating up the colorful plastic holds with the lightness of a feather. After Amos lowered her down on the rope, they switched places, the curvy, 101-pound Coco now tending Amos's line. Amos charged the slab like a Cape buffalo and heaved and grunted his way to the "top," then was amazed when the wispy yoga master effortlessly lowered his corn-fed bulk to the ground. By gum, the system worked as advertised!

By the end of class, Amos and Coco had a workable understanding of the equipment and the basic safety system, and had tasted enough of the magic of ascent to know they intended to pursue the sport with ambition.

Taking Jules's advice that their first purchase should be a credible instruction manual to review techniques learned in class, as well as a harness and a pair of rock shoes, Amos and Coco agreed to meet at the local shop to buy these items before their next class, scheduled to meet at a local practice crag the following Saturday morning.

some equipment, and protection techniques are used by most mountaineers.

5. **Technical rock climbing, commonly called "free climbing."** A rope, and specialized equipment and techniques are always used to protect against a fall. Fifth class climbing is the subject of *How to Rock Climb!*

6. **Rock so sheer or holdless that ascent by using hands and feet is impossible.** The equipment is used directly to aid the ascent, hence the common usage names for sixth class climbing: artificial, direct aid, or simply, aid climbing. Recall the hoary image of the intrepid climber hammering his way up the rock, his

weight suspended on a succession of creaky pins. Things have changed, but the old notion still best illustrates what aid climbing is all about.

It is commonly agreed that technical rock climbing starts at fifth class, and the bulk of this book will deal with fifth class climbing. Fifth class climbing varies from low-angle slabs, where only the beginner will relish a rope, to 125-degree face climbs so extreme that world-class climbers might fall fifty times before they work out the entire sequence, if indeed they ever do. In the early 1950s, fifth class climbing was designated as "easy," "moderate," and

World Rating Systems

West German (UIAA)	American (Decimal)	British	Australian	East German (GDR)	French
	5.5	4a / vs			
	5.6	vs / 4b			
5+	5.7	4b / 4c · hvs		VIIa	5a
6-	5.8	4c · hvs	16	VIIb	5b
6	5.9	5a	17		5c
6+	5.10a	5a · E1	18	VIIc	
7-	5.10b	5b	19	VIIIa	6a
7	5.10c	5b · E2	20	VIIIb	
	5.10d	5c	21	VIIIc	6b
7+	5.11a	5c · E3	22	IXa	6c
8-	5.11b	E3	23	IXb	
8	5.11c	6a · E4	24	IXc	7a
	5.11d	6a · E4	25		
8+	5.12a	6b · E5	26	Xa	7b
9-	5.12b	6b · E5	27	Xb	
	5.12c	6b			7c
9	5.12d	6b · E6	28	Xc	7c
9+	5.13a	6c · E7	29		8a
10-	5.13b	E7	30		
	5.13c	7a			8b
10	5.13d	7a · E8	31		
10+	5.14a	7b	32		8c
11-	5.14b	7b			
	5.14c	7c · E9	33		
11	5.14d	7c			9a
	5.15				

Though ratings vary from one area to the next, the fifth class decimal system is pretty uniform throughout the U.S.: A 5.8 in Yosemite would most likely be rated 5.8 at Tahquitz Rock as well. Climbers rely on the rating system being consistent, lest they are misled by guidebooks and end up on climbs either too hard or too easy for their fancy. Once a climber travels to a foreign area, however, he must become fluent in another rating system, for every country has an individual method of rating the difficulty of rock climbs. The attending chart plots comparative difficulties relative to various national rating systems. It is reasonably accurate but not unequivocal. All rating systems are open-ended, but the differences in difficulty between various number or letter ratings vary from country to country. There are other differences also: The British system factors a seriousness appraisal into the rating that precedes the standard technical rating (E5 6a). Note that the seriousness ratings overlap each other considerably in relation to the difficulty rating, as represented in the chart by the dashed lines.

"advanced." As climbers got better and the climbs harder, a decimal system was adopted to more accurately rate the levels of difficulty within the class.

Devised in the early 1930s by the Rock Climbing Section of the Sierra Club, this system is principally used as an index of difficulty. The original scale, 5.0 through 5.9, was intended at the time of its adoption to cover the whole range of humanly possible rock climbs, anything above 5.9 being regarded as impossible. Standards are made to fall, of course, and shortly that one did.

The decimal system ceased to be purely "decimal" when aggressive pioneers sought to rate climbs harder than established 5.9s. Like other rating systems used throughout the world, the decimal system has evolved into an open-ended system that now includes climbs from 5.0, the easiest, to 5.15, to date, the most difficult leads achieved. Climbs of 5.10 through 5.15 are in the realm of the advanced or expert climber; to better shade the nuances of these advanced levels, the letters a, b, c, and d were tacked onto the rating. For example, 5.12d represents the extreme end of the 5.12 standard, whereas a 5.12a or 5.12b is an "easier," low-end 5.12 (however, not one climber in fifty consistently manages this grade).

Modern routes tend to be rated somewhat softer than older routes, meaning you can normally count on an old 5.10 to be more exacting than one established last week. Convenient bolt protection, the earmark of the sport climb, at once removes much of the psychological factor while reducing the physical strain of hanging by fingertips and frantically trying to place gear in the rock. Because most sport climbs are first and foremost physical challenges, they likely will seem "easier" than older climbs of the same grade that feature psychological trials as well.

The standardized rating system was intended to provide uniformity. That is, a 5.7 route at El Dorado Canyon, Colorado, should correspond in difficulty to a 5.7 route at Suicide Rock, California. This is the theory, but not the reality. Ratings should be considered area specific only. Entire areas, such as Joshua Tree National Monument, a world-renowned desert climbing area in southern California, are widely know to have "stiff" ratings, meaning a 5.10a route

at "Josh" would likely be rated 5.10b or even harder at other areas. Other popular locales such as Red Rocks outside Las Vegas are known to have "soft" ratings, and folks flock to the place to shore up their self-esteem as well as enjoy the divine sandstone. A few questions to locals (who might lie) or, better yet, a few introductory routes at any area will generally give you a feeling about an area's tendency toward soft or stiff ratings. Either way, it's good to get straight on an area's rating biases from the get-go, especially when trying to push your limits.

There are often significant (at least one full grade) differences from area to area and gym to gym, especially at the easier levels. You must also include the "sandbag" factor, the shameful practice of underestimating the actual difficulty of a given route ("sandbagging"). The desired effect is that the sandbagger looks good and us hackers feel bad about finding a route far more difficult that its rating. Both individuals and entire climbing communities might systematically underrate everything by an entire grade, even more. Unfortunately, sandbagging remains a petty form of arrogance from which the climbing world has always suffered. Inasmuch as human nature is more constant than ratings, we can expect at least 10 percent of all ratings to be sandbags. An almost certain indicator of a sandbag rating is when a plus (+) is affixed to routes in the 5.7 to 5.9 range. That is, a 5.7+ route is almost always going to be a solid 5.8.

A related point worth mentioning is that in years past you would only call yourself a 5.10 leader if you could consistently lead any 5.10 route, including thin faces, roofs, finger cracks, off-widths, et al. Today, many climbers who have hangdogged up a 5.12 sport climb tend to consider themselves 5.12 climbers. Put them on a 5.9 adventure climb, where the runouts are grim and the required techniques manifold, and they might back off at the first difficulties. The point is: Since the rating system was first devised, climbers have been preoccupied with bandying about high numbers in the most cavalier manner. Don't be swayed by such "smack," and wait until you get out on the rock to form your opinions about potential climbing partners. Many sport climbers are fairly inexperienced, and can perform only under very circumscribed conditions. The danger here is that many of them don't realize this themselves, and they subsequently can make sketchy partners outside a climbing gym or practice area where every yard of every climb is chalked and bristling with bolts. The difference between a difficult toprope climb in an indoor climbing gym and a long, complex free route in the mountains is the difference between a candle and a blowtorch.

Sixth class, direct aid climbing is divided into five rating classes: A1 through A5, depending on the difficulty of placing protection anchors and their precariousness when placed. Put figuratively, this means you can hang your van from an A1 placement, but falling on a tenuous A5 thread of bashies will surely result in a harrowing 100-foot "zipper."

Grade

The decimal system tells us how difficult a climb is. The attending grade rating tells us how much time an experienced climber will take to complete a given route.

> I. One to three hours
> II. Three to four hours
> III. Four to six hours—a strong half day
> IV. Full day—emphasis on full
> V. One to two days—bivouac is usually unavoidable
> VI. Two or more days on the wall

The decimal rating is a relatively objective appraisal of difficulties, usually arrived at through consensus. The grade rating is posited as objective, but it uses the hypothetical "experienced" climber as the measure of how long a given route should take. Compare the grade rating with the par rating on a golf course. A par five means a honed golfer can probably hole the ball in five shots, rarely less, but a hacker will smile at a bogey six. Likewise, a couple of good climbers can usually crank a grade V in one day, whereas the intermediate climber had best come prepared to spend the night. World-class climbers can sometimes knock off a grade VI in an inspired day, depending on the amount of difficult direct aid

on the route. The more hard aid, the less likely that any team can "dust" a grade VI route in a day.

Free Climbing

Normally speaking, there are two types of individuals who climb without a rope: the world-class climber whose experience is extensive and who knows her capabilities and limits perfectly, and the sorry fool who doesn't know any better and is courting disaster. More will be said on this topic in Chapter 5: The Art of Leading, but let it be clear that, with rare exceptions, a rope and equipment are always employed in modern fifth class climbing. Accordingly, the layman often assumes that equipment directly assists a climber's ascent. It does, in the advanced realms of aid climbing, but not in the form known universally as free climbing.

Free climbing is the basis of all sport climbing and can be loosely defined as upward progress gained by a climber's own efforts—using hands and feet on available features—unaided, or "free" of the attending ropes, nuts, bolts, and pitons, which are employed only as backup in case of a fall. Rock "features"—the irregularities on the stone such as cracks, edges, arêtes, dihedrals, and flakes—provide the climber his means for ascent. The variety is endless, and even uniform cracks of the same width have many subtle differences. It is precisely this fantastic diversity that gives climbing its singular challenge, where each "route" up the rock is a mental and physical problem-solving design with a unique sequence and solution. Because every climb is different, discovering what works, for what climb and for what person, is the process that keeps the choreography of ascent fresh and exciting.

But it's not all ad-lib. There are numerous fundamental principles that apply to all climbing: The smooth coordination of hands and feet allows fluid movement; balance, agility, and flexibility are often better weapons against gravity than brute strength; endurance is generally more important than raw power; preservation of strength is accomplished by keeping your weight over your feet, rather than hanging from your arms; and the best execution of any climb is that which requires the least effort.

Featuring . . .

Arête: an outside edge or corner of rock, perhaps as large as a mountain ridge.

Buttress: much broader than an arête, a buttress is definitely mountain-size.

Chickenhead: a bulbous knob of rock.

Chimney: A crack of sufficient size to accept an entire body.

Dihedral: an inside corner, formed by two planes of rock.

Headwall: a much steeper section of a cliff, residing towards the top.

Horn: a flake-like projection of rock, generally of small size.

Line: the path of the route, usually the line of least resistance between other major features of the rock.

Rib: a narrow buttress, not so sharp as an arête.

Roof or ceiling: a section of rock that extends out above your head like a roof or ceiling.

Slab: a section of rock or gentle angle, sometimes a relative reference when it's a part of a vertical wall.

Finally, staying relaxed is half the battle. Much of climbing is intuitive, and the moves come naturally to the relaxed mind. Likewise, a relaxed mind allows you to find and maintain a comfortable pace, neither too fast nor too slow. A common situation with both beginners and those pushing their limits is for the leader to tighten up and become rushed in response to the difficulty and the effort required. Learning to stay relaxed, especially in the midst of great physical and mental strain, is one of the priceless boons of free climbing.

Climbing requires certain techniques that are not obvious and must be learned and practiced before you can hope to master them. Climbing is one of the most primal activities a person can undertake, but unlike Java man, the modern climber usually wears shoes.

Rock Shoes

The following discussion might seem longer than is necessary. Believe me: It is not. Since all climbing is done in rock shoes, which can absolutely crucify your feet if the fit is poor or the style is wrong for your feet or your climbing, you should understand the basics from the start and avoid the torments. Just as a ballerina does not dance in moccasins, climbers do not climb in loose shoes. And with anything that fits snugly, one wrong aspect (width, length, et al.) can turn your reunion with nature into a hardship from hell.

For your first couple of outings, try to rent a pair of rock shoes if at all possible. Most mountain shops and guide schools have rental gear. Climbing shoes make the experience much more enjoyable and considerably easier for a beginner. The old practice of going with tennis shoes for your first few outings has largely been junked. Should you choose to pursue climbing, your first purchase should be a pair of shoes. Entry level shoes go for about $80 to $100, while top-end shoes can run upwards of $150. Keep in mind that climbing shoes can be resoled (for about $40) when they wear out. Also, watch for notices posted on the bulletin boards of outdoor equipment stores. You can buy a perfectly good pair of used climbing shoes for a fraction of what they would cost new. Otherwise, consider buying a pair on sale. Even world-class climbers look for shoe deals. Particularly for beginners, who can grind the sole off a new rock shoe in a matter of days, forget about getting the most "advanced" model till your footwork rounds into form.

Rock shoes have steadily evolved from the days of clunky, lug-soled boots to the advent in 1982 of "sticky rubber" soles. These shoes were so effective that many old-timers claimed it was "cheating" to use them—and they should know, since they were

Amos and Coco #2:
Harnesses and Italian Slippers from Hell

Amos met Coco at the neighborhood mountain shop and the two were shown a wide variety of harnesses by a discerning saleswoman. Aware that Amos and Coco were just starting out, the saleswoman suggested a generic harness, modestly priced, that would serve them well on all venues. The saleswoman mentioned that once they came to learn their preferred style of climbing, they could buy a harness targeted specifically for traditional or sport or alpine or big wall climbing. But because most harnesses are basically the same, they would probably find that the recommended generic item would fill the bill no matter if they ended up in the New River Gorge or the Himalaya.

Coco chose the cheapest model in the store. It fit well and had all the required features, including convenient loops for racking gear and a double pass-through buckle. Amos would hear nothing of a generic model and wanted the most advanced specimen on hand, something Tarzan the Apeman might wear, had he been a climber. The saleswoman gladly sold Amos the store's best model—at twice the price of Coco's harness.

Next, rock shoes. Coco went with a pair from the sale bin. Like her harness, the shoes were made for women and fit well, and though not a highly specialized model, they would work fine on any old rock. Meanwhile, Amos was eyeballing the poster of a world-class Italian climber muscling out the underside of a huge limestone overhang in Crete. Pointing to the

Mediterranean's footwear, Amos said, "I want those!" They fit funny, torquing Amos's dogs into unnatural and tragic positions. And they cost four times as much as Coco's shoes. But Amos wanted the cutting-edge units, and in ten minutes he had them. When the two budding climbers exited the store, Amos had spent nearly $250 while Coco had been touched for only $90.

the first to buy them. Built on orthopedically perfect lasts, with a glovelike yet bearable fit, modern rock shoes are a remarkable innovation. Since the first super rock shoes arrived in 1982, advances in fit, materials, and rubber have kept pace with advances in technical achievement. Currently, there are countless brands available for both men and women. The choice for the beginner is mainly a matter of price and fit. For the expert, the choice is usually an attempt to match a specialized shoe to a particular kind of rock or a specific technique. Some shoes are stiffer, good for standing on minuscule footholds but poor for pure friction. There are shoes for cracks, for limestone "pocket" climbing, and for gym and sport climbing, and shoes designed to fit inside insulated high-altitude boots. In short, an expert will often have a whole quiver of boots for various applications, much as a champion skier will have various skis for different conditions and uses.

A beginner can get confounded, but each manufacturer has a generic, all-around rock climbing shoe best suited for the novice. As mentioned, since a beginner's footwork is generally careless, he will trash his shoes much faster than an experienced climber, so consider that when plunking down money for your first pair. Most manufacturers are continually redesigning their shoes. If you shop around, you can often buy last year's models at considerable savings. Again, a beginner can benefit most from a low-tech boot. In an effort to always have the latest, most far-fangled design, shoe manufacturers sometimes miss the mark with experimental or limited edition models that are so fantastically colored, so painful, so perfectly useless that you couldn't off

these duds to a barefoot climbing bum standing in a campfire. Such designs invariably end up in the discount bin. Leave them there.

While a general use shoe is the novice's most practical choice, you will eventually want the shoe best suited to the type of climbing you prefer. For lower-angle face climbing, a soft sole and supple, low-cut upper is best. For steep wall or pocket climbing, you'll want a tight-fitting shoe with good lateral support, a pointy toe, and a super low-cut upper for ankle flexibility.

Many advanced climbers do most of their climbing in "slippers." While most modern rock shoes are not "boots" at all but are cut at or below the ankle, slippers have also done away with the laces (though perhaps half the models feature velcro tighteners) and offer far less support.

Slippers require strong feet, but offer a sensitivity on rock not found in regular shoes. Slippers are excellent for bouldering, steep sport routes, and indoor climbing. However, slippers definitely underperform on traditional routes, and can downright punish your feet in cracks, so beginners might do well to stick with a normal rock shoe—for that first season, anyway.

Optimum performance in a slipper requires a painfully tight fit lest your foot roll around inside as though the shoe were a bathroom slipper. This often results in a pronounced callus or "corn" on top of the big toe. The only compensation here is that slippers are easy to remove, so most climbers take them off between each route. Also, to keep them light, many slippers are straight leather with no liner. Normally worn without socks (common with regular rock shoes as well), slippers—and in fact almost all rock shoes—usually take on a fierce bouquet. Air them out and store them in a cool, dry place.

Climbers have traditionally worn shoes painfully tight. If not, the foot would rotate inside the boot when standing on small holds. Thankfully, climbing shoes have a tendency to stretch with time (although many models have stitched/glued-in liners meant to remedy this), but the perfectly fitting shoe can be quite snug when new. Modern climbing shoes—unlike the shoes of old—are constructed on anatomically correct lasts and are contoured to fit the foot. But you must try them on and climb in them to know if they fit your foot.

Some brands may favor a wider or narrower last, so try on an assortment of different shoes until you find the perfect fit. As a novice it is probably more important to your climbing to have a good fitting shoe than one that is specifically designed for the type of climbing you intend to do.

The foot should not rotate in the shoe; neither should the toes be dreadfully curled in the toe box—unless you're climbing at a very high standard. Climbers wear their shoes with and without socks— sans socks for a better fit and increased sensitivity. Others prefer to wear thin socks, citing better comfort. Try it both ways. A floppy pair of shoes are frustrating to climb in, and you don't want to spend to the tune of $150 and waste all that technology on a sloppy fit. Shoe manufacturers often run demos in climbing gyms and at bouldering competitions so you can test drive their various models. Do so and learn what you do and do not like.

Climbing magazines routinely have an equipment review that rates the relative merits of each brand's wares. These are usually reasonable guides in a sweeping kind of way, though many assessments are tainted by the individual preferences of the reviewer and her considerations to particular manufacturers. Rock shoe manufacturers are big advertisers in climbing magazines, and you might suspect the rags would be averse to publishing critical reviews even if certain shoes are so shoddy you could barely make it across the street in them without falling on your ass. Whatever, remember that despite significant advances in both rubber and shoe con-

struction, there's no magic in shoes unless you know how to use them.

Dirt, grime, oil, tree sap, and such can dramatically affect a sole's performance, so always keep your shoes clean. Limit walking around in them to a minimum. Most climbing soles are not rubber at all but TDR—Thermo Dynamic Rubber—a petroleum-based synthetic. Regardless, the TDR oxidizes and hardens just like rubber, and though this is only a surface condition, it can affect performance on all but the so-called "stealth" rubbers. An occasional wire brushing is the solution for both grime and hardening. Hot car trunks loosen the glue bonds of the rands and soles. Superglue can fix this, but it's better to avoid excessive heat. Foot powder helps avoid stitch rot from sweaty feet.

Chalk

The use of carbonate of magnesium—or gymnastic chalk—to soak up finger and hand sweat became standard practice over thirty years ago. Arguments pro and con used to be waged, but for climbers the world over, chalk has become accepted as a necessary evil. The advantage is that chalk increases your grip, especially if your hands tend to sweat. On coarse sandstone, in forty-degree shade, the advantages are minimal. But stick a climber on a greasy, glacier-polished Yosemite crack in midsummer swelter and his hands will sweat like he's going to the electric chair—and chalk can make a huge difference. The arguments against chalk are many, almost all true. The golden rule for all climbers is respect for the environment: You leave the place as you found it. Though not permanent, excessive chalk buildup is not only an eyesore, it telegraphs the sequence of holds to subsequent teams, diminishing the factor of discovery so vital to the climber's experience. Also, too much chalk on the holds can make the grip worse than no chalk at all, a common condition that has caused many climbers to carry a toothbrush to uncake chalky holds. Knowing that an afternoon thundershower usually returns the rock to pristine status, and in light of the real advantage chalk affords, chalk has become required tackle the world over. But there are a few (very few) exceptions. On

Steve Petro proves the virtues of a heel hook while turning the lip of an overhang, Priest Draw, Arizona. Bill Hatcher photo

cliffs so steep rain never touches them, any chalk will be there until Jesus comes home. For this and other reasons, climbers at a few areas have, through consensus, decided chalk will not be tolerated, and visiting climbers should respect the local custom.

Some years ago several manufacturers began making chalk in colors, intending to match the color of local rock. This chalk was slimy, however, and on the wrong rock it looked worse than white chalk, so it never fell into widespread favor except in a few isolated places where its use was for a time mandated. A newer, environmentally unobtrusive product called X-Factor was introduced to replace chalk, but those with sweaty hands continued to prefer chalk, and X-Factor went the way of the *X-Files*. Perhaps in time the right chemistry will be found, and the cliffsides will not be peppered in white paw marks. In the meantime, climbers will continue to use white chalk.

Helmets (a.k.a. brain buckets)

In pure rock climbing areas like Yosemite, Colorado's Eldorado Canyon, Tahquitz Rock in California, or the 'Gunks of upstate New York, you can climb all year and rarely see anyone wearing a helmet. The reason is that in these areas, rockfall is rare, and while it is certainly possible to injure your head in a fall, for some reason serious head injuries rarely happen. Most climbers have eschewed wearing helmets be-

cause they feel awkward; others consider them unstylish and gauche. These days there is not much to advance either claim. The old helmets were seemingly lifted off Spartacus, weighed ten or so pounds, and looked silly. Fashioned from modern composite materials and borrowing styling from mountain biking, the modern helmet is a fashionable and functional unit. That much said, a number of head injuries (primarily from rockfall and leader falls) do occur each year in rock climbing that could be avoided through the use of helmets.

Perhaps the most compelling argument for using a helmet is that, with the huge influx of new climbers on the cliffside, the hazard of dropped gear has increased significantly. A carabiner dropped from two pitches above you (300 feet) can have the velocity of a major league fastball by the time it strikes your bean. Regardless of popular opinion, wearing a helmet does not make you a doddering old sap, nor does it make you a "safe" climber. Many Yosemite veterans are wearing helmets on walls. In the mountains, where the rock quality is often poor, only the certified madman doesn't wear a helmet. It's your choice. If you feel better wearing a helmet, do so. But avoid the tempting delusion of thinking a helmet makes you a "safer" climber than a person going au naturel. Acts of God notwithstanding, safety largely lies with the climber, not in his or her gear.

CHAPTER 2

Face Climbing Skills

Picture a climber on a steep wall of orange sandstone. Above her, the rock sweeps up like a cresting wave, without a single crack in which to lodge her hands or feet. From the ground you can't see hold one, just a polished wall; yet she moves steadily up—high stepping, counterbalancing, reaching, ever fluid and graceful. She's face climbing, and to the beginner it looks harrowing. But you'll soon learn that face climbing is the most natural form in all the climbing game. It varies from low-angle slabs, where balance and the friction of good shoes are all that's required, to 120-degree overhanging test pieces where simian strength and precise technique are required to even get off the ground.

The cardinal rule for face climbing on walls up to about eighty degrees (and oftentimes beyond that angle) is to keep your weight over your feet. We live much of our lives on our feet; they are much better suited for load-bearing than our arms, which tire quickly regardless of their authority. Keeping your weight over your feet is the result of proper body position. On face climbs less than ninety degrees (or dead vertical), your body should remain in the same upright posture as when you're walking at the shopping mall, with your center of gravity directly over your feet. The reasons are these: First, the vertical posture is the only one that is naturally balanced. If you've ever balanced a stick on your finger, you'll remember it is only possible when the stick is vertical. Second, when your body is vertical, gravity forces your weight straight down onto your shoes, which is best for maximum friction and purchase. A beginner's initial reflex—to hug the rock—may feel more secure, but this actually throws the whole body out

of balance; and when all the unbalanced weight is transferred to the feet, the shoes tend to skate off. Lastly, when the body is vertical, the climber's face is not plastered against the rock and his field of vision is open to see how and where to proceed.

Most instructors will tell you that many, if not all, bad habits are accompanied by either breath holding or rapid breathing, or combinations of both. If you can pay some attention to keeping your breath slow and steady, you can avert the frightened response to paste yourself close to the rock. So strive to breathe easily, stand up straight, stay in balance, and keep your weight over your feet. These are easy concepts to understand, but until you can consistently perform them on the rock, you will never advance beyond beginner's status.

Footwork

Good footwork is one of a climber's most important assets. Except on overhanging rock, you will climb basically on your feet, your arms acting only as a support mechanism to maintain balance as you step up from one foothold to the next. It's magical how well sticky rubber rock shoes adhere, but even so, a beginner will need some time before learning to trust her feet. Once you prove to yourself that the shoes do indeed stick, you can begin exploring the various ways to stand on holds. With practice you'll find that even the tiniest footholds can provide some support.

The variety of different footholds encountered is almost infinite, but aside from pure friction, where you simply paste the sole flush to the rock, there are basically two different ways to stand on footholds: by smearing and by edging.

Smearing

The name derives from the action of "smearing" that part of the sole (generally, but not always, beneath the big toe) onto a slightly rounded hold (imagine the back side of a spoon). You will generally want to smear as much of the sole over as much surface area as possible, thus maximizing the friction. Beginners may have to consciously think about pushing down with the toes to hold the smear. Much of the art comes from your ability to choose just the right place to step, having a keen eye for any irregularities, rough spots, or dents. Even the most flawless face usually has slight ripples, and above these ripples is a lower-angled spot—if only a single degree less than the mean angle. The experienced climber scours the face for these. In smaller dishes and scoops, the heel is oftentimes kept rather high, which increases the frontal pressure on the sole. On more uniform slopes, a lowered heel means more surface area of sole rubber contacting the rock. More rubber means increased friction. The lowered heel also puts the calf muscle in a more relaxed position. Try a variety of heel positions and find what works through experience. And always concentrate on consciously pushing the foot against the rock to increase the friction/purchase.

Perhaps more than in any other type of climbing, keeping your weight correctly balanced over your feet is absolutely essential when smearing. A good exercise is to get on a slab and, starting from the upright posture, slowly lower your torso closer to the rock. You will immediately feel that the closer you get to the rock, the less your shoes will stick. Different rock has different friction properties. Polished limestone is desperate even at forty-five degrees, while the coarse quartz monzonite at Joshua Tree allows pure friction well into the seventy-degree realm. Given some supporting handholds, smearing can be useful even on overhanging rock. If your foot slips, experiment with foot position: high heel versus low heel. You might also try to push into the rock more by moving your center of gravity out, away from the rock, or by pulling out slightly on the handholds.

Discovering just how steep an angle you can smear on and picking the optimum foot placement is a function of experience, but as with all face climbing, smearing is natural and readily learned however insecure it may at first seem. In the bygone era of hard-soled rock shoes, particularly when many rock shoes had marble-hard cleated soles, smearing was a risky practice, rarely done. With today's sticky rubber soles, smearing has become the favored means of using ill-defined footholds.

Edging

The practice of placing the very edge of the shoe on any hold that is clear-cut—the serrated edge of a flake, a cluster of crystals, a pronounced wrinkle—is called edging. "Edge" applies not only to the shoe's running edge, but also to the "edge" that forms the top of the hold. You usually edge when the hold is sharp. The edge of the shoe is placed directly on the best part of the hold and the sole finds purchase by conforming and biting onto the edge once the shoe is weighted. On vertical and overhanging terrain, edging allows the climber to get her lower body closer to the wall and distribute more weight onto her feet, reducing the strain on the arms. Edging is the most basic method of standing on holds, but it takes practice to become proficient.

You generally edge with the inside of the shoe, near the outside of the big toe. Both your foot and most modern shoes are designed to stand most easily on this section of the shoe. Also, when edging on dime-sized holds—and you will—it is necessary to feel just how good or bad the shoe is holding, and the area around the big toe is the most sensitive and best suited for this work. However, it is not unheard of for people to prefer edging off the ball of the foot, which requires less foot strength; and many times it is necessary to edge with the shoe pointing straight on the hold (called "toeing-in"). Toeing-in requires strong toes and is especially useful in the small pockets so common on limestone and volcanic crags. While we normally climb directly facing the rock, many times you will find it necessary to step one leg inside the other, particularly when traversing. Knowing how to edge with the outside of the shoe is essential here. How essential? The ability to edge

Toned to the bone, Tiffany Levine backsteps an outside edge at Sinks Canyon, Wyoming.

Bill Hatcher photo

expertly with the outside of the shoe is many times the very technique that separates the intermediate from the advanced climber. It is simply impossible to reach advanced status without knowing how to outside edge.

Back-stepping, a technique particular to steep rock, also makes use of the outside edge. It increases your reach and forces your hips in. Outside edging is almost always done just back from the origin of the small toe. The foot's bone structure makes that section of the foot fairly rigid as opposed to the rest of the outside part of the foot, which is fleshy and flexible and gives the shoe edge every reason to "butter off" the hold. Back-stepping is another technique that has become popular and invaluable on sport climbs. Until you master this technique, the more difficult overhanging routes will remain out of reach. Like all other footwork techniques, practice on the boulders, inches off the ground, will greatly hasten your prowess with what at first may feel awkward and unnatural.

Edging is an exercise in precision. Many edges are so small they can't be seen until you're at them.

Careful placement of the foot is essential, and once the shoe is weighted, it is equally important not to change the attitude of the shoe lest you pop off. Thus, one key to proficient face climbing is isolating the movements of your legs and upper body from the rigidity of your foot placement—in short, knowing how to keep your foot perfectly still on the edge while the rest of your body carries on. This is especially key when extending the leg, or "pressing out" the hold, which is where it is most difficult to keep that foot rock solid. Change your foot's orientation on the hold, even a fraction of an inch, and you're off.

Contrary to common sense, a razor-sharp shoe edge is not ideal for standing on small holds. Because rubber stretches once weighted, a slightly round edge is less likely to "buttress," or fold off of, dinky footholds. Most shoes feature a sole that is beveled back underfoot, resulting in more stable edging and less "buttressing." The old notion of honing your edges with emery boards and so forth is hogwash.

Edge holds will appear at various angles, and few are formed perfectly for a foothold. Here, it is

Hanging out from the rock, Melissa Quigley maintains a vertical body position to keep her weight directly over her feet on the Wild Iris Wall, Wyoming. Bill Hatcher photo

critical to exactly match the shoe's running edge with the rock's edge. Again, once it is lined up, do not move it. Since holds often slant you will commonly find yourself applying pressure at oblique angles, which requires ankle flexibility; foot attitude must be maintained perfectly while the edge is weighted. With extreme edging, when the holds are very small indeed, many such edges are "time-bomb" in nature, meaning the climber cannot "camp" on them too long without the shoe "blowing off" from either toe fatigue or the fact that even the best shoe cannot work marginal holds indefinitely. More about this will be discussed in Chapter 5: The Art of Leading.

It is sometimes best to smear an edge ("smedging"), especially if the edges are puny or the moves dynamic. Remember, you can smear an edge, but you can't edge a smear.

A common and practical way for beginners to gain trust in their feet is to toprope (explained shortly) a low-angled slab and practice climbing with one or no hands. A no-hands climb is almost certainly going to be friction all the way. But with one hand you can quickly learn that edging is largely a matter of body position and precise footwork, and that when both of these factors are rock solid, your feet can truly do most of the work on less than vertical rock.

Rest Step

Often on sustained face climbs, your calves will become vastly pumped, one factor that can evoke the dreaded "sewing machine leg," where the tired limb will shake as though you have the palsy. To rest your calves, try the rest step: Find a good edge and stand on the heel of the foot, with the leg straight, the center of gravity directly over the heel, and most of your weight on that foot. If possible, use the rest step whenever you have to stop to place protection, or when you need a rest. Imaginative resting is one of the keys to efficient climbing.

Another important prevention against "sewing machine leg" is fluid, relaxed breathing, a factor often overlooked by beginners and experts alike. Conscious, fluid breathing relaxes the climber and ensures the muscles get sufficient oxygen. Beginners typically climb "tight," with the muscles tensed, especially in the gut and chest areas (which is where anxiety physiologically manifests). The result is shallow, rapid breathing that can border on hyperventilation, or the opposite campaign of holding your breath till you're blue in the face. Direct a little of your attention to your breath and your body will relax considerably. Shallow, panicked breathing and breath holding have caused as many needless falls as poor footwork.

Sandy Litchfield pulls over a big roof on #1 Super Guy (11b) at Shelf Road, Colorado.

Stewart M. Green photo

Footwork Tricks and General Technique

The technique of footwork is one of subtle precision and is tough to explain, let alone illustrate; but if you understand the principles, practice will bring to light what good technique can do for you. Here are some general steps toward good footwork.

1. Scan the rock to find the best possible foothold. Don't move your foot until you know where you're going to put it. The size and location of the foothold determine its utility. When possible, place your feet directly beneath your hands to minimize the strain on your upper body.

2. Place the foot precisely on the best part of the foothold. "Zero in" on the foothold like an archer to a bull's eye. Concentrate on the foothold as you bring your foot to it.

3. Fluidly transfer weight to the new foot placement.

4. Hold the foot absolutely still as you stand/move on it. Use the ankle as a hinge to cancel upper body movement. Foot movement can cause the foot to ping off its hold. Focus on keeping the feet still and maintaining fluid movement and weight transference between holds. With experience this will become second nature. The directions given here plant the seeds that will soon blossom into intuitive movement.

Amos and Coco #3:
Amos Finds His Flow

On the afternoon during their first day at Mt. Gorgeous, that granitic maestro Jules Pinkus moved the topropes over to a steeper part of the wall, roughly eighty degrees and flecked with sharp edges, pockets, and a few big sloper holds. Amos huffed and flexed and broke wind—and sent Coco up for a go.

Rather than rely on upper body strength she didn't have, Coco maintained a fluid pace splaying her supple legs out in unlikely configurations, smearing her feet onto the sketchiest holds, bracing her body here, bridging there, and high stepping somewhere Amos couldn't even see, and heaving only when necessary and for brief spurts with her incense-stick arms. At the anchor she yelled, "Okay, lower me," and Amos did as much, lowering the yoga master to the deck, smooth and steady as church music. Coco leaned back on the rope, keeping her torso upright and her elastic legs at a forty-five-degree angle to the rock, and walked down in graceful strides, arriving at the base none the worse for wear. "Nice work," said Amos. "It's not too bad if you just look around for the holds and trust your feet," said Coco.

The two switched over, and as Coco belayed, hale and hefty Amos charged up the wall like a bull attacking a cape, his feet skedaddling over the ample holds as he yarded with his meat-hook hands. Despite missing most of the gigantic handholds and footholds, Amos powered his way to the belay anchors on top, sucking down half the sky, grinding about six months worth of rubber off his boots, and rasping his fingertips down to the wood. When Coco lowered Amos back to the ground, he looked like Marlon Brando at the end of *On the Waterfront*. Jules suggested that he straightaway re-climb the pitch, knowing that for Amos to succeed in his exhausted state—and Amos would perish before he'd up and quit—he would have to slow down, husband his energy, plot his moves, get his body in the upright position, and use his feet and hands on the big holds, which he did.

"Ain't that something?" Amos said after his second lap. "You looked like you found your flow," Coco commented. "My what?" said Amos. "You want to use the least amount of energy," said Jules, an expert mountaineer by any measure, "not everything you have. When you slow down, use your head and the available holds, everything comes together for you." "You got that right," said Amos. "That's when I start flowing like the Nile in flood." Jules laughed, glanced at Coco, and asked, "Where'd you find this guy?" "Up at Esalen, at a conference on ki gon movements and holotropic breathing techniques," she said. "You've got to be kidding," said Jules, eyeballing Amos's blocky form. "I sure am," said Coco.

Too Fast!

The common problem with most novice climbers is that they rush their moves. They hug the rock, their feet are kicked toward (but aren't placed on) the holds, and because they don't trust their shoes, their limbs quake and their shoes are often skedaddling all over. To climb fluidly and under control, you must settle in and relax. The frantic climber is the first to make a mistake, to miss a key hold. You must choose your holds carefully and always follow the line of least resistance. This sometimes means passing a good hold that is off to the side and would require awkward, more arduous moves to get to. Maintaining balance often means using smaller steps and smaller holds rather than awkward, off-balance strides between huge holds. The climber should move methodically and with precision, placing his feet carefully, staying balanced, and easing up onto doubtful holds rather than jumping upon them. The aim is to climb smoothly and gracefully, and to use as little energy as possible. A good rule is whenever you reach a solid hold, pause and compose yourself, if only momentarily. Three slow and conscious breaths are often enough to steady up. Use the rest step when the chance arises. This takes the strain off the calves and puts it onto the skeletal system, which never tires.

Sloppy footwork is generally the result of impatience and anticipatory fear, most often unjustified. If fluid footwork seems impossible, if your shoes simply keep skating off even large holds, practice on slabs low to the ground. Get used to standing on marginal holds, keeping your weight over your feet. Experiment and learn. Traverse along the base of the cliff, where a fall means slipping mere inches to the ground, and where you can try even the most improbable sequences. Practice walking over little slabs with no hands. Always aim to climb precisely, fluidly, and relaxed. Striving to meet goals of control, rather than for success at all costs, will help build solid technique. And always fight the initial instinct to only look up for holds. Many times the beginner

Torque between the toe and heel placed in a hole or horizontal crack below an overhang can keep the body from swinging out and provide stability and reach.

will look down only to gauge the distance he is above the ground. You must pay attention to the climbing at hand. If you watch an experienced climber, you'll quickly see that she is looking down at her feet at least half the time, scanning for holds and placing them with keen eyes.

Heel Hooking

Heel hooking is the attempt to use the foot as a hand and is rarely used on climbs less than vertical. Basically, you hook the heel of your shoe over or behind a flake, knob, corner, or any feature that will accommodate such a move. Most often, the foot is actually extended sideways, and sometimes kicked over the head, where it is hooked behind and/or over a shelf or ledge. You then pull with the foot, folding the chest in and up until you can reach the hooked or desired hold. A heel hook is often a way to avoid throwing a strenuous and risky dynamic move, and in isolated cases a climb is impossible without using this technique. Though it is sometimes possible, even necessary, to hook something other than the heel (the toe, perhaps), try not to

hook anything above the shoe's rand (the strip of rubber that circles the shoe above the sole). The rand is made from the same compound as the sole and grabs the rock well, whereas the leather upper is prone to shoot off even a jagged flake. Rock gyms provide a perfect, controlled setting to develop and master heel hooking for the simple reason that many overhanging gym routes are unclimbable without this technique. When you have to heel hook, you will. And the more it's used, the quicker it's mastered.

When lateral movement is required on steep climbs, the body will often feel like it's set to hinge out and away from the face. Climbers often look for a side hold or flake at or below waist level to hook a heel on, thus holding the body in place while the hands are arranged on other holds. Heel hooking requires good flexibility and moxie. The applications and variations are many, but it's normally a technique used to employ a "third arm," or to stay in balance where otherwise it would be impossible. Words can take us only so far. Experiment and learn.

Handholds

There are as many different kinds of holds as there are ways to grab them, but there remain five basic techniques: the open grip, the crimp, the vertical grip, the pocket grip, and the pinch grip. In addition to these grips, there are three other basic techniques often called upon in face climbing: mantling, the undercling, and the sidepull. Again, as with footwork, a calm and deliberate manner, coupled with trying different ways of using the hold, will result in confidence that you're using the hold most efficiently.

Open Grip

The open grip is the way you latch either a big hold or a rounded hold. (Once you master this grip, you can also use it on thin holds, which many experts prefer to do.) Your fingers conform to the natural curvature of the hold and you pull. The notion is to grab the best section of the hold and feel around for the most secure position, rather than just pulling straightaway the moment your hand is placed. With big holds, this is not so important, but when a hold

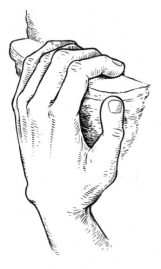

1. The Open Grip

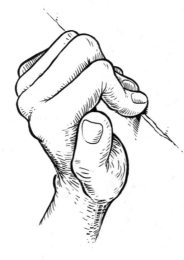

2. The Crimp

3. The Ring Grip, using the thumb to reinforce the fingers

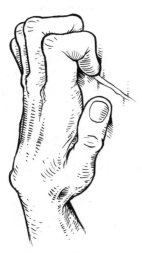

4. The Vertical Grip

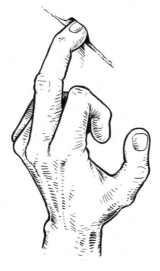

5. The Pocket Grip

6. The Pinch Grip

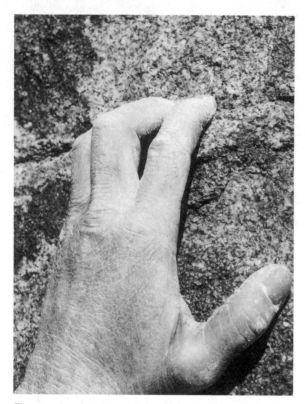

The open hand grip—a favorite among experts

Kevin Powell photo

forearm muscles work overtime to keep the fingers from straightening out, and if the climber hangs too long, the forearms are sure to get "torched." The reason many experts utilize this grip on almost all manner of holds is that they are so honed from bouldering, sport climbing, and gym climbing that their forearm muscles are as strong as wild horses. They go with the open grip whenever possible because, over the long haul, this grip is easier on the joints and ligaments than crimping. But understand that this is a learned technique, and even those who know it well can only perform it relative to their immediate level of fitness.

Crimp It

The crimp, one of the most useful handholds, is used most commonly on flat-topped holds, be they minute edges or inch-wide shelves. The fingers are bent at the second knuckle and the thumb is wrapped over the index finger if possible. Sometimes the thumb is braced against the side of the index finger, but whatever position the thumb ends up in, it's your best friend, as it's considerably stronger than any of your fingers. Remember that the thumb lies close to the rock, negating any leverage effects, while the fingers often project 1 or 2 inches away from the edge, which forces them to work counter to their own leverage. Crimping works much like a shoe does when edging. Once weighted, the fingers dig into the rough contours of the hold.

As a result, and because the second knuckle is locked off while your fingers are reinforced by your thumb, crimping allows you to apply magnificent torque to a hold. You can also shred your fingertips on sharp edges, and the overly ambitious climber can incur finger injuries owing to the sharp angle the tendons make and the stress the knuckles absorb. Regardless, crimping is most often the chosen technique when clasping sharp holds.

Some experts claim that crimping is a natural posture, but most beginners find it otherwise. It's a foreign configuration, and it takes time for the knuckles to get accustomed to the stress. Because you don't want your fingers to rip off the rock, you'll need to feel around for the best part of the

is both small and rounded, the slightest shift in hand and finger position can make a huge difference.

With the open grip, the hand functions like a claw. The core arm muscles fight the tendency of the fingers to straighten out, but if the hold isn't incut the friction of the finger pads supplies the actual purchase on the hold. Accordingly, you try to cover the most surface area possible, increasing the friction at the power point. As with any handhold, if the hold is too small to accommodate all your fingers, give priority to the strongest digits, starting with the middle finger, on down to the pinky.

Experts in biomechanics insist that the open grip is least stressful on both joints and tendons and should be used whenever possible, especially when training on fingerboards. The difficulty with the open grip is that on severely rounded holds, the

hold, which might also be the most painful. Only practice can reveal exactly how this all works, but you've got the basic notion.

Vertical Grip

The vertical grip involves bending the first and second knuckle and pulling straight down on the hold, oftentimes with your fingernails behind the tiniest of edges. This grip is used exclusively on micro flakes found on steep slab climbs, is painful, and is said to be the climbing equivalent of *en pointe* in ballet. At 205 pounds, I've never fancied the vertical grip. Perhaps if you're skinny as a broom straw, your fingernails can take the strain. Mine never could.

Pocket Grip

The pocket grip is most often used on limestone and volcanic rock, which is typically pocketed with small holes. Many sport climbing areas feature this kind of rock, and "pocket pulling" has become a re-

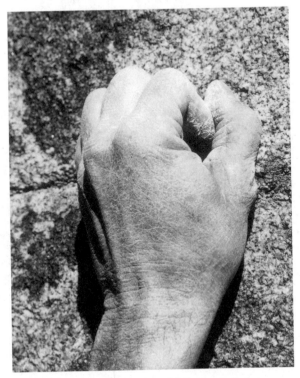

The crimp grip—secure but stressful Kevin Powell photo

quired technique for the modern climber. The ultimate form of the pocket grip is one finger stuck into a hole (a "mono-digit" or "mono"). Because it is rare that a pocket will accommodate all of your fingers, the first choice is the strong middle finger, next the ring finger, then the index finger, and so on. Using the middle and ring finger in a two-finger pocket better balances the load on your hand. The initial tendency is to use the index and middle finger for two-finger pockets. With practice, the middle and ring finger combo is almost always a better option.

It is sometimes possible to stack the fingers on top of each other for increased torque. Feel the pocket for any jagged edges that can cut into the finger. Also, keep the pull in line with the axis of the finger, not pulling side to side, which is like bending a hinge—your knuckle—the wrong way. This is advice you will invariably have to shun should you someday tackle the really grim sport routes. Just be prepared for some sore joints and a few layoffs when a tendon goes.

Though sport climbing tricks are not the domain of this book, pocket climbing has become so ubiquitous these days that many beginners actually break in on volcanic and conglomerate crags, where the majority of holds are pockets. For any number of reasons, pockets are rugged on the tendons and the soft, fleshy part of the fingers, especially between the first and second knuckle, which is where the fingers usually crank over the edge of the pocket. When the pocket edge is sharp (very common), you are essentially mashing both the tendons and the tissue over a blunt knife, something that takes some getting used to. Consequently, the number of finger injuries from pocket climbing far outnumbers those sustained on other venues. For the beginner, whose fingers are not accustomed to the strain, let alone to pulling on two-finger holes in the wall, caution is advised. Many climbers, from beginners to world-class wonders, try and safeguard against bruising and outright injuries by taping their knuckles from the first knuckle down. This inhibits finger flexibility, so it's a trade-off. Many experts, however, are always nursing a sore finger or two, and these are routinely taped. Bottom line: Pockets are hard on the fingers and always will be, no matter how strong or experienced we may be.

Pinch On

The pinch grip is the action a lobster does with its pincers, and what a climber does when pinching a knob, flute, rib, flange, or other protuberance. Though the basic technique is self-explanatory, a climber will often need to feel around quite a bit to find just where his thumb and fingers fit best. On small knobs, the most effective pinch combines the thumb with the side of the index finger. Few people outside the ranks of brick layers have much natural pinching strength. For the most part, it has to be developed.

Mantling

A mantleshelf is a rock feature, typically a ledge (small or large) with scant holds directly above. The act of surmounting it is called mantling. Picture a youngster heaving himself up and onto the top of a wall, then standing upon it. This is the basic form. Mantling is often performed on large features such as shelves or knobs, but when the face offers only one hold, you might find yourself mantling—albeit gently—a mere pencil-width crease.

The technique has four components. After placing both hands on the mantleshelf, inspect the shelf or hold for the best place to mantle on, usually the biggest, flattest spot. If the spot is to the left of your face, you mantle with your left hand, and if it's to your right, then you mantle with your right. The second step involves hoisting the body up high enough to enable cocking one or the other arm on the mantleshelf. Use available footholds to get this upward impetus and ease the requisite arm power. On steep mantles, it is important to get the torso as high as possible before cocking the arm. If the arm is cocked low, with your weight checked only by skeletal tension, it is beastly strenuous for the triceps to initiate upward thrust from this "bottomed out" position. The third part is the press, which is typically the most strenuous phase of any mantle. Whenever your free hand can grab a hold and pull, do so—this helps initiate the press. Keep pulling with that free hand until the mantling arm is straightened and "locked out." The concern is to make sure the palm doesn't skate off the shelf, a real possibility on a rounded or slick surface. Most climbers find that the bottom, or heel, of the palm is best suited for mantling. Once you have "pressed out" the mantle, try to find a handhold above for the free hand. This makes it much easier to execute the last phase: the step up and leg press into the standing position. For balance, you'll want the foot close to the supporting hand. Often the hand must be moved to free up space for the foot. Using the knee is tempting here, but only makes it more difficult to get into the standing position and often results in grievous "rug burns." Rock your weight from your mantling hand to over your raised foot and try to stand up smoothly and without jerking motions, which can dislodge the foot.

In extreme cases, you must mantle using only your fingertips in the cling position, or perhaps with the thumb in a small divot. Many times you will step onto a hold different than the one you have pressed out. Regardless, the basics remain the same: staying balanced, utilizing footholds, not getting stuck in the bottomed out position, avoiding use of the knee, finding a handhold above for the free hand, and smoothly stepping up.

One element of mantling often used as a stabilizing influence on slabs and in corners is called "palming." In its usual form, you lean off a straight arm and palm that has been placed below and to the side of the torso. The palmed hold, if sufficiently "rosy," can often bear enough weight to allow you to reach above or to shuffle your feet up onto higher holds, or both. Keep in mind that tough mantles are almost impossible to reverse, and it's not unheard of to get "mantled out" with no place to go. But good mantles can provide much-needed rests, so take advantage if you have the opportunity.

Years ago, when the majority of climbing was done on granite and sandstone, top climbers were also skilled mantlers. They had to be. As sport climbing has gained popularity, mantling has fallen out of prominence because the routes are often too steep for it and also because volcanic and conglom-

Feet press down, right hand pulls up off the undercling as the left hand reaches for the higher hold.

Extending off the feet to gain height to counter pressure off the hands in the undercling position Kevin Powell photos

erate rock—the common stuff of sport climbing—requires more pocket work than mantling.

For this reason many leading sport climbers are "hosed" on old climbs featuring hard mantles. Again, the best place to hone your mantling skill is on the boulders. It's a skill worth knowing and obligatory if you ever hope to crank the old "trad" routes.

Undercling

Anytime you grab a hold with your palm up, whether you have your fingers behind a flake, or you're grabbing the underside of a small roof or step in the rock, you are underclinging. The technique is often used as a balancing tactic until a free hand can

reach above to a better hold. In its pure form, it functions through the opposing pressures of the hand (or hands) pulling out from the hold under which you are clinging and the force that is directed onto your feet. Counterpressure, in simple terms. The technique is intuitive and self-explanatory, but the following points are worth mentioning.

On a full-blown undercling, where you must traverse under a long flake, try to keep your arms straight, as this transfers some of the load off your biceps and deltoids and onto your bones. Utilize footholds as much as possible to ease the load on your "guns." Rather than undercling off the very quick of your fingertips, try to get as much of your

Tim Powell belays Darrell Hensel up the crimpy Voodoo Child *(5.11a), Sunshine Face, Suicide Rock, California.* Kevin Powell photo

hand as possible behind the hold. Difficult underclings can involve lots of shuffling and crossovers of both hands and feet. Only experience can show you the how and why of it all. On long underclings featuring few footholds, it's often better to move briskly and to keep moving. Dallying in the middle of a bleak undercling is a sure way to "flame out" in no time flat.

Sidepulls

When a handhold is oriented vertically, or near vertically, it's difficult (if not impossible) to pull straight down, so you'll most likely use it as a sidepull. The idea is to lean away from the hold, with your hands and feet working in opposition, similar to liebacking a crack. If the sidepull faces right, you'll want your body to be left of the hold so you can lean away from it. Ideally you'll find some left-facing footholds below and slightly right of the sidepull to provide the opposition. You can often make a longer reach from a sidepull than you could from a horizontal handhold.

As mentioned, a sidepull is similar to the crack technique of liebacking, with your hands and feet working in opposition. The strength to pull the walls down is not so crucial as the ability to "juke" your body into a posture in balance against the oppositional force of the sidepull. In fact, most sidepulls simply keep the upper body attached to the wall, while the legs provide the upward thrust. Trying to heave yourself up off a sidepull without the aid of footholds is truly bleak duty.

Movement: The Upward Flow

While we have discussed hands and feet separately, the aim of all climbing is to choreograph the different moves into fluid upward movement. To settle into this flow requires combinations of holds and techniques. Looking closely at different types of face climbing is the best way to understand the dynamics of this upward flow. Three basic ways exist for using your legs to propel your mass upward against gravity.

Static Step

The static step is generally the most strenuous and therefore least efficient way to move. The static step involves statically pressing your weight up on one leg while simultaneously bringing your other foot up to the next hold. On difficult slab and friction routes, where the weight transfer must be extremely smooth, the static step is almost always used.

Spring Step

The spring step takes advantage of dynamic movement to efficiently move the climber's weight. The technique comes into its own on vertical to overhanging rock. At the moment just before bringing a foot up, "bounce" off that foot to dynamically propel your weight upward. The bounce may be subtle or exaggerated, depending on the move, the individual climber's style, and the relative security of the hold. Many times it's no more than a little juke with the calf muscle. Depending on the terrain, this move should be used most of the time for efficient upward movement. If you watch experts use the spring step, you'll note it gives them the appearance of being light on their feet. It takes practice to do this move smoothly and controlled enough that you don't shock-load the foothold and blow off it, or change the attitude of the shoe on the hold and ping off that way. Lest you get the wrong idea, the spring step is rarely, if ever, an explosive movement. Also, it's an all but worthless technique when delicate weight shifts are required between small or marginal weight-bearing holds.

Frog Step

The frog step entails bringing one foot up, then the other, while the torso stays at the same level. After the second foot comes up, the climber is essentially in a crouched, or "bullfrog," position. At this point both legs can work together to push the weight up. Supple, flexible hips are desired to enable adequate "turn out" of your legs, and to ensure that your hips remain close to the wall. The frog step is useful on all forms of face climbing but is especially availing on vertical climbs.

Eric Hörst crimps small holds on Diamond Life (5.13a) at West Virginia's New River Gorge.

Stewart M. Green photo

The corn-fed male "jock" is likely to be about as flexible as Michelangelo's *David*, and the frog step can put grievous strain on the groin and other ticklish software. For this reason many climbers start each outing with a few minutes of stretching intended to loosen up those muscles. Over time even *David's* muscles will start to relax. The trick is to stay consistent with the stretching. A few minutes before each climb can make a difference over time.

Slab Climbing

Slab climbing refers to smooth rock "slabs," usually ranging from fifty to seventy degrees. Beginning climbers are always startled to see a honed slab climber move over seemingly holdless rock. Slab climbing requires the application of every face climbing technique: smearing here, palming there, edging, mantling, and so on. The ace slab climber is fluid and rarely stops, lest he interrupt the rhythm of ascent. The body is kept well away from the rock, eyes ever scanning the wall for usable features, stopping only when a good hold allows. A baseball player watches the ball all the way to where it meets the bat. Like-

wise, once a climber has chosen a hold, he watches the hold until he gains purchase with his hand or foot. Because you can only watch one hold at a time, you only move one limb at a time. Keep this in mind and you will naturally assume the "tripod" position, maintaining at least three points of contact with the rock while shifting your weight accordingly as you move each limb. Your feet will mostly be smearing on slabs. A series of small steps is generally most efficient for movement up a slab, but occasionally the footholds will be far apart and you'll be forced to high step.

Because slabs are relatively low-angled, climbing them is much more a process of balance and friction than of the "Tarzanesque" strength required on steeper climbs. Consequently, slabs are far and away the best place for a beginner to get accustomed to the nuances of footwork, body position, handholds, and general movement.

While slab climbing is usually thought to be more fun than toil, there are exceptions. Extreme slab climbing occurs when the angle is too steep to just friction, yet the rock is devoid of holds—the classic "bald face." On these, balance, precision, unwavering concentration, and a dash of magic are most often your ticket to ride. "Micro-edging," often painful and always nerve-wracking, is surely one of the most absorbing forms of climbing. Even the experienced expert is astonished at just how small a hold it is possible to stand on. Unlike other forms of climbing, intricate sequences are rarely necessary to ascend slab and friction climbs. There are usually several ways to make upward progress, and this characteristic has led some climbers to label all slabs as boring. Slab climbing has fallen out of favor with many top climbers, who are ever becoming more specialized and seeking steeper and steeper rock. Many advanced slab routes, however, feature protection thin as the holds, and the critical climber might find himself eating his words when facing a teetering, 5.10 high step with his quaking boots 30 feet above the last bolt.

For the beginner, there is no quicker way to hasten climbing prowess than to spend an initial few weeks (or months) doing "slab duty." Assuming the upright posture, keeping the weight over the feet,

Amos and Coco #4:
Coco Floats, Amos Pops, and Jules Shines

For day two of his beginning climbing class, Amos blasted to the venue in his fire-breathing, two-ton Chevy crew truck, meeting Coco (in her pearl-white Geo Espris) and the rest of the class at the trailhead of the local practice cliff, appropriately named Mt. Gorgeous. Close on the heels of the dauntless Jules Pinkus, the group walked five minutes to a variously angled sandstone wall, 80 feet high and twice as wide. Jules rigged four topropes over a section of clement, seventy-degree slab. The class broke into four groups, two to a rope, to review the belay techniques learned at the gym. One student climbed as the other belayed, all under Jules's watchful eyes.

Maintaining upright body position, weight well over her feet, Coco quickly mastered the slab as Amos belayed. Amos then cinched on his $160 fire-engine red "Italian" slippers, grimaced, and started up. Amos pawed rabidly at the scant holds, hugging the rock and suddenly yelling "Fudge!" as he slipped onto the cord.

"For one thing," said Jules, "those shoes are all wrong for slab climbing, and they probably so punish your feet that you're leaning in to stay off them." Jules pulled a knackered old pair of shoes from his pack; Amos traded out his "Italian" slippers, then bicycled up the slab. Only after Jules had Amos climb it one-handed did he learn to get his husky body upright where the shoes worked their wonders. The firefighter then understood the nature of friction climbing as opposed to muscling his way up on nothing holds.

"Nicely done," said Coco, lowering Amos back to the deck. "Thanks," said Amos. "You're pretty handy with that belay." "The belay device does all the work if you let it," said Coco. "I'm pleased to have you working it, just the same," said Amos. "And just what do you mean by that?" asked Coco. "I'm not sure," said Amos, admiring the scenery. "Ain't it gorgeous out here!" Coco gazed down a rolling green valley that gave way to the ocean, a vast blue plain wrinkling far in the distance. "Divine. . . ."

learning the various holds and grips, and moving precisely while relaxed are all essential things that are learned much faster on the less strenuous arena of slabs. Trying to break in on steep rock is a bad practice, and tends to foster bad habits that are difficult to unlearn. This has been proven time and time again by my good friend Bob Gaines, who runs a climbing school in southern California. During his longer seminars, Bob has found that spending an initial two days honing up on slabs helps students transition to the steeper climbs considerably faster than if he straightaway threw the same folks onto vertical terrain. He's tried it both ways, and without exception, starting on slabs has proven the way to go.

Steep Face Climbing

Many of the recent strides in technical expertise are due to climbers venturing more and more onto the steep faces that past generations wrote off as either impossible or too contrived. Before the mid-1970s, a climbing route normally followed a prominent weakness, or "line," up the cliff—for instance, a crack system or an obvious dike or intrusion. As most of these natural lines were climbed, later generations, wanting the same notoriety and thrill of exploration that past climbers enjoyed, turned to the steep and often hold-bereft faces. Climbers no longer only looked for natural lines but often chose the blankest, most difficult way up a cliff in their quest for the limits of technical difficulty.

But steep face climbs need not be extreme.

Many are rife with big holds and ledges, and they can be technically easier than difficult slabs. It's not simply the angle, but also the size and position of the holds that determines difficulty. Steep face climbs, however, even if they have bulbous holds from bottom to top, are invariably more strenuous than lower-angled climbs. They require much more from the arms and, in their most extreme expression, can involve hoisting the body up off one finger stuffed in a shallow, rounded "bullet hole."

The overall strategy of climbing long and sustained steep faces will be discussed in greater detail in Chapter 5: The Art of Leading. For now, understand these basic principles: Unlike slab climbing, you will often see the steep face climber sucking his hips and chest into the wall, trying to get the weight over his feet. Keeping the weight off the arms is essential to climbing steep faces efficiently, for you are often called on to make a strenuous upper body move, and if you've been needlessly hanging off your fingers, the strength might not be there when you most need it. The steeper the angle, the more the arms come into play; but try not to overpull. Try to only hang on, and rely on the legs for upward thrust. The importance of this principle cannot be overstated. The genuine expert is oftentimes not the strongest on the block, but rather the one who knows how to use the least energy to do a given move, sequence, or climb. Overpulling comes not only from hasty, ill-planned movement but often from impatience. Take enough time to recognize the

Like a crab clawing up a barnacle, Mike Tupper boulders up a pocked wall at City Rock, outside Guadalajara, Mexico. Bill Hatcher photo

"Watch me here!"
Paul Piana powers
out a limestone wave
on the shore of
Halong Bay, Vietnam.
Bill Hatcher photo

best sequence for you, and then try and finesse your way over the rock.

It's often better to make two small moves than one long one. Try to avoid getting your body too stretched out because this compromises your balance and decreases the efficiency of your muscles, making the moves more strenuous. Avoid getting scrunched up, or any body positions that require yogi-like contortions; if you have to execute them, get into a more natural position quickly. And never pass up a good rest hold.

If you cannot find a decent foothold to snatch a breather, at least stop at the best handhold and alternately drop each hand and shake out. Again, the skilled steep face climber is the one who exerts the least energy figuring out the easiest, most natural way to the top.

A beginner can benefit greatly by watching an expert climb, but in the case of steep face climbing, this can be misleading. The expert may appear to be, and may well be, simply hauling himself up on his arms. What you might not know is that this expert climbs 200 days a year and has done so for a dozen years. As a result, he has developed phenomenal endurance and cardiovascular strength, and at the moment can't be bothered to fiddle with footholds. But put the same climber on a route at the very limit of his ability, and you can bet your bottom dollar that he'll be observing the basic principles I've mentioned above. The reason is simple: The climber has not been born—nor ever will be—who can hang indefinitely on his guns. Given enough stress, even the mightiest arms will flame out.

Overhanging Face Climbing

Owing to the development of areas like American Forks, Rifle, Echo Cliffs, and Hueco Tanks, as well as the hundreds of climbing gyms now available to the cragsmith, radically overhanging climbing has become all the rage among the elite climbing set. While the realm of sustained, overhanging climbing is strictly the expert's turf, most climbing areas have moderate routes that feature an overhang, or a short overhanging section. In the Shawangunks in upstate New York, there are numerous moderate overhanging routes, moderate only because the holds are

Amos and Coco #5:
Pliant Gams, Titanium Hamstrings

As the sun dove toward the distant Pacific, peerless Jules Pinkus set a toprope over a steep and occasionally overhanging route that worked through a series of steps and small roofs via long reaches on bucket holds. Most of the class had made various laps up the friction and steep face climbing routes and had, through direct experience, become fluent with belaying and lowering as well as reckoning sequences and using their feet on merciful holds, all the while maintaining upright body position. Climbs which that morning seemed as insolvable as the Rosetta stone slowly gave up their secrets as the students relaxed and discovered the intuitive nature of the work. Jules Pinkus was hardly surprised that as the students tired, they came to depend less on strength and more on finding the most efficient technique for scaling a given route. Everyone from Mordecai, seventy years old if a day, to little Ruthy, barely seven, had the basic procedures down cold.

As a finale to a royal day, Jules had strung this last and most demanding toprope problem for anyone who still had the voltage to give it a go. The chant "Amos, Coco, Amos, Coco" rose from the class, and the stout and genial firefighter and the ethereal yoga teacher knew they had been volunteered to represent the class in tackling the incredible. As in most classes, those with a bright technical future tend to shine, however dimly, from the very start; in fact, the unlikely couple were the only ones left with sufficient steam to even try this last climb. Amos massaged his forearms, which felt like two bowling pins. Then he spit forcefully into his hands, rubbed them together hard and fast enough to start a fire, and grabbed the belay. Coco tied into the "sharp end," gazing overhead and trying to mentally climb the imposing overhang. "Do it up tiger," said Amos, and Coco pulled for glory.

A natural technician, Coco wove her way up the steep wall, using her pliant gams to bridge off paltry holds and keep her weight off her arms. She progressed swimmingly until she came to a bulge featuring several small pockets and no footholds. The kundalini was no longer rising. Hanging onto a bucket hold with her dwindling arms, she'd reached a point where she no longer could thieve her way up with fancy footwork. She'd have to clasp the scant handholds and power her way past the difficulties. To do so she'd have to tap an inner fierceness she previously had scorned as anti-spiritual. All the flexibility in Calcutta couldn't see her through just now, and unless she accessed that innate aggression, she was finished. "Quit hanging about and get after it, woman!" Amos bellowed from below. But the idea of raw power and aggression, and using it, was so alien to the tofu-fueled Coco that after dangling for several minutes off the bucket hold, her arms finally turned to butter and she slumped back on the line, letting Amos lower her to the ground.

"Sugarplum," said Amos, "I think you got too much stardust in your eyes. You need to cowboy up and pull down." "Show me how it's done, buckaroo," Coco said sarcastically. Amos tied in and cast off as Coco belayed.

Owing to titanium hamstrings, Amos was unable to stem his legs out and utilize many of the holds Coco had employed, leaving the firefighter to try and heave his way up the holds with sheer gun power. By the time he reached the point where Coco had flamed out, his arms were full of lead—but this didn't stop Amos from pressing on. He grasped the first small pocket and yanked it to eye level, stretched to the next pocket, and shot off into space. Coco lowered him down in an exhausted heap. "You need to find your center and breath, then take it from there," said Coco. "You looked like you were trying to pull the wall over on us." "I was," said Amos.

That crack mountaineer, Jules Pinkus, now tied in and cast off. The students watched in awe as Jules combined both flexibility and strength, aggression and poise, resting here and powering through there. He never hurried but never dallied, always looking about for the best holds and climbing methodically and smoothly. Jules had something of both Coco and Amos, and both qualities were required on this route. But he had something extra as well, a pattern of moving in which everything seemed to issue from his center, as opposed to hauling and boosting his center up the wall with arms and legs. It was a slippery process for Amos and Coco to grasp—this business of moving from the center—but seeing it in Jules had made a little bit of it their own, if only as an idea.

As it happens, Amos's battery was dead and he snagged a ride back into town with Coco. Despite their differences, they were both the same in one crucial respect: Neither could gracefully accept defeat on something they thought was somehow possible, if only in the future. Coco needed strength and aggression; Amos needed to center himself, slow down, and loosen up. To that end Amos agreed to attend one of Coco's yoga classes the following night, after which Amos would go over some strength routines for her benefit. Little did they know that the climbing bug had bitten them hard and deep, and that both their lives would take off in directions impossible to have imagined.

terrific and the climb resembles swinging around on a big jungle gym. The technique does not differ radically from that required on steep faces, save that everything is more strenuous. Almost all overhanging climbs go from one good hold to another. However, "good" here might only mean "not as bad" as the "bad" holds.

Climb the difficult stretches aggressively, but not so fast that you feel rushed. While you cannot get your weight directly over your feet, footwork on overhanging rock is a surprisingly crucial factor, for even the poorest foothold takes more weight off the arms than common sense would tell you. When you bungle the foot sequence, you're left to hang on longer and harder, which on a route nearing your max will usually spell failure.

A cardinal rule is to always try and keep your arms straight; when bent, the muscles are working hard and the arms tire much faster. Ideally, the hands and shoulders act only as a hinge, holding your body to the wall as your legs push you upward. Because this is not possible much of the time, it is essential to do so whenever you can to relieve the strain on the arms.

Throughout this process, body position should be: head back, shoulders wide, hips in, legs bent, arms straight. Constantly try to walk the feet up. When it's time to get the next handhold, first choose

the hold with your eyes. Then push yourself up with your legs till you can reach the handhold and return immediately to straight arms.

Try to avoid extremely long reaches, for this requires the other arm to be locked off, and the locked-off position, on overhanging ground, is probably the most strenuous position in all of climbing. When you must lock off a hold, try to keep the hand close to the shoulder and the elbow close to your side. This is easily confirmed on a pull-up bar. Try letting go with one hand and keeping your chin above the bar. You'll quickly realize your only chance is to assume the locked-off position just described. The geometry of the body makes it so. In rare instances on exceptionally arduous climbs, you might see a climber briefly locking off a hold well to one side of his body ("flagging") and reaching up quickly to a hold on the other side. Be consoled that such a maneuver is limited to the very best and, owing to the bleak leverage required, requires a degree of strength unusual in even world-class climbers. It is also the quickest way to torch a deltoid (shoulder), especially the rotator cuff, which requires months to heal following a thorough tweaking.

Back-stepping often beats locking off when you must make a long reach on steep rock. A classic back-step move reaching left, say, would have the

In flight! All limbs dislocated from the holds, Mike Paul slaps for the sloping top on Saturday Night Live, *a difficult dynamic boulder problem at Joshua Tree, California. Having generated momentum off lower holds, Mike must fly upward and stick a one-handed latch, not letting his lower body swing him off the top.* Gregg Epperson photo

outside edge of the left foot on the rock, opposing the right hand, which is ideally sidepulling. The right foot is splayed out right and propels the body as the left hand reaches for the faraway hold. Back-stepping has steadily become an invaluable technique for ascending formidable overhanging routes. We will take up this topic in greater detail in Chapter 3: Crack Climbing Skills.

Dynamic Climbing

A dynamic move is another way to describe a lunge, where a climber vaults off a hold and is propelled to another. Dynamic moves range from 6-inch slaps to all-out jumps, where a climber is completely detached from the rock before quickly clasping holds above at the apex of his leap. Twenty-five years ago, dynamic moves were virtually unheard of on all but practice rocks. As climbs got more and more difficult, dynamics ("dynos") became a requirement on many of the harder test pieces. Properly performed, dynamics are climbing's most athletic expression, requiring deluxe coordination, raw power, and precise timing.

Usually, dynamic moves are "thrown" on overhanging rock to span long stretches between good holds. But not always. Sometimes dynamics are thrown from a poor hold to a pathetic hold. While it is occasionally necessary to generate the thrust solely with the arms, with the feet dangling in space, dynamics are usually performed by an explosive pull from the arms, aided by propulsion from the feet as they kick off footholds.

Start by hanging straight down from your arms, with your legs crouched and ready to spring. Some experts will tell you not to waste energy by pumping up and down on your arms as you set up for the lunge. Others find that small preliminary bounces can increase their spring. In any case, eye the hold you're firing for and see yourself latching it, then catlike, launch single-mindedly for the hold. Once the lunge is underway, one hand shoots up and slaps onto the "target" hold. Ideally the climber exploits the moment of weightlessness that occurs at the apex of the leap—the dead point—to grab the hold with accuracy. But remember, the hold you're lunging for may be far poorer than it appears from below.

Sometimes a hold is too greasy or rounded to lock off and reach above, but while hanging below, it is possible to generate enough momentum to literally fly to that upper hold. This phenomenon is difficult to explain but is obvious when you encounter it. Rounded holds, even on very overhanging rock, are often tolerably secure when your arms are extended and your bulk is hanging directly below them. But the higher you pull up, the worse they become because your body position forces you to pull increasingly out, rather than down on the hold. This is one reason that jumbo "dynos" are usually initiated with the arms fully extended.

This is the basic form of the intentional dynamic. Much more common is the dynamic thrown out of desperation, where a climber has worked himself into an irreversible fix, and just before peeling off, he slaps for a hold. Another situation is: You pull up statically to a certain height; there is a hold right above your face, but if you let go, you'll fall off. You let go with one hand and hope you can slap the hold faster than gravity rips you off.

Practice—normally on boulders—can bring to light many more examples of dynamics. One of the most difficult concepts to master is that dynamic climbing requires total commitment. It also requires time and experience to successfully hit a hold and apply instant power as your weight shock-loads down following the dynamic. Again, practice makes perfect. Remember that, except on upper-level routes, only one climb in fifty requires any dynamic climbing, and the place to practice dynamics is not on a long climb, but inches off the ground, or on a steep sport route with a bolt at your nose.

The standard line on throwing dynamic moves is that almost every dyno is "do, or fly." Since there is little chance of staying on the rock after misfiring a dyno, you either stick the dyno, or you fly off the rock onto the rope.

Move from Your Center

One of the most obvious things about climbing is totally lost on 99 percent of all climbers. That is, in terms of the actual body mechanics, the arms and

Randy Vogel slots lean hand jams on the classic Right O'Kelly's Crack, Joshua Tree, California.
Kevin Powell photo

legs are serving to transport the torso up a piece of rock. What is lost here, however, is the visceral sense of moving the torso, or center, distracted as the climber is by the intricacies and toils of the movement itself and the taxing strain placed on the fingers, hands, and forearms. The center, roughly from mid-thigh to lower chest, contains the "core strength" that regulates the movement of the limbs. In a strange and unexplainable way, this core strength is the key to good climbing, and is probably more important than anything else on steep to overhanging routes. Without good core strength the torso sags

Amos and Coco #6:
Expanding Perspectives

Over the following several months, Amos and Coco hit the cliffside some dozen times and had become regulars at the climbing gym as well. Under Coco's supervision, Amos had worked his way up to Yoga 1 class, and though his legs were still two Doric columns, he was beginning to relax, had learned to connect his breathing to his movements, had lost twenty pounds of grizzle (no more burgers or barhopping), and was learning to move from his center with poise and precision. Coco had broken her rigid trance of being identified with a soft and indulgent spiritual perspective, and this freed up her previously disowned aggression, allowing her to start kickboxing classes and a casual weight lifting regime twice a week (after climbing at the gym, which had cross-training facilities in-house). She'd also introduced other foods into her diet beyond lentils, carrot sticks, and green tea.

Climbing and its special demands were causing both climbers to take stock of long-defended, second-hand perspectives they had come to accept and cherish as core identities. It was not a matter of right or wrong per these perspectives, rather that the perspectives mechanically imposed inclinations onto their lives, biases that kept them low on the cliffside. Once they struggled past the trap of defending what was keeping them gravity-bound, the sky opened up and they had real choices that led to increased performance and consciousness. As prisoners to these perspectives—which seemed objectively real, superior, and imperative solely from the narrow terrain of the perspective itself—they had been closed off to repressed aspects of themselves that were now required where their boot rubber met the rock. At first, embracing these opposite tendencies was scary and felt "unnatural"—even taboo—but once they understood that this was merely conditioning, rather than the "way things really and truly are," their whole personas seemed to relax into the process. In fact, Amos and Coco were expanding by the minute, and neither could have envisioned that climbing would have impacted their lives this way.

under the arms, and the legs are essentially moored to a flimsy base instead of counterpressuring off a taut and robust core. Once a climber changes her orientation from hauling and thrusting herself up the rock to moving her core over the rock, technique rapidly improves. At first this takes practice and conscious effort—which is difficult to do because you get lost in scanning and pulling and stepping. The trick is to keep some attention on your core and intentionally climb as though your core is dictating what to do with your arms and legs. This way you get a feel for climbing *from* your core as opposed to hauling your core up the cliff. In a sense, your core leads the way. This will confound you at first, but stick with it and be amazed. The chief deterrent is that virtually all of us live from our heads and climb the same way, as though it were our heads alone that we were transporting up the rock. When you move from your core, your center of gravity shifts and so does your experience. You can practice this simply walking down the street—which is as good as anyplace to start because this concept is as counterintuitive as all get out. But once you get a taste for it, you're only one step shy of a "Brave New World."

CHAPTER 3

Crack Climbing Skills

The most visible and tangible weakness up a cliff is a large crack that runs from bottom to top. When you walk to the base of the rock and your partner asks where the climb is, the answer is self-evident. A climbing route is often referred to as a "line," a term derived from the line the crack forms on the cliff, though a "good line" doesn't necessarily follow a crack. A good crack line may pass over steep, otherwise featureless rock, be clean, and offer exciting locations, heroic exposure, and a straight, or "plumb line," topography. A "bad line" might wander all over a rubbly cliff, through vegetation, and up dark and dripping recesses. But good or bad, a crack line is a route waiting to be climbed, if it hasn't already been climbed. A prominent crack system is nature's way of telling us where to climb, and when expeditions are mounted to big, faraway cliffs, or when a beginner studies a crag for the first time, eyes naturally home in on any crack system the cliff affords.

While sport climbing has moved away from cracks and onto the bald and open faces (some 5.12 sport climbers could no more climb a 5.9 crack than they could jump over the moon), a beginner's program that neglects crack climbing is a very poor itinerary indeed. The fundamentals of placing and removing equipment and establishing belays are learned on cracks. And if someday you should aspire to tackle the world's long and classic climbs—from Chamonioux to Patagonia—you will need fluency in cracks because such routes are predominately crack climbs and always will be.

While face climbing might be a natural movement, few face climbs follow natural lines, and while cracks are natural lines, crack climbing is a very unnatural campaign. Crack climbing requires subtle and strenuous techniques where the only hope of mastery lies in rote experience. All crack climbing involves either jamming or torquing the limbs or body inside the crack. Just as in face climbing, the idea is to keep your center of gravity over your feet as much as possible. On low-angled climbs, the hips and torso should remain back away from the rock; as the angle steepens, the hips move closer to the rock, a technique that holds true no matter the style of climbing.

There are two types of "jamming." With the classic "hand jam," the hand is placed in an appropriately sized crack, and the muscles expand the hand inside the crack. The various counterpressures result in a locked, or "jammed," hand that can be very secure when properly placed. The second method involves torquing and camming the appendage in a bottleneck or constriction in the crack. In wide cracks, the limbs are often twisted or stacked, and in very wide cracks you'll find that wedging and cross pressures are the only way to get up. Most jams use a little of both torquing and camming, so to label these as separate techniques is a bit artificial.

Since no two climbers are exactly the same size, where one climber might pull fist jams, another might get hand jams, and so on. Again, anyone with aspirations toward big, classic climbs will soon discover such routes predominantly follow crack systems. So if you dream of the big traditional classics, you must become proficient at crack climbing. No way around that. . . .

Amos and Coco #7:
With the Staying Power of Stone

Seeking to broaden their curriculum beyond toproping at Mt. Gorgeous, Amos and Coco took a three-day intermediate seminar from none other than Jules Pinkus, that sage of the High Lonesome. This time the class was held at a traditional, or "trad," cliff sporting hundreds of routes—mostly crack climbs—established over three-quarters of a century by the icons of American climbing. Scaling this staunch granite, Amos and Coco knew they were a new link in a chain of adventurers reaching back to the days of manila ropes and soft iron pitons. As such, they felt part of something that lived on through time with the staying power of stone, something that would continue on, far into an indeterminate future, when their very bones were dust. "Such is the impermanence of all things," said Coco. "But lust . . . er . . . love is forever," Amos said. "Ain't it?" "That depends," said Coco.

Whereas the beginning seminar had focused on basic rope work and face climbing, the intermediate class was all about crack climbing, which was brand new to Amos and Coco. The first route, over which the valiant Jules Pinkus had strung a toprope, followed a thin crack bisecting a high-angled slab. As Coco tied into the line, Jules noticed the yoga master had toned up her upper body considerably since the first class, two months before, and said so. "That's my influence, thank you," said Amos. "He'd take credit for the stars in the sky," cracked Coco. Judging from the straightforward snap in her voice, she'd apparently off-loaded a little of the precious New Age fluff she so thoroughly embodied during the beginning seminar. "Got me?" Coco asked Amos, who was set to belay. "Not yet, but give me time. . . ." Coco laughed. Amos said, "Get after it, girl," and Coco started up the thin crack.

Slipping her tapering digits into the hilt, Coco waltzed up the fissure, pausing only to arrange jams and chalk up. Jules noticed she was mostly face climbing the crack and he suggested she get a good finger lock and hang all her weight on it to experience just how good, or bad, it really was. The finger jams felt strange and precarious, and Coco didn't trust them; but after experimenting a bit and trying things this way and that, she found the jams were good enough. At the top anchor she said, "Lower me," and Amos obliged. "You made it look easy," said Amos, as Coco untied. "You'll make quick work of it, big man," said Coco.

Amos gathered his energy and began balancing his chi with several elaborate hand motions, looking somewhat like a lumberjack experimenting with ki gon movements. "What the hell you doing?" asked Jules. "Dicking around," said Amos. "I could be shining my shoes for all it matters, but so long as I gather my focus and calm myself first, I seem to climb a lot better." Jules glanced at Coco, who said, "Don't look at me. He just makes up those silly moves as he goes along." "Watch and weep, cupcake," said Amos. "Remember to breathe, Tarzan," said Coco.

Amos started up. Only the very tips of his summer sausages found purchase inside the slender crack. The jams felt sketchy, like they could rip right out, but owing to his sessions in the climbing gym and dozens of laps up face climbs at Mt. Gorgeous, he had learned to keep his jumboness over his feet as he milked the jams and made do.

After several laps apiece, Amos and Coco were getting a feel for the work and had learned how to slot their hands thumb up or thumb down, depending on available jams, body position, and footholds. Finger jamming would take time to perfect, said Jules Pinkus, but they were on their way thanks to mastering basic body movements on the cracks.

The names and different techniques do not correspond to any standard crack dimension (though a "hand crack" generally refers to a 2-inch crack) but describe the method you must use based on how your fingers or hands fit a given crack. Climbers with slender hands enjoy advantages on thin finger and hand cracks but work at a disadvantage on most wider cracks. Regardless of crack size, a smooth rhythm is preferred—hand, hand, foot, foot, repeat. In its purest form, crack climbing is a mechanical drill, with the climber repeating essentially the same move over and over, ad exhaustion.

Finger Cracks

Finger cracks vary in width from shallow seams into which you can only get the tip of your pinky to a crack that swallows your fingers up to the third knuckle. Halfway between pure crack climbing and pure face climbing, thin cracks require styles from both forms. Consequently, finger cracks are often technically demanding.

Except in the Wingate sandstone of the Canyonlands and other such desert areas, it is a very rare crack that is absolutely parallel-sided. Most cracks, thin and otherwise, vary in size, if only barely; it's these constrictions that you look for. The knuckles are the thickest part of the finger, particularly the second knuckle. It is possible to jam the knuckles above constrictions in the crack, and when the wrist is bent and the arm pulls down, the knuckle becomes locked like a chock in a slot—the standard "finger lock." This practice may prove as painful as it sounds, and it's crucial to first wiggle the fingers around to attain the best fit before weighting them. On steep thin cracks, the fingers are often inserted so that the thumb is down, but this will vary depending on circumstances.

As a general rule it is preferable to use the thumb-up jam whenever possible (no matter the size of the crack). Two reasons: One, you can reach farther from jam to jam. As you push down on a thumb-up jam, you are not uncamming it as you do with a thumb-down jam. Two, because the hand is aligned anatomically correctly, the thumb-up jam doesn't require twisting to get the digit to lock/cam

in the crack. For these two reasons, thumb-up jamming is less strenuous than the thumb-down variety.

Many times it is better to jam the shank of the finger—the fleshy section between knuckles. Find the appropriate slot, insert as many fingers as possible (in the thumb-down posture), then pivot the wrist and pull downward. This will naturally create a camming torque on the stacked fingers, so the fingers will stick even if the crack is nearly parallel. Remember that the thumb is stronger than the fingers, so always try to brace it against the index finger in whatever position feels best. This reinforces the jam to prevent it from rotating out.

For ultra-thin, less-than-first-knuckle cracks, you most often assume the thumb-up position to utilize the thinnest digit—the pinky—and any other parts of your fingers that you can snake into the crack. "Pinky locks" are marginal jams at best and function well only if the pull is straight down. Though in theory the thumb-up jam is better, oftentimes a straight-in crack (a crack splitting a uniform face) requires a combination of thumb-up and thumb-down jamming.

When the constrictions are slight and the jams are loose or marginal, leaning to one side or the other will often add a degree of stability to the adventure. Look for any footholds for counterpressuring. If the crack is offset, where one side of the crack is raised above the other, the thumb can apply opposite pressure against the offset edge.

Such are the basic positions for vertical cracks. But many thin cracks slant one way or another, and just as many weave around in the course of even a short climb. The trick is to try and keep your body in an anatomically natural position, where your limbs are not corkscrewed round each other and where you don't need excessive core (abdominal) strength to compensate for an out of kilter corpus. As the crack leans, your body will inevitably be below the crack, and this pretty well dictates that the upper hand will have to be kept in the thumb-down position and your lower hand in a thumb-up position (except when reaching through). With leaning thin cracks, it is sometimes possible, even desirable, for the lower hand to be thumb-down. But should

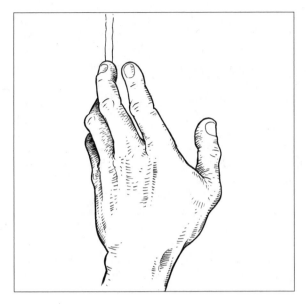

"Pinky lock"

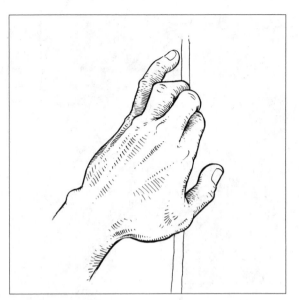

Standard finger lock

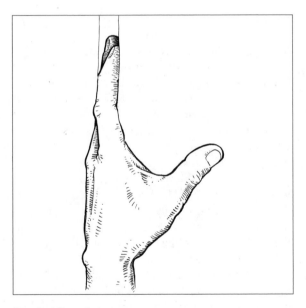

Standard finger lock

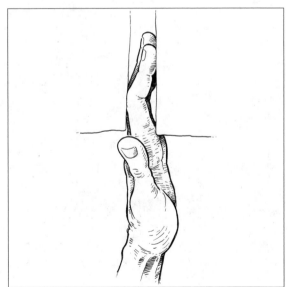

Off-size fingers

Mort Guzman "milks" a Devil's Tower (Wyoming) thin crack for the best jam. Bill Hatcher photo

the crack lean to your right, to place the right hand thumb-up means to crank against the knuckles the wrong way, since slanting thin cracks are usually a combination of jamming and pulling down on the lower edge of the crack. Extended sections of finger jamming, especially if the rock is sharp, can gnarl your knuckles, so you may want to run a couple wraps of 1-inch tape around the joints. The torquing action of extreme finger jamming can result in tendon damage, so lay off if you feel your fingers getting "creaky."

No one can climb a thin crack without feet. Even the best jams pump the forearms quickly, and without good footwork, you're soon "hosed." Like face climbing, thin cracks are usually a matter of finding hand positions that best support the upper body, while your legs supply the upward thrust. Thin cracks get progressively more difficult as the footholds evaporate. Always scan the face for footholds. Thin cracks are strenuous, so never pass a rest spot, even if you're not tired. Leaning off the jams puts the climber to one side of the crack. If there's a foothold on that side, use the outside edge of the upper foot on that hold because it keeps you more balanced and in a far less twisted attitude.

Thin cracks occasionally open up and allow a flared "toe-jam." Most rock shoes feature low-profile toes tapered particularly for this. Twist the ankle and get the sole of the shoe vertical, then jam the toe in above the constriction and try to keep the heel low. When there are no footholds and no pockets for toe-jams, climbers will sometimes stick the outside edge of the shoe vertically in the crack. Though marginal, this works surprisingly well because it creates a foothold of sorts and invariably takes some weight off the arms. The last choice is to simply use friction, with the sole flat against the rock, the foot pushing in somewhat to gain purchase. Here, keep the heel low if at all possible, getting as much rubber on the rock as you can.

Save for a substantial shelf to stand on, "stem" holds are a thin crack climber's best friend. These are holds on each side of the crack that slant in and on which the climber can "stem," or bridge, his feet. A good stem provides a solid base for the lower torso

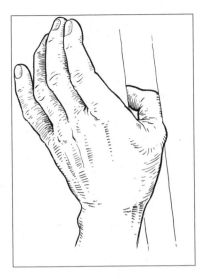 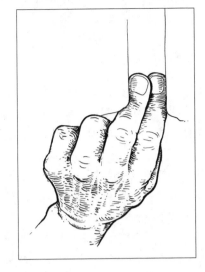 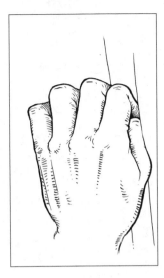

The thumb stack: 1. Place the thumb.   *2. (From above) Curl fingers over and pull down.*   *3. Step 2 seen from front.*

and often allows the climber to shake out a pumped hand, sometimes both hands. On a steep thin crack, you hope for two good finger locks within reach. Keeping your arm extended (remember, a bent arm tires quickly), suck your chest in and get your weight over your feet. Shake out one arm at a time until you've recovered enough to carry on.

When climbing thin cracks in corners, it is often possible to stem between the two walls using pure friction. If you find a stem hold, look to paste one foot in the corner and back-step the outside foot onto the stem hold.

All these descriptions may sound straightforward (if a little confusing without studying the illustrations), but climbing a thin crack rarely is. The best—or only—workable solution is usually a subtle blend of all these techniques. The correct sequence is rarely obvious, requiring patience and a certain amount of scratching around to discover what best works for you. Hasty moves can result in painful abrasions, so climb fluidly.

I have broken down the variety of individual moves likely to be encountered on thin cracks. Putting these moves together, with tips on strategy

and approach for all crack climbing, will be taken up in Chapter 5: The Art of Leading.

Off-Finger Cracks

An off-finger crack is too big for the fingers and too small for the hand, where the third knuckle butts into the crack and the fingers rattle around inside. Cracks this size rarely allow good toe jamming—just a tad too thin—so you're doubly cursed. For most climbers this is the hardest size of crack, save for the notorious off-widths. Everything's wrong about this size, and there are no easy solutions. One approach is to keep the fingers straight and together and stuff them in to the hilt, thumb up. You lever the fingertips off one side of the crack and the back of the fingers, or knuckles, off the other side—sort of a crowbar effect. This "bridge" jam is terrifically strenuous, difficult, and worthless most of the time (save for transitional moves). Another way is to insert the hand thumb down, overlap the middle finger over the index, over crank with the wrist, and pray to God that it doesn't rip out. Far and away the best method is the "thumb-stack"—or "butterfly" jam. Place the thumb near the outside of the crack, the

Amos and Coco #8:
Hell and Devils

On the second day of the intermediate seminar, the insuperable Jules Pinkus set topropes over several hand cracks. These climbs slashed walls much steeper than the thin cracks they had climbed the previous day; indeed, some were dead vertical.

Several of the cracks were a tad too wide for Coco's hands, and with the unfamiliar jams required, she chafed her hands in several places. Jamming her feet in the cracks also felt weird.

Amos found hand cracks much to his liking, and after a few laps on the easier units, he took a shot at a vertical article. "Probably too hard for you just now, but go ahead," said Jules. "Just don't thrash." "You got it," said Amos, who did a few peculiar motions to balance his vital energies and connect with his center. "Lose another 200 pounds and you might start levitating," said Coco, ready to belay. "Steady on that cord, fruitcake," said Amos.

Amos deftly moved up the vertical crack. Being so new to the practice, he didn't know if the jams would hold or how long he'd last, but he kept on, torquing his meat hooks and twisting his feet into the crack. After 20 feet he was tiring; after 40, he felt like he had an anvil in his knickers, and his forearms were singing from repeatedly making the same flexing motion with his hands.

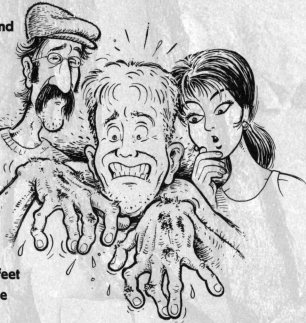

. . . the backs of his paws were covered with punctures and flappers.

Apparently, these cracks used muscles in different ways than face climbs. Another few moves and the firefighter was on his last gas, but then the old, hard-charging Amos McCoy sprang back to life, slugging his hands into the crack, wobbling, and flailing. Finally Jules yelled up for him to rest on the rope or he'd ruin his hands for sure. But it was too late. When Amos finally pitched off a moment later, the backs of his paws were covered with punctures and flappers. "Hell and devils!" Amos shouted, and Coco lowered him off.

"You lost your center, maharaja," Coco said. "I lost more than that," Amos grumbled, eyeing the tragic abrasions on the backs of his hands. "When you get pumped," said Jules, with the authority of Solomon, "that's when you have to start climbing ever more carefully, or you'll soon regret it." "I do," said Amos. Coco applied various herbal poultices to Amos's lesions, and in a few minutes the pain eased and his vigor returned.

As the day was still young and most of the class was still game for more, Jules Pinkus demonstrated how to tape hands for jamming, and soon all the students were taped up and working the toprope cracks with alacrity. With each voyage up the various cracks, the students got a little more familiar and comfortable with jamming. Climbs that seemed awkward and insecure that morning were starting to feel reasonable, though still challenging. "Some take right to cracks and others need more time to get dialed in," said Jules. "Whether you start off fast or slow rarely determines how good you will eventually get if you just stay with it. The main thing is to get that mileage in."

first knuckle against one side, the thumb pad against the other. (For this to work effectively, the crack must be thinner than the link of jammed thumb. The thumb is inserted at an angle, the pad higher than the knuckle.) Curl the fingers over the thumbnail and pull down, effectively wedging, through downward pressure, the thumb between the two walls. At first this technique feels strange and impossible and about as reliable as a felon on bail, but it's really the only viable technique (with practice). All told, this technique is much more about "feel" than strength, and is probably one of the toughest maneuvers to master. Without it you can bank on getting humbled on exacting off-finger cracks.

Because off-finger jams are always cammed or wedged, they're invariably less secure and more strenuous than a good finger lock. Hence, footwork

(as always) is key. It will help to wear tiny (i.e., painful) slippers with a thin toe profile. The drawback is that while these might be perfect for a short pitch, they won't cut the gravy on a longer route. With luck, the crack will open up enough to allow at least marginal toe jams. If not, you're essentially face climbing with your feet. If there are no face holds, your world is all shook up.

Hand Cracks

Most climbers regard hand cracks as the last word in crack climbing. The crack is perfectly suited for both hands and feet, the technique is readily learned and very secure, and vertical (or even overhanging) hand cracks are often readily "hiked." An added boon is that (for reasons only a geologist can guess) hand cracks often bisect spectacular sections of rock, and

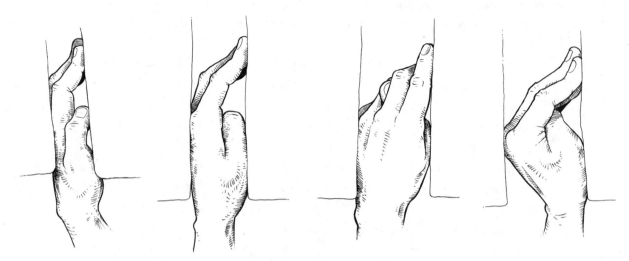

Hand jams

many of the world's classic climbs involve extensive hand jamming.

Hand jamming is usually done with your fingers bent at the palm, or third knuckle. The thumb-up hand jam is a tripod configuration, with the fingertips and heel of the palm on one side of the crack and the back of the hand and knuckles pushing against the other. In a tight hand jam, increase the outward pressure by bridging the thumb off the index finger. If the crack is large enough, wedge the thumb into the palm to create additional outward pressure. The importance of squeezing the thumb, though neglected in most climbing manuals, cannot be overstated. It's the expanding action of the hand and the wedging of the thumb that create the actual hand jam, which when properly performed is the most powerful jam of all. Once mastered, an experienced climber will often prefer to hang off a "bomber" hand jam than off an equally good shelf—though most uninitiated sport climbers would prefer the shelf.

When climbing straight-in, "splitter" hand cracks, most climbers prefer the thumb-up position, though in some situations the thumb-down jam works better. When the crack jags, or is a little slim, the thumb-down jam is normally—but not al-ways—employed. With the thumb-up jam, the wrist is straight. The wrist twists with the thumb-down jam, and the result is a torquing action that can sometimes add authority to a thin or bottoming jam. As you move up, try keeping your arms straight and penduluming from jam to jam, leapfrogging each hand jam above the previous one to increase speed and efficiency.

With slanting hand cracks, or in corners, you will generally jam the upper hand thumb down and the lower hand thumb up, shuffling rather than reaching through with the lower hand. When you find it necessary to lean off the crack, the top hand is often thumb down, the bottom hand thumb up. There are exceptions to these examples, and climbing even the most peerless, straight-in hand crack may require all these techniques, if only to vary the stress and to use other muscles. A hand jam is often tight, and the back of the hand is frequently set against coarse rock. Ghastly abrasions can result from hasty jamming or rotating the hand in the crack, which is a common mistake as you pull up and past a poor or insecure jam. To avoid this, whenever possible place the jam so the fingers are pointing straight into the crack. As you pull up, rotate your wrist—not your hand—keeping the jam locked tight. Even with suave technique, extended sections of hand jamming can trash your hands if you don't protect them with tape. Tape also adds confidence by allowing you to jam a little harder without feeling excruciating pain. Check the end of this chapter for details on taping.

With hand cracks, which readily accept feet, turn your foot on its side so your inside ankle faces up. Slot the foot in the crack—keeping the heel low—then pivot the foot toward the horizontal. As you weight it, keep trying to rotate it tighter in the crack. Properly set, such foot jams easily support the bulk of your weight. It's a mistake to think the foot jam improves the deeper you set your shoe, however. Keeping the foot as far out of the crack as can be easily secured allows quick removal and keeps your center of gravity away from the rock and a bit of your weight off your arms. You rarely have to stick the shoe in past the ball of the foot. Any constrictions make foot jams that much more secure. Always try to keep the feet relatively low and the legs somewhat straight while crack climbing. The higher your feet, the more your rump hangs out and the more you hang on your arms. The low heel position lays more rand and sole rubber along the crack, resulting in added friction. Also, the increased surface area available for contact on the rock minimizes the pain quotient (and to be sure, jamming can put a hurt on your feet).

Lastly, understand that at first it feels very insecure and downright weird to twist your feet into cracks. It feels as if you might break a foot bone or the foot jam might suddenly blow out. Neither are true. As with all jamming, learning to be comfortable and secure with jammed feet is a matter of feel, which readily comes from experience. Like riding a bike, once you learn how to climb cracks, the technique is yours for life.

Cupped or Cammed Hands

As the crack opens up too wide for tight hand jams, the security of the jams begins to diminish, peaking at the point just before a fist jam fits in the crack. For these wide hand jams, try "cupping" the hand by pushing the fingers forward into the crack and stuffing the thumb into the palm, or "camming" the hand by rotating the hand sideways until good purchase is made on both sides of the crack. For cammed hands, it is necessary to keep the hand torqued to maintain the stability of the jam. The hazard here is that the more radically the hand is cupped, the less of the hand (back) is contacting the rock. Pushed to the max, the back of the hand becomes convex, and only the bit of flesh just back from the base of the middle finger will be catching the rock. Accordingly, that small area can be abraded down to the wood with a single ill-placed jam or slight shift or pivot. For that reason, if you are cupping at the max, tape your hands. I can look down at my hands and see pink marks that bear painful stories, some twenty years old, of ripped flesh from cupping.

Fist Jamming

Even experienced climbers find fist jamming a precarious technique, in part because it's seldom used, but mostly because the fist jam rarely feels quite right. The jam is set by clinching the fist, which enlarges the small fleshy muscles on the outside of the hand; since these expand very little, the best fist jam is usually a matter of matching fist size with crack size. When the fit is snug, the fist jam can, with practice, be made very secure.

Look for a constriction to jam above. If the crack is parallel-sided, choose the spot where your fist fits snugly. Sometimes you will slot the fist straight in, like a boxer throwing a slow-motion jab. The fist is then flexed as the hand is rotated into the vertical position. Other times the fist is simply placed vertically and the hand flexed. Depending on the crack, the fist, once slotted, can assume several basic forms. With a glove fit, the thumb is wrapped across the index and middle finger. The thumb may be tucked across the palm on a tight fit. On an ultra-thin fist jam, let the middle and third finger float above the index finger and the pinky, which narrows the profile of the fist. This "ball jam" can be expanded very little and is only "bomber" above a constriction. (A wide hand jam is usually preferable over the "ball jam.") An even less reliable position is sometimes (though rarely) used when the crack is too wide. Keep the thumb on the outside of the fist, braced over, or against the index finger. This is a painful, and most often makeshift, jam, which will rarely bear much weight. Sometimes the flex of a forearm inserted into the crack will add security to a loose jam.

On straight-in fist cracks it is often possible to jam the entire crack with the back of the hands facing out. However, many climbers prefer to jam the lower fist palm out, finding the strain is distributed over a greater range of muscles. Picture yourself picking up a beer keg, then tilting the keg horizontally. Your arms would form a circle, with your lower hand palm up, supporting the keg. If your lower hand was palm down, the keg would be resting, no doubt precariously, on the back of your hand. Turn your hand over, and you kick in the full power of your shoulder, back, and biceps. With extreme fist cracks, by jamming the lower fist palm up, you form a sort of ring of power; using this configuration, many scandalous fist cracks have been tamed. When the crack leans, you will invariably use this technique.

Unlike jamming thinner cracks, you will seldom reach above the upper fist with the lower one. It's just too awkward most of the time. It's usually better to shuffle the fists up the crack, locking off the lower jam and reaching above for the next one. The aim is to keep your body in an anatomically natural position. Example: On a leaning crack, the upper fist will palm toward the ground and the lower fist will palm toward the Milky Way.

Fist cracks are often quite strenuous, and even crack masters are inclined to rotate their jams. Again, rueful abrasions can result. Many climbers tape their hands for even moderate fist cracks.

Since the breadth of your hand and foot is roughly the same, if your fist fits, so will your feet. Look for a constriction. Otherwise, the foot goes straight in. If it's loose, torque it laterally for stability. As with all jamming, try to keep the feet low and the weight over them. Resist the temptation of booting the shoe into the crack or jamming it too deeply. The shoe can get stuck, and it's rugged and scary trying to crank it free.

Faculty

Crack climbing faculty depends far more on technique than strength, a truth frequently proven by gym-trained climbers who devour 5.12 plastic like birthday cake but who get perfectly spanked, say, on

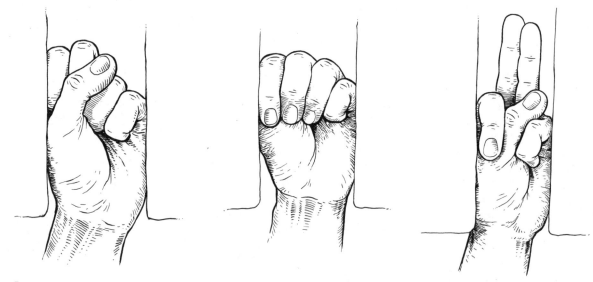

Fist jams

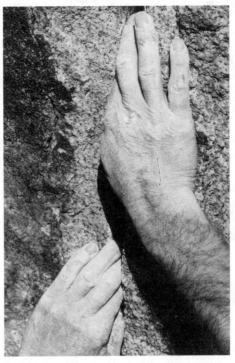

Fingertip jamming

Fingertip jamming

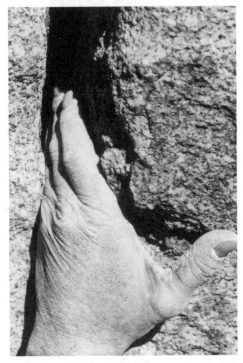

Sinker finger jams

Stacked finger jams Kevin Powell photos

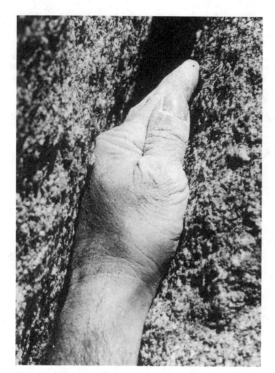

Thin hand jam (marginal)

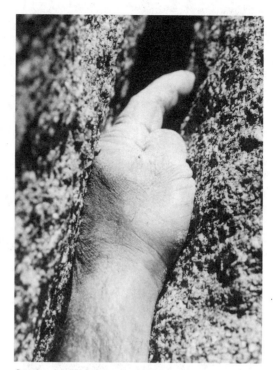

Bomber hand jam

Perfect-size hand crack gobbles the whole hand.

Wire hand jam Kevin Powell photos

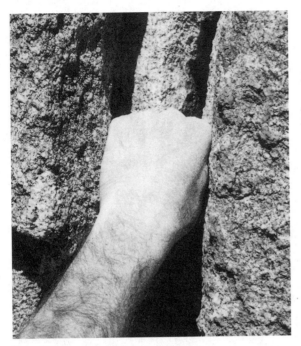

Tight fist jam—palm in

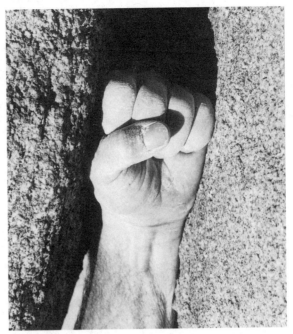

Locker fist—palm out

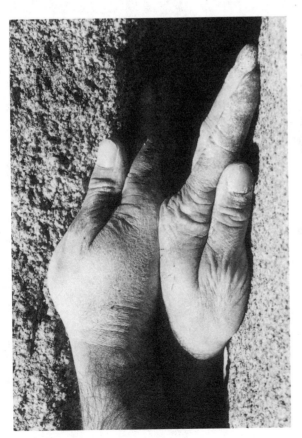

Stacked hands

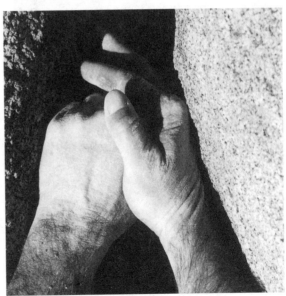

Stacked hand and fist Kevin Powell photos

Fists torqued tight, Nic Taylor punches through Twilight Zone *(5.10d), Yosemite Valley.* George Meyers photo

Two routines can drastically hasten your learning curve, if you're willing to put in the work. First, you must log enough crack time to feel comfortable with the moderate grades, perhaps up to 5.9. Most dedicated climbers can accomplish this in a year. Once you are fluent with the fundamentals, spend a day or two each month trying to climb as many cracks as you can in one day. Obviously you need to climb at an area featuring crack climbs, hopefully ones that are centrally located. This practice caught on at Joshua Tree National Monument in the late 1970s, and quite a few climbers joined the "Century Club," having bagged at least a hundred crack climbs in one day. Another drill, one especially effective as you broach the upper grades, is to first lead a difficult crack, then drop down on toprope and lap it to failure. Take breaks. Rest and eat. Even leave and come back. It's amazing how what seemed like death on the lead will (if you're in shape) seem pretty casual after a few laps. When I used to frequent Yosemite, I must have climbed *Butterballs* and the last pitch of *New Dimensions,* two notorious 5.11 cracks, at least fifty times apiece, mostly on toprope. The technique and confidence I picked up doing this was invaluable. By normal climbing standards I have very large fingers, and through doing laps on these test pieces, I learned to compensate for finger size, discovering easier, or at least possible, ways of doing things. I rarely bothered pulling this drill on hand or fist cracks because few of these ever gave me pause. Do the laps on that size that gives you fits and improve by leaps and bounds.

Off-Width Cracks

Off-width, or off-sized, cracks are too wide for fist jamming and too narrow for anything but the knee, if that. The extreme off-width crack is far and away the most feared prospect in all of climbing. There is simply no easy means to climb off-widths, and success often involves more grunting and cursing than finesse and elegance because very few climbers have taken time to master this, the most awkward technique of all. The reasons are several. Few climbing areas feature many off-width cracks, and if you can't practice, you'll never master them. The technique is

a 5.9 fist crack. Clearly, the strength is there, but not the craft. Without practice you cannot develop a feel for the jams—what works best, how to quickly set reliable jams, plus getting to where all the countless body nuances become second nature, allowing you to ascend a stern crack with the liquid flow of a waterfall rolling in reverse. Again, crack climbing is mostly about feel, learning how to place your fingers and hands in ways that allow you the most efficient, secure, natural, and least painful jams that a given crack affords. In face climbing, a keen novice can often make valiant strides, sometimes skipping entire grades. Not so with crack climbing. Proficiency comes from rote learning, which means mileage. No climber masters cracks without his share of pain and failures, and without logging many miles up cracks.

Amos and Coco #9:
Arm Bars, Pink Tights, and Brazen Hussies

Day three of the intermediate seminar moved to off-width cracks, chimneys, and flares. Instructor Jules Pinkus, that rugged veteran of El Capitan and K2, first strung a toprope on an 80-degree, off-width crack and demonstrated the foot stacks and various arm bar configurations as he climbed the 50-foot pitch. Jules made it look like so much cheesecake, but the first student up the crack—a svelte and brassy triathlete named Rose—found the crack a rude affair, and she barely made it 10 feet before falling back onto the rope.

After Jules offered a little coaching, Rose had another go, and she quickly learned to get her feet stacked and knee lodged securely, allowing her lower body to form an adequate platform for her upper torso. But she couldn't quite get the arm bar figured and came down after 15 feet.

Jules changed strategies. He had everyone stand at the bottom of the 6-inch-wide crack and work on arranging their arm bars until they learned how to brace the inside arm in the crack while pulling on the lip of the crack with the outside hand and arm. It felt awkward at first, less so after a few minutes; but when the students tied into the rope and had to put the moves together, combining both upper and lower body movements, everyone struggled. Amos heaved so hard with his outside hand he almost opened the crack up a few more inches, and Coco rasped the knee off her pink tights. By noon, however, all the students had made several trips up the crack. Things were starting to fall into place.

"Like any other sport, mastery on off-widths comes only with practice," said instructor Jules Pinkus. "If you think otherwise, you're selling climbing short." "I did that with yoga and paid the price," said Amos. "Took me several months to squeeze the magic out of that one." "Listen to him," laughed Coco. "Tarzan can finally touch his toes and now he's talking like Yogananda." "Who?" asked the firefighter.

That afternoon, Jules arranged a toprope on a dark and steep chimney. Compared to the counterintuitive moves involved in climbing the off-width crack, the students found the chimney much to their liking and comparatively easy. With his back pressed against one wall and his hands and feet jack-knifing off both walls, Amos made quick work of the chimney, marveling at how he could take his hands off the wall and wave and make faces at Coco belaying below. "Quit showing off, you big galoot," she said. "Big fella looks pretty solid up there," Rose put in, glancing up at Amos gracefully ratcheting up the chimney. Coco had noticed Rose eyeballing Amos throughout the day and tried to ignore the intrusion.

Soon Coco was moving up the chimney as Amos belayed. She found the work at once strenuous but fun and gleefully bounded out from the wall as Amos lowered her off. At the base, Rose was busy flirting with Amos, variously placing her hands on his shoulders and chest to emphasize a point. Coco flushed and said, "Quit pawing him, you brazen hussy!" Amos tried to draw Coco aside but she'd hear none of his guff and kept after Rose. Finally Amos dragged her off, and after walking a minute into the forest Coco said, "What?!"

"Chimneying up that thing, well," Amos paused, "well you wore clean through them leotards, creampuff," said Amos. "Thought you might want to know that." Coco reached back and felt her bare bottom. "If we was alone I'd let it slide 'cause I'm like that," said Amos. "But I don't want that Pinkus getting i-d-eers." Then they both broke out laughing.

Late that afternoon Jules Pinkus rigged a rope over a vertical lie-back that soared into the sky some 120 feet and looked hard and intimidating. Amos powered up the climb with polished skill, utilizing available footholds and, when those ran out, flushing his boots off the polished wall and motoring to the next good foothold. Coco made the long lieback look easy, attributing her success to her strength training, to which Amos gave her full credit. The contrasting styles were apparent—Amos basically relying on power and coy footwork, Coco using pace, flexibility, balance, and power only when needed. Both climbers played toward their strengths, witnessed in their mutual styles. The key to improving, said Jules Pinkus, was to work on your weaknesses. To that end, he had Coco try and climb the whole thing without pausing, using pure power; while Amos was asked to climb very slowly, stemming whenever possible, and to use as little force as possible. Both climbers found the drill enlightening and now had something to shoot for on future expeditions. And as Jules knew, there would be many more climbing trips for this duo.

Max Plank arm-barring up a flaring off-width crack at Joshua Tree National Monument. Kevin Powell photo

thinner cracks, the nasty off-widths were gratefully overlooked, and today, most climbers simply avoid the technique because they lack the requisite experience for the climb to be anything but a pitched battle. If one of the international climbing competitions were staged on an overhanging, 5.13 off-width, we'd probably see contestants trying to paw up the bald face on either side of the crack.

The most arduous off-widths are about 4 inches wide, where you cannot get your knee in. Upward progress involves locking off the upper body, moving the legs up, locking them off, and then jackknifing the upper body back up. Repeated ad nauseam, this sequence makes the Eight Labors of Hercules seem like raking leaves.

You must first decide whether to climb with your left or right side in—and forget about changing sides halfway up. In a vertical crack, if the gash is offset, you will probably climb with your back against the raised edge, which may provide a little extra leverage, allowing you to stem outside of the crack. If the crack edges are uniform, or flush, you find what side of the crack has the best edge and/or footholds. While the outside arm grips the outside edge, the inside arm is locked inside the crack. In thin off-sized cracks (normally 4-inch and 5-inch), the back of the upper arm is held in place by pushing the palm against the opposite side—the classic "arm bar." The outside arm can add torque by pulling out on the crack's edge. For optimum leverage, place the arm bar diagonally down and away from the shoulder. This kicks in the front deltoid and upper chest muscles, and adds to the fulcrum effect of the arm bar. If the crack won't accept your knee, jam your inside foot (and if necessary your calf), usually by torquing it horizontally. If the crack is slightly larger than the width of the foot, torque the foot diagonally across the crack so the toe jams against one side of the crack and the heel wedges against the other side to create opposition across the crack. The heel is placed on the side of the arm bar.

Usually it's best to use the outer foot to propel the body upward, while the inside leg and arm stabilize the body. Make sure to use any edges or stem holds for the outside leg. Once the feet are set, the

more battle than dance, and in an era of tri-colored tattoos and diamond belly rings, off-width cracks are about as popular as walking barefoot in the snow. History also plays a part in the disdain climbers have for off-width stuff. In the early 1960s, most of America's greatest climbs were in Yosemite Valley, and most featured off-width climbing. When up-and-coming climbers wanted to bag the big-name routes, they had no choice but to tackle these off-width test pieces. The first few encounters were desperate, thrashing, villainous affairs; but they stuck to it, and one long summer was usually enough to master the technique. As the newer generations turned toward

Bruce Bailey sets an arm lock on the rugged Twilight Zone (5.10d), in Yosemite. Note the foot bridged out right and the mammoth chock slotted above his head. John Sherman photo

outside hand moves up and pulls hard against the lip of the crack, then the arm bar is quickly shuffled up and locked off, usually level with, or just beneath, the outside hand. Then the process is repeated. If the crack is overhanging and you can't get the knee in, the hardest part is moving the arm bar up. Sometimes this is only possible with little dynamic hops, shuffling the arm bar up and quickly locking it before you pitch out backwards.

Once the crack opens up enough to get a knee inside, the technique is much more manageable. While the jackknife motion may still be necessary to move your upper body, your lower body can now be securely jammed. The inside leg is in a vertical version of the arm bar, with hip, thigh, knee, heel, and toe all torqued and counterpressuring. Both the outside and inside foot should be in a heel-toe jam. Keep the toes lower than the heel, which allows the toes to be smeared for better purchase. The outside leg is usually set above the inside leg, with the knee pointed up and out of the crack. If you are either wafer thin or remarkably flexible, or if the crack opens up enough, the arm bar can be replaced with the arm lock, or "chicken wing." Much like the arm bar, you simply fold the forearm back and palm against the opposite side of the crack. If the crack is tight, your elbow will point into the crack; with a slightly wider crack, the elbow will be pointing nearly straight up, with the triceps resting against the rear crack wall. Many times, the natural muscular tension in your arms and a little upper body English will make the arm lock so snug it's hard to even move it. Some climbers swear by the arm lock and use it whenever possible; others only use it to augment the arm bar, and some find it too awkward and only use it to rest. Some don't use it at all. When the crack widens too much to use the heel-toe jam, you must start foot stacking, the most called-upon stack being the "T-bar."

The best sequence of when to move what is a matter of what the crack dictates, and what process works best for you. Experience is the best and only teacher, but remember the following points. Resist the natural temptation of sticking your body deep into the crack. It may feel more secure, but it inhibits

The T-bar

your mobility. So stay outside of the crack as much as possible. And don't thrash (advice that, to the beginner, is virtually impossible to follow). Set each limb solidly, and keep it locked as the others shuffle up. Don't rush, pace yourself, rely on small movements rather than drastic lunging, and never skip the chance to rest. Always scan for face holds inside or outside the crack. Often a couple of face holds will get you around the nastiest part of an off-width.

Wear sufficient clothing to protect against the inevitable scrapes. Remember that most off-widths are rated for people who know exactly what they are doing. As a beginner you may find even a moderate off-width climb the hardest thing you've ever done. Most climbers do. After you have a few under your harness, go back and see what a huge difference experience and technique make. Lastly, this writing will make little sense till you have checked the illustrations and thrashed up a few off-width climbs. After that, return and reread this, and it will make a whole lot more sense.

Hand Stacking

Also known as "Leavittation" (after Randolph Leavitt, pioneer of this technique), hand stacking supplants the strenuous arm bar with a variety of two-handed jamming configurations: fist against hand, hand against hand, fist against fist. This technique should work anywhere that hands can be stacked and the lower body can at least momentarily support the whole body via knee jams and/or calf locks. Leavittation is particularly efficient on straight-in, off-width cracks so desperate or overhanging that a pure arm bar is prohibitive, if not impossible. Only practice can show you what kinds of hand stacks work—there are no rules or "best jam" guidelines. It's the jammed legs that are the real trick.

The basic sequence: Find a hand stack, then a knee lock as high as possible below the hand stack. This "active" leg will soon bear your full bulk, so work it in as securely as possible. The "passive" leg is heel-toe jamming below and is mainly a balance point. You must then release the hand stack and es-

tablish another above, the high knee jam supporting your weight while your abdominals keep you upright. Then repeat the process.

The knee lock is key, though tough to master, and is usually where even experienced climbers fail with Leavittation. The secret is to keep it as high as possible. For optimum torque, once your knee is completely inside the crack, bend it back so it locks and allows you to bring your foot back out of the crack. Your foot is in turn placed against the outside of the crack, supplying a sort of brace effect that allows you to let go with both hands and set up the next hand stack.

A straight-in crack allows a choice for the active, or jammed, knee; the leaning crack does not. If the crack leans right, jam the left knee; if left, jam the right one. Leavittation is a very advanced technique that takes practice to even understand. Its normal application is on off-width cracks at the very top of the scale and in a fairly narrow range of size, though the technique is occasionally fitting on moderate routes and in cracks that fluctuate between sizes.

Squeeze Chimneys and Flares

By definition, any crack too wide to heel-toe jam but only wide enough to barely accept the body is a squeeze chimney. They may be easy to slide into, but usually they are strenuous and almost claustrophobic to ascend. A bottoming, or shallow, squeeze chimney is a flare. Once it is too wide to use an arm lock, or "chicken wing," it becomes a chimney. These techniques often overlap on a given climb, but we'll look at them separately to focus on the various methods of climbing these types of cracks.

Squeeze chimneys are climbed using off-width techniques with a few additional antics and variations. The arm lock is the standby for the arms, though a wide arm bar and even an inverted arm bar (elbow higher than the palm) is often used. You can typically get inside a squeeze chimney, so the arm lock and arm bar variants can be used with both arms. The normal configuration sees the arm lock for the inside arm and the inverted arm position (or "chicken wing") for the outside arm. Sometimes, both arms are using the inverted arm bar.

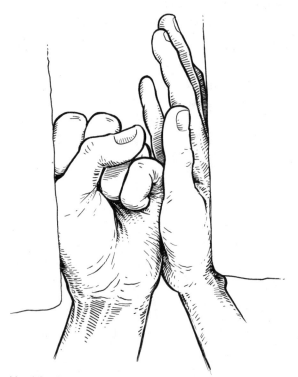

Hand Stacking

The leader jams, her shadow liebacks. Susan Ward flashes Scar Face, Canyonlands, Utah.

Bill Hatcher photo

With knees, chest and hands pressing off one wall, and arse, elbows and back thrust against the other, Yosemite legend Jim Donini is a study in counter-pressuring as he chugs up the ancient gullet of Ahab (5.10a), Yosemite, California.

George Meyers photo

Foot stacking (the T-bar) should be used if at all possible. If the chimney is too wide, press both knees against the front wall, with both feet torqued flat against the back wall. The opposing pressures between knees and feet keep the lower body in place. Like off-width cracks, the lower and upper body move up alternately.

Many squeeze chimneys are so slim you have to exhale to move up. Most chimneys narrow the farther you enter them, so fight the urge to work

deeper—albeit more securely—into the bowels of the crack, and instead stay toward the outside, where movement is easier. You'll probably find that staying lodged is easy, but moving up is tough duty. Just climb slowly, work it out, and never get frantic—which is sage advice no novice can ever seem to follow.

Flares are wide enough to get inside, but too shallow to do so very far. They can be nasty undertakings, very strenuous and insecure, and technical riddles. At once grueling and confounding, grim flares are perhaps the most technical climbs of all. Because every flare is a little different, they defy much generic explanation. Still, almost every flare requires the inside arm to be arm locking, and often the purchase of elbow and palm is marginal. The outside hand needs to exploit any handhold, or at least vigorously palm off the flare to augment the arm lock. The feet are bridging—inside foot backstepping the back wall, outside foot pressing off any footholds available, or simply frictioning flat against the face. Sometimes you alternate these tasks between the outside and inside feet. The outside foot is key, for it presses the arse and back against the back wall, so the decision on which way to face often depends on where the footholds are. Many times you won't know which way to face until you try (though with notorious flares, there is usually a traditional direction climbers face: toward the wall or with their backs to the wall). If the flare is extremely shallow, very steep, and devoid of footholds, you're looking at a nasty piece of work, where anything goes.

Arduous flares, especially on granite (or any polished rock), are a handful even for experts steeped in the work. We tend to think that overhanging face climbs, with their stratospheric ratings, are the last word in technical labor, but they have nothing over the nasty flares. Though dreary flares often require considerable overall strength, you cannot simply muscle them because the purchase of the various arm locks and foot stacks are ever so marginal. Protection is often lacking, rests are few, and five moves might be required to move a few precious feet. The good news is that once you acquire a feel for the work, you have the technique for life and don't have to continuously work at keeping your edge, as you do with face climbing. But gaining that technique in the first place is, for most climbers, so difficult and frustrating that many don't bother at all. The drawback with this is that many of the great classics require fluency with this technique, and if you're ever interested in establishing big new routes, what will you do when you encounter a grisly flare?

Chimneys

When cracks widen enough so that they are easily entered, they may lose some degree of security, but they are usually much easier to climb. Knee chimneys are just that: Bridging is done between knees and back, and different sizes are accommodated by flaring the knees to varying degrees. Movement is a ratcheting affair, with the arm usually in the inverted arm bar position. Knee chimneys are usually secure. Knee pads can prevent hateful bruises (and pain) to the kneecaps, and a long-sleeved shirt will protect the shoulders.

When the chimney is wider than the distance between your knee and your foot, you push your feet against one wall and your back against the other. To move up, one foot back-steps off the back wall so your legs form a bridge via opposing pressures. The hands are either pressing off the far wall or bridged between both walls, like the feet. In either case, the

Rest position in a wide chimney—feet and legs pressing the butt and back against the opposite wall

To move up, one leg comes back, counterpressures off the opposite leg, the hands do the same, and the torso scissors up. Repeat. Kevin Powell photos

back is released and the legs extended; the torso moves up and the back is again pressed against the back wall. Opposing pressures between hands and back allow the feet to either shuffle up or to exchange positions—front foot now back-stepping, back foot now pressing off the far wall. Always let the legs do the pushing. Foot-back chimneys should never be strenuous for the arms.

If the chimney is wider than the distance between your hips and feet, you can "bridge" it using one hand and one foot on each wall, each limb pressing directly out. If your purchase is attained by pure friction, this is sketchy work, so keep an eye peeled for any footholds or shelves to bridge off of.

In chimneys too big to bridge, it is theoretically possible to use the alarming full body stem: Lodge yourself dead horizontal, facing straight down, with both feet on one wall and both hands on the other—like a clothes rack in a closet. Most expert climbers have done this for a couple of moves somewhere. I've heard climbers claim they had done this on long routes, up vertical shafts for hundreds of feet, and I don't believe a word of it. I can't imagine not falling if you had to do the "clothes rack" for more than a few feet. Don't believe everything you hear. And if something sounds absurd, it probably is.

Liebacking

"Hanging on for dear life" is often the description given for the full-blown, all-out lieback. Fortunately, few liebacks are all-out, but most are athletic and strenuous. Liebacking is perhaps the most exhilarating technique (outside of roofs and dynamics) in the climbing game. You can span amazing sections of rock. It's also the quickest way to find hell in a handbasket for, owing to the great opposing pressures, if your hands fail you fire off like you're spring-loaded. In its pure form, the technique is used to climb arêtes, cracks in right-angled corners, or cracks that are too shallow for jamming. In its partial form, anytime you lean off a hold you are liebacking, for you are lying back off the face hold, the jug, the edge of the crack, or whatever your hands are on. It's a means to use holds that are other than simple horizontal edges.

The basic motion is pulling with your hands and pushing with your feet, one in opposition to the other. A typical lieback will find your side flush against the wall. Your hands are clasping the near edge of the crack, and you are liebacking off them. Your feet either are pressing against the crack's far edge, balanced on small holds, vigorously pushing off a corner's far wall, or maybe even jammed in the crack. There are many quasi forms of liebacking, but all involve the upper torso leaning off to one side and the arms pulling to create opposing pressure against the feet.

The purest and most typical lieback occurs on a flake leaning against the wall or in a crack in a ninety-degree corner—a dihedral, or "open book." Here, your hands are pulling directly out, and your feet are pushing the opposite way, directly against the face or far wall. Since the technique is strenuous, try to keep the arms straight, which again lets the skeletal system, rather than the muscles, absorb at least some of the strain. Many times it is possible and desirable to leapfrog the hands, one over the other, but often the top hand will remain on top throughout, with the lower hand shuffling up to it, and then the top hand reaching above. On steep liebacks, you'll never want the hands to lose contact with the liebacked edge, so the hands are slid up. Also, leapfrogging your limbs can sometimes get you crossed up, throwing your balance out of whack. Try and keep your feet as low as possible, using any footholds. The closer your feet are to your hands, the more strenuous the lieback becomes. Of course, the feet stick best when they are kept close to the hands, as most of your weight is counterpressuring off the soles of your boots. However, that same weight is also taxing the daylights out of your fingers and guns. It is much less strenuous with the feet lower, but with the decreased pressure, the feet will skid off much easier, so watch out. There is a fine line—often a matter of a half inch—between just right and too low.

The full-blown, or "Frankenstein," lieback is most often found in a steep or overhanging corner. The crack's edge might be rounded or the crack is so thin it will accept only fingertips. The opposite

To the wonder of all who have tried to follow, Ron Kauk smears, liebacks, and miraculously stays pasted to Magic Line *(5.14b), Yosemite, California.*   Jim Thornburg photo

Now what? One small move at a time, Andy Petefish ratchets up a flared dihedral on Devil's Tower, Wyoming.
Bill Hatcher photo

wall may be overhung, slanting away and smooth as glass. So your feet gain purchase only through the friction of direct pressure. The Frankenstein lieback entails drawing your feet up by your hands and "swinging" into the all-out, liebacking posture. The problem is, not only is this extremely strenuous, but there's often the tendency to swing completely out, like a door opening on its hinges. This "barn door" effect can be countered either by increasing the torque to both hands and feet (which makes things more strenuous still), or by bridging the outside foot out and pushing obliquely off the far wall, hoping to stall the swing and regain equilibrium. Sometimes you must momentarily palm off the opposite wall to halt the swing. Sometimes it is possible to jam the inside foot in the crack, keeping the other foot stemmed wide to provide a hinge-proof base. If

you're fortunate, the opposite wall will be peppered with big footholds. If not, it's you and Frank all the way.

Most liebacks require a clever mix of all these techniques; when to use what is fairly intuitive once you've swung into the lieback. Your body responds automatically to changes in equilibrium and variations in angle. As much as you can, strive to keep the arms straight. Feel the edge of the lieback as much as possible, and crank off the sharpest, most defined spot. Look for any stem or rest holds, but don't stop if it's more strenuous than carrying on. Climb aggressively, and don't hang about looking for footholds that aren't readily apparent. The exhortation "go for it!" was invented for the climber swinging into a lieback. Once committed, don't hesitate: Power over it quickly.

Stemming

"Stemming," or bridging, normally occurs in right-angled or oblique corners, where the crack is non-existent or so thin as to be of little value. Many times it is necessary when the crack momentarily pinches down. Even when the crack is good, your lower body may stem the whole way. In any case, stemming is essentially face climbing in a corner.

Many difficult climbs involve stemming, and the extreme stemming problem can require creative sequences and improbable, marginal counterpressures. Consider the stemming corner as an ultra-flared chimney. In its pure form, the feet are pasted on opposite walls, perhaps frictioning, maybe back-stepping and smearing on footholds, but always counterpressuring against themselves and/or the hands. The hands may also be cross-pressuring, palming off the slightest irregularities, or pawing holds. Essentially, your body is like a spring lodged between two sloping walls. The only thing keeping the spring in place is the purchase at both ends, and the tension between. Moving the spring up, then, is the hard part, for this requires the tension to go lax, at least momentarily—yet it never can. Usually it's the diagonal pressure of one hand and one foot that keeps the climber in place, and the climber alternates this bridge in moving up. This can involve a dozen little moves to gain even a meter of upward progress. Sometimes you may actually chimney the corner, back against one wall, feet smearing off the other. You may back-step with one shoe, edge with the other, palm with one hand, and mantle with the other. The possibilities are endless. Flexibility, balance, and the ability to exploit any and all features are a stemmer's best tools. For some reason many climbers forget to breathe when stemming. This can not only make things more strenuous but can freeze you up after only a few body lengths. Staying fluid and loose is key to this technique.

As a final note, I mentioned earlier in the chapter that once you learn jamming technique, you need not relearn it. Crack climbing, however, is a matter of feel, and you can lose that feel if you haven't climbed cracks in a while. The intuitive, no-thinking movement that earmarks great crack climbers is attained from familiarity. If you're out of crack climbing form, take a few days to get dialed back in, and the feel will quickly return.

Protecting with Tape

Perfect technique does not eliminate hand abrasions altogether. Some cracks are lined with crystals; others require awkward, shallow jamming, notorious for shredding even expert hands; and overhanging fist cracks are almost always good for a few "gobies." A popular solution is taping. There are dozens of taping patterns, none so good to preclude all others, but certain tips apply to all taping methods.

First, remove hair from your hands and wrists (and the palms, too, should you have any there). Shaving will work, but singeing the hair off with a low-level flame is even better. The tape will adhere well only if you apply a chemical taping base, such as tincture of benzoin or Cramer's Tuf-skin, both available at sporting goods stores (although many climbers forego this step). Apply the taping base only where the tape will go, otherwise the bald areas will collect dirt and the skin will feel greasy. Also, don't use waterproof tape, only cloth, or coaches, tape (commonly available in 1-inch width).

Following the procedure outlined in the photos, start with half-inch strips, pinched at the center, that loop the base of the fingers. Next, bind these to the wrist. Finally, should extra reinforcement be necessary, apply selected lateral strips to tie the finger strips together. As you tape, flex the hand and wrist to stretch the skin, otherwise the tape will limit hand expansion and decrease jamming force. Tape loosely, especially around the wrist. Tight taping cuts circulation and hinders flexibility. Should you already have some gobies, place a small piece of tape upside down over the abrasion to avoid ripping the scab off and losing your mind when you yank the tape off.

Crack gloves are available and they seem to work great. Fingerless, sheathed with an ultrathin layer of sticky rubber, and secured round the wrist with a Velcro strip, these gloves are required tackle for doctors, dentists, and other professionals who cannot afford abrasions.

Multiple parties mount the laser-cut fissures on Devil's Tower, Wyoming. Bill Hatcher photo

CHAPTER 4

Ropes, Anchors, and Belays

We have reviewed the salient points of physically climbing rock. The psychology and strategy of putting it all together, in conjunction with the process of safe rope management, can be done only after we have a working knowledge of equipment.

No climber ever gets "honed" without falling, and the falling climber is quickly killed without a solid, dependable protection system. The protection system combines bombproof anchors, ropes, connecting links, and alert partners to provide a sort of safety net that, in the event of a fall, keeps him from hitting the ground. When a layman sees a climber lashed to the cliff, all the odd-looking widgets and knots and whatnot appear complicated enough to vex Solomon. Actually, the system is quite simple once you understand what the gear is and how it all works.

We see the climber moving up the dark cliff, secured by a rope and partner above. Who got that line up there? Somebody had to go first, and had he fallen, he would have died a horrible death—right? Wrong. The whole point of the rope and the attending gear, along with the hundred years that went into refining both technique and equipment, is to safeguard the climbers in the event of a fall. Rock climbing is not the pastime of nihilists or madmen, at least not in the mainstream, and when an ace climber starts an extreme climb at the limit of his ability, it is likely he will fall, perhaps dozens of times. And he doesn't expect to get hurt. When the beginner starts up her first climb, the aim is entirely different than that of the ace. She is not looking to push her limits, rather to slowly and comfortably learn how to move over rock, and to bone up on what the gear is and how it is properly used. But for both the ace and the novice, the larger aim is to have fun, not to cheat death. Of course, both climbers can do so only if they are confident the safety system is fundamentally reliable. And it is.

In a nutshell: Two climbers are tied into their respective ends of a 150-foot or 165-foot rope (200-foot ropes are standard tackle at sport climbing areas). Starting from the ground, one climber secures (anchors) himself off to a tree or a big block, or perhaps arranges an anchor with some of his specialized gear fitted into a handy crack. In any case, the anchor is not what it should be unless it is fail-safe (meaning it cannot be wrenched loose no matter what happens on the cliffside). The climbers then double-check themselves and each other to make sure harnesses, knots, and anchors are properly arranged. Having decided on a particular passage, or "route," up the cliff—say a prominent crack—the other climber (the "leader") starts up, scaling the crack using hands and feet. The person on the ground (the "belayer") is meanwhile paying out the rope, using a technique or mechanical device that can stop the rope cold if need be.

Now the leader has gained a difficult section. She removes an appropriate piece of gear from her harness, places it in the crack, tugs it to get a good seating, clips a carabiner (snap link) through the gear, then clips her rope through the carabiner. The leader now has an anchor that "protects" her for the climbing just overhead. On sport climbs the anchor is usually a permanent bolt, drilled and set into the rock. Say she climbs 3 feet above the anchor and falls. The

Moccasins won't get it here! Mike Waugh and Mary Ann Kelley seek truce with Indian Giver (5.11), Joshua Tree, California. Kevin Powell photo

belayer checks the rope; the leader falls twice the distance she has climbed above the anchor, or 6 feet. Since the rope stretches, she might fall inches more, but the belayer, lashed to his anchor and holding the fall, doesn't budge. The leader gathers her wits and tries again.

A question: If the leader was only 3 feet above the anchor, why did she fall 6 feet plus the odd extra inches? First, for several reasons, the belayer cannot effectively take in the rope when the leader falls. His duty is to lock the rope off, so when the leader's weight comes onto the rope, the rope is held fast. If the leader is 3 feet above her anchor—or "protection"—she must first fall 3 feet to that protection. She still has 3 feet of slack out. So she falls 3 more feet, past the protection, for a total fall of 6 feet plus, depending on rope stretch. Hence the equation: The leader falls twice the distance above her last protection—and then some.

Carrying on, the leader places protection as she sees fit, always placing something before a difficult section. Sixty feet up the crack, she might have placed six or eight pieces of protection, depending on the difficulty and how secure she feels. Once the leader gains a convenient place to stop—say a ledge or a stout tree—she arranges an anchor that is absolutely fail-safe. In this case, that means an anchor strong enough that, no matter what the other climber does, no matter how far he falls, he cannot cause the anchor to fail or come out. Now it is the leader's turn to "belay," or to take the rope in, as the other climber, or "second," follows the "pitch," or rope length. As the second follows he removes all the protection that the leader placed, so it may be used on the next pitch. Since the belayer is taking up the rope as the second climbs up to her, the second can only fall as far as the rope stretches.

The amount a typical rope will stretch totally

Scott Milton claws up a slanting flute, Halong Bay, Vietnam. Bill Hatcher photo

Amos and Coco #10:
Absolutely Bombproof

Over a period of several months, and often one piece at a time, Amos and Coco purchased a decent collection of nuts, SLCDs, free biners, quickdraws, and slings. They learned that building a rack was something like furnishing a house; unless you're a tycoon, it is much more of a process than a one-shot deal. They saved a little here and sacrificed a little there and purchased gear as greenbacks allowed. Being partners, they didn't have to double up on stuff and could assemble, between them, a workable all-purpose rack without mortgaging their souls. It was from Coco, who had a thrifty streak, that Amos learned to scout for deals, and he saved $50 off the retail price by buying a discounted rope. Eventually they'd both want full racks, because even the tightest partners never always climb together, but the buddy system worked fine to get started.

After six months, the two climbers together had a rack that would allow them to go to most any area and tackle most any climb. The immediate task was to learn how to use the gear safely and efficiently. Aside from rigging a toprope at Mt. Gorgeous, the local practice crag, neither Amos nor Coco had any practical experience with gear placement, so they took a one-day seminar on equipment and anchors from that redoubtable mountaineer, Jules Pinkus.

Unlike the beginning and intermediate climbing seminars that Amos and Coco had taken, the accent of the gear and anchor seminar was not on climbing, but on gear placement and anchor systems, and the exercises were somewhat dry and painstaking. The payoff was that once they understood gear placement and could construct absolutely bombproof anchors—which is the foundation of all sane climbing, according to instructor Jules Pinkus—refinement would come through practice, and they could henceforth climb without the nagging doubt of possible system failure and certain death. In other words, gaining a solid working understanding about the gear and the nuances of arranging solid anchors could only enhance their climbing pleasure.

So for two days Amos and Coco practiced placing tapers and hexes and SLCDs, and constructing anchors of every imaginable design. All this work was carried out at ground level. Jules Pinkus convened the class at the start of a handful of centrally located climbs, and each student used the cracks at the start of these climbs to experiment with placing gear and, on the second day, to construct anchors. It was not exciting work, but absolutely essential for those students looking to start leading. Students would critique each other's placements and anchors; instructor Jules would do the same and demonstrate the pros and cons of various configurations. Amos was somewhat deft with things mechanical and took to setting anchors with ease. Coco had a nice touch with gear placement, and though not particularly mechanically minded, she too began to feel comfortable with the basics. To be sure, both Amos and Coco would continue to learn more about both placements and anchoring constructs, and would eventually develop an eye for what to do and where to do it and how to arrange things efficiently. Their initial anchor setups took nearly an hour, but by the end of the seminar, they both had the basic principles in hand. Amos declared himself ready for El Capitan, but Coco suggested that he might want to learn how to lead first before jumping on the Captain.

depends on the amount of rope that is "out." Body weight stretches a standard, dynamic climbing rope about 6 to 8 percent of the length in use (this ratio will increase slightly as the rope ages). In other words, say you are the second (following) on the rope and are presently 100 feet below the belayer overhead. If you fall, the rope could stretch as much as 8 feet, meaning you could fall 8 feet. This rarely happens, however, because rope stretch is reduced by the various frictions along the rope—namely, the assorted protection devices the leader has placed and through which the rope runs. Generally, though not always, the above scenario would result in the second falling only 2 or 3 feet. The point to remember: The more rope that is out (the distance separating the second from the leader), the longer the potential fall.

Once the second reaches the leader's anchor, or "belay," he in turn takes over the lead while the erstwhile leader continues belaying, and the process is repeated until the team finishes the route.

This is free climbing; note that the gear is not used for upward progress. The leader does not hang from the gear he places, rather he climbs using only hands and feet. In free climbing, the gear is used only to safeguard against a fall. The sport is to climb the rock using your own physical abilities. Rope and gear are what make the process sane and allow you to push your limits, saving your life should you fall off. Since falling has become an integral part of sport climbing, both the system and the gear are very reliable but, once again, it's all in how you use them, and the most fundamental item, the rope, is no good if you're not on it or it's not anchored.

The Rope

The rope is your lifeline, the primary piece of equipment to any climber. There is not a single serious climber whose life has not been saved by the rope many times over. Climbing ropes are extremely

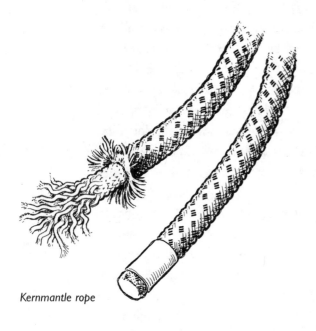

Kernmantle rope

good condition has no reason to break whatsoever, no matter how severe a fall you may log. But the fact that many ropes have been severed by a sharp edge, and dozens killed in the process, cannot be minimized. That more climbers don't perish from severed ropes is not a testament to the false conclusion that this cannot and will not happen, rather it speaks of climbers' heightened caution in that regard. In short, when there are sharp edges about, when there is anything in your orbit that can possibly cut into the line, beware!

All modern climbing ropes are "kernmantle" (or jacketed-core), comprised of a woven braided nylon sheath over a braided, plied core. (This refers to loose springlike bundles. Think Slinky.) Prior to 1970, one viable alternative to kernmantle was "goldline," a nylon rope of twisted, or hawser-laid, construction, where three or four main strands were twisted around each other. Though goldline handled poorly and stretched like a rubber band, it was plenty strong, and at half the price of kernmantle, it was widely popular. For several reasons, goldline became a forgotten commodity, and though many of America's most noted climbs were accomplished on goldline, I haven't seen anyone climbing on one since the early 1970s.

The standard dimensions of a modern climbing rope are 50, 55, and 60 meters (165, 185, and 200 feet, respectively) in length, and 10, 10.2, 10.5, or 11 mm in diameter. There are 8 to 9 mm ropes that are intended to be used as twin and double ropes (see chapter 5: The Art of Leading). The 55-meter ropes are basically nonexistent these days. You might still find a few lines of that length in Canadian ice climbing circles, but probably nowhere else. The new long ropes presently used by many sport climbers are 70 meters (230 feet). The new diameters for the ultra-skinny single rope range from 9.4 to 9.6 mm.

For decades, a 150-foot rope was the standard. You can still purchase one of this length, but why? Most routes have been engineered to require a 165-foot rope, and ropes in the 185- to 200-foot range will get you down in fewer rappels. At many popular sport climbing areas, where 95 percent of the routes are less than 100 feet, a 200-foot rope allows

dependable. Modern ropes have evolved a long way from the horsehair cords of the Carthaginians and from the dicey hemp lines the climbing pioneers used around Zermatt and other alpine villages, where accounts of ropes snapping were many and tragic. Those early hemp ropes were replaced, first by flax, then with cotton varieties from European-grown fibers. Philippine manila and sisal from Mexico in turn succeeded these, and by World War II, a dense, three-strand "balloon" manila and a similar four-strand yachting rope (white line) were the only choices for an alpinist. During the war, Arnold Wexler of the U.S. Bureau of Standards concluded that for strength, elasticity, and durability, nylon was superior to all natural blends. Since 1945, all viable climbing ropes have been fashioned from nylon, or perlon, a continental trade name for a plastic similar to nylon.

Though there are isolated cases of ropes being cut over sharp edges or chopped by rock fall, a modern climbing rope has never been known to simply break from the impact of a fall. Not in the United States, not in Europe, not anywhere. There is so much overkill built into the system that a rope in

you to lead the climb, clip the top anchor, and lower back to the ground. Hence, a 200-footer, or the emerging favorite, 230 feet, is often the preferred length for sport climbing.

Experts have conducted exhaustive studies on the various qualities of kernmantle ropes and have presented complicated graphs and formulas that seem impossible to understand. All the rare terminology and physics actually pertains to basic concepts, easily understood if simply explained.

The easiest way to understand the mechanics of a climbing rope is to think of a Slinky. When you twist steel, you turn it into a spring. Nylon works the same way. If you tie an object to a Slinky and drop it, the Slinky will stretch until it takes up the load, then contract. Climbing ropes, just like Slinkys, lose their capacity to recover their elongation (return to their original shape/form) after time and use. The harder the use, the faster a rope's dynamic qualities will be compromised. Of course, there are many tests and measurements that determine the capacities of a given rope, a technical science administered by the Union Internationale des Associations D'Alpinisme—UIAA—an international organization that sets minimum standards for commercially available rope. Rope manufacturers provide the UIAA findings and anything else they have been able to independently prove that might give them a marketing edge, but only a few specifications relate directly to performance.

The first relates to the number of falls sustained before the rope breaks in a UIAA-simulated drop test. In this drop test, they tie an eighty-kilogram iron block to one end of a 2.8-meter length of rope. The other end is secured to a fixed anchor, using 0.3 meters for the anchoring setup. They then raise the iron block 2.5 meters above the anchor point and drop it for a total free fall of 5 meters (a X2, or times two, fall). Common sense would tell us that a far longer fall would better gauge a rope's strength, but this is untrue. Kernmantle ropes have fantastic dynamic qualities, meaning they stretch when fallen on. Consequently, the longer the fall, the more rope there is "out" to absorb the dynamic energy generated by a falling climber. So generally, it's the short

falls, where the rope stretches comparatively little, that most stress the rope.

To recap: It is not the length of the fall that determines the impact, or the actual amount of stress that is placed on the cord. The impact force is determined by the ratio between the length of the fall and the length of the rope that arrests the fall. The equation reads: Fall factor equals distance fallen over length of rope. The maximum fall factor is two (X2), precisely the kind of fall the UIAA does in their lab tests. In the field this can occur, for example, when a leader has climbed 10 feet above a hanging belay (explained later) and has not placed any protection; he falls and is stopped that (10 feet) distance below the belay. Since he is 10 feet above the belay, he falls 10 feet to the belay and the same distance past it for a total distance of 20 feet, which is twice the distance of the rope that he had out (10 feet), resulting in a fall factor of two.

Experts all agree that, for many reasons, the UIAA test is more severe than any fall you could possibly take in the field. Technicians insist that the impact force during the first lab test fall (on an 11 mm rope) is equal to driving a truck at thirty miles per hour directly into a stone wall. This force comparison was worked up by Howard Wright, marketing director of Maxim Ropes. He "wanted to [find] a real world example of a similar force to the average impact force that you see reported for climbing ropes. I mean, just what the hell does 9kN *feel* like? So what I did was pull a random piece of 11 mm from the floor and run a UIAA drop test. The impact force was around 8kN or 1,800 pds/force. I did a little research and found crash test data that showed the driver would be subject to the same amount of force, 1,800 pds, if they crashed a Ford F-150 into a wall head-on at thirty miles per hour." Keep in mind that a rope must withstand five UIAA test drops to be approved.

Various manufacturers have gone on to make ropes they claim can withstand up to thirteen test falls, but since the UIAA approval means a rope is stronger than you'll ever need, the thirteen-fall figure is somewhat superfluous, though it may indicate improved durability of the rope in extreme uses. The original kernmantle ropes were approved if they held only two UIAA drops, yet in actual practice none of these ropes ever broke. Never broke on an actual climb, that is. In the lab, a two-fall rated rope broke after the third test fall! But since we don't climb, or fall, in the lab, you might ask: If a two-fall rope never broke in the field, why would I need a thirteen-fall rope? Because the thirteen-fall rope is more durable, that's why. In other words, the original two-fall ropes were amply strong, but tended to wear out faster than the newer models. And this is no small advance, since a rope can wear out in a flash if you're climbing on rough rock.

The shape a rope maintains, when in use, also plays a key role in that rope's durability. The rounder the rope—or more accurately, the more a rope holds its round shape—the better the rope wears because it presents less surface area and lower friction. The downside to a super round rope is that it's harder to tie knots into, has stiffer handling qualities, and has somewhat lower strength/performance when running over a severe edge (and holding a fall) because it concentrates the falling force over a rounder, and therefore smaller, area than a rope whose shape flattens when weighted over an edge. In short, the flatter the rope, the better severe edge performance due to more surface area to dissipate force. A looser weave in the rope also translates to suaver handling. It is more limber and can change shape somewhat, but this also increases the surface area; hence the line will wear out faster due to increased friction. Several European ropes are extremely soft (and extremely expensive), handle like a dream, and are a joy to use, but for today's fall-intensive sport climbing, they are the first lines to wear out.

The next spec is weight, which would be an important consideration if ropes of the same dimension differed much. Of the six leading rope manufacturers, the lightest 11 mm rope is seventy-two grams per meter; the heaviest, seventy-nine grams per meter; so weight is a negligible factor for ropes of the same diameter. If a climber is concerned about weight (a real concern on desperate free climbs), he will simply use a smaller diameter (and less durable) line.

"Static," or "working elongation," basically refers to how much a rope stretches when weighted with an eighty-kilogram iron block. The leading ropes vary little here. "Impact force elongation" (I.F.E.), how far the rope stretches when fallen on, is far more important but seldom listed in the statistics, probably because it requires very sophisticated equipment to measure. I.F.E. is a real consideration, since the longer a rope stretches, the farther you fall, which increases the likelihood of hitting something. Conversely, more stretch means less impact force on the line, so it's a trade-off. The available specs from most leading manufacturers vary from about 6 to 7 percent I.F.E. Negligible, you say? Maybe, but the difference might be 6 inches in a 40-foot fall; and as rope physicist Dennis Turvill has pointed out, "A fall 6 inches longer can mean the difference between a good bar story and a compound fracture." Hopefully, impact force elongation will soon be a required statistic for all ropes.

"Impact force" pertains to the degree of shock the body receives at the end of a fall, a crucial factor since a greater force means a more jarring, painful stop. The UIAA specifies that the maximum impact of force on the climber must be less than 2,640 pounds for a single rope. Different brands can vary as much as 25 percent, so some thought should be directed to this statistic.

Another factor is whether a rope has been treated with a waterproofing compound. Compounds differ among manufacturers. Some are paraffin-based and come off the rope quickly. The better coatings are silicone or various fluorochemicals, the latter being the best for durability. Though nothing can keep a rope dry in a deluge, tests prove that coated ropes are approximately 33 percent more abrasion-resistant than uncoated ropes. Also, coating greatly reduces the ability of the rope to absorb damaging ultraviolet rays; and for these two reasons, coatings do more for a rope's longevity than the number of falls they allegedly can sustain.

Different sheath characteristics—the tightness of the weave and whether the sheath, or "cover," moves much—directly affect how a rope handles. Sheath slippage is the result of core and cover balancing/stretching, not the core and cover shifting. The cover works like a Chinese finger lock, meaning it is not going to shift when loaded. Remember that the UIAA spec calls for less than 1 percent sheath slippage, which is less than 2 feet for a 60-meter rope. Whenever a little sheath creeps off the end of a rope (which happens), cut off the excess and reseal with a hot knife.

Ropes that are prone to excessive kinking, that are stiff and hold knots poorly, and that twist and spin a suspended climber, are really dastardly things to use. Unfortunately, it is difficult to determine a rope's handling characteristics (the rope's "hand") when it is brand new, and there is little objective information that honestly pegs these qualities. Moreover, a rope in the retail shop that handles like silk might prove to be a "corkscrew" once you have used it. The sheath might stiffen or soften up after only moderate use. Ultimately, a climber is left to review the available literature and experiment with other ropes, drawing conclusions accordingly. Fortunately, most of the ropes currently available work very well.

Since any UIAA-approved rope is stronger than you'll ever need, most climbers tend to buy the cheapest UIAA-approved rope they can find. The majority of climbers don't understand, or care, about all the attending statistics. The ideal rope would stretch little when weighted, have a low impact force, handle like a mink's pelt, weigh one pound, fit in your back pocket, and cost around $50. But no one rope is close to having all these characteristics. Ropes range in price from $130 to $200. Traditionally, most of the ropes sold in North America were imported from Europe. The popularity of sport climbing has, over the last fifteen years, spawned a plethora of American and Canadian manufacturers who fashion top-quality climbing ropes, usually at a lower price than the imported models.

Climbing ropes are both durable and fragile. Despite the astronomical tensile strength of kernmantle ropes, they are made of supple nylon, which is easily damaged when even slightly abused. Since you're hanging your all on the rope, you'll want to pay extremely close attention to the use and care of your lifeline.

Caring for Your Rope

Never step on the rope. Debris can work through the sheath to cut and abrade the core. Stepping on someone's rope is an extreme breach of decorum.

Never lend your rope to anyone. Never buy a used rope. They don't fetch much money, and there's probably a good reason why someone wants to deal it. It may have been used to tow a backhoe out of a snowdrift.

Protect your rope from unnecessary exposure to the sun; save for huge falls that result in sheath damage and careless abuses, U.V. rays are the single most destructive force your rope is exposed to, so the more time spent in sunlight, the faster it will deteriorate. Always store your rope in a cool, dry, shady place.

Contrary to common opinion, alcohol, gasoline and other hydrocarbon solvents do not affect nylon chemically; and though you should avoid exposing your rope to any foreign substance, a little gasoline is not disastrous to your rope. Battery acid and other corrosives spell instant death to your line, however.

A certain amount of grime is unavoidable. When the rope become obviously dirty, machine wash it in cold or warm water and mild soap. Use the delicate fabric setting and rinse it for two cycles. Avoid the dryer.

Instead, string it up in a shady place, or flake it out on a clean floor and let the water evaporate naturally, normally accomplished in a couple of days.

Periodically inspect the rope for frays and soft spots by folding the rope carefully between your fingers and working it from one end to the other.

Regarding a rope's life expectancy, the following general rules are worth considering. Retirement guidelines just issued by the UIAA give a modern rope ten years of life if it's used rarely or not at all. Traditionally, for normal weekend use, you chuck a rope after two years no matter how "good" it looks or feels. For multi-fall use, retire a rope after three months of constant use or up to a year of part-time use. Any rope suffering a long fall of great severity should be retired immediately. Howard Wright of Maxim Ropes nods to these rules but stresses that the primary criterion in determining a rope's condition "is accomplished through visual inspection (look for wear, cuts, discoloration, and chemical exposure) and tactile inspection (feeling for damage to the core, including lumps, twists, or breaks)." And beware of rope fattening. Remember that nylon absorbs water and will fatten. In short, the best retirement guidelines are visual inspection and feeling the line in your hands. And remember the Slinky metaphor: The more you use a rope, the less it stretches back to its original length and the less it is able to elongate and absorb energy.

A rope bag is an inexpensive and practical way of storing your rope. There's a lot of garbage rattling around the normal pack, car, or closet, and the rope bag protects your cord from it until the moment you start climbing; the rope is re-bagged once you're done. Some climbers use them to store the slack during a climb, but most will find this a bit much. In extreme instances—say, climbing just above a wind-whipped ocean—a rope fed out of a rope bag is a saving grace. For sport climbing, a rope bag (one that rolls out into a rope tarp) protects the rope from the dirt and makes it convenient to move the rope from route to route. Rope bags have been standard gear for more than a decade.

Webbing

Originally used to batten down gear on PT boats during World War II, nylon webbing (flat rope, or "tape") is an integral part of a climber's equipment. When tied into a loop (forming a "runner," or "sling"), its applications range from gear slings and

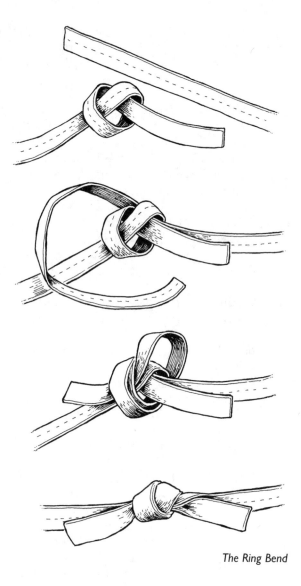

The Ring Bend

extensions for anchors to makeshift harnesses, all to be further explained. For now, understand that for fifth class climbing, webbing comes in four widths: $\frac{9}{16}$, $\frac{11}{16}$, 1, and 2 inches. Webbing is most often tubular (hollow inside) and is incredibly strong. Utilizing modern fiber technology, super strong Spectra webbing (as well as several less popular blends) is also available.

The most common use for webbing is for quickdraws and runners. Quickdraws come pre-sewn with a carabiner loop on each end, and are used to connect the rope to chocks or bolt anchors. Runners are tied or sewn in single loops (about 4 to 6 feet of 1-, ⅝-, or ⁹⁄₁₆-inch webbing) and are often carried over one shoulder and under the opposite arm. (This is often a problem, however, as the loop length in doubled slings is always changing and entangling with other slings and gear, one loop hanging down to your crotch, the other tight as a noose. Many prefer to triple the sling, tie it in a knot, and clip it onto the gear sling or side of their harness.) The length will vary according to your size. The runner should never be so long that the bottom hangs below your waist, where it can easily snag on the rock, or even on your foot during a high step. Runners and quickdraws are used somewhere on virtually every climb, and it is a common error not to have enough. Some sources advise you to carry upwards of a dozen runners, but such wisdom invariably comes from those hawking climbing gear. Most climbers consider ten to twelve quickdraws and four or five runners more than adequate for all but exceptional cases. On short (one pitch) sport climbs featuring bolt protection exclusively, the leader will usually count the bolts and take the exact number of quickdraws needed for the route.

Sewn slings and runners have long become the norm. The sewn joints dispense with the knot, which is sometimes a hindrance. Their disadvantage is that they cannot be untied and connected with other slings to form a king-sized runner should the need arise, and it will.

Be cautious when using any sewn gear. In their original state the stitching is stronger than the webbing. However, the stitching abrades with use, and the overall strength is then significantly reduced. It is a good practice to inspect any sewn webbing periodically. Most climbers carry a collection of both sewn and tied slings.

Webbing is generally sound until it becomes abraded or stiff to the touch from exposure to sunlight and general wear. If there's any doubt, pitch it. Though it's rare, old slings have broken. And never

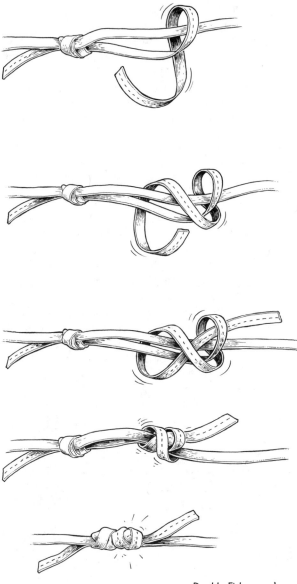

Double Fisherman's

use a sling you have found or fleeced off the crag. A sling is usually left because someone "bailed," or decided to retreat. The runner was secured to an anchor, the rope doubled through the runner, and down they went. To retrieve the rope, they had to pull it through the sling; and pulling even 50 feet of rope through a nylon sling can generate sufficient friction and heat to greatly diminish the strength of the webbing by melting the nylon. Visual inspection can tell you much—faded color or notable stiffness, for instance—but not all. Some climbers like to date their slings with a felt pen, and pitch them after one year of use. Treat your slings with the same respect you give your rope.

A ring bend or water knot has been the traditional knot to tie runners together. Nylon webbing is slippery, however, particularly when new, and it's not unheard of for the ring bend to loosen with time and come untied. A good practice with any gear is to routinely check your knots, especially the ring bend. A much more secure (albeit permanent and bulky) knot for both rope and webbing is the double fisherman's, or grapevine, knot. Though it is possible to untie this knot, it becomes increasingly tighter as the runner is weighted and stressed. Since the grapevine knot is a "cinch" knot—meaning the tighter you pull, the tighter it gets—just a few climbs

is usually enough to make this knot more or less impossible to untie. Should any knot prove difficult to untie, roll the knot quickly between your palms or under a foot. If the knot has been sucked down to the size of a pea, however, these methods won't work. Try some gentle taps with a smooth rock, which will often loosen the knot enough to get your fingers in. There is more on runners in Chapter 5: The Art of Leading.

Connecting the Climber to the Rope

For decades, climbers tied the rope directly around their waists. It was a simpler era. Climbers also avoided taking falls. The main disadvantage with the bowline-on-a-coil, the standard knot used years ago for tying in, is that when weighted or fallen on, it cut into a climber's vitals or worked up the rib cage like so many pick axes. Other disadvantages: The knot uses a lot of rope, is a hindrance on long pitches, and

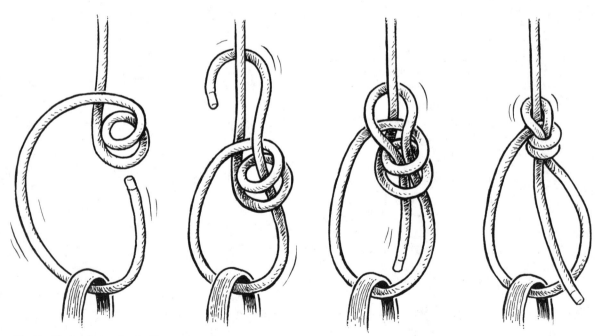

The Double Bowline with a half-hitch check knot

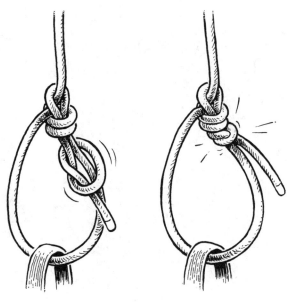

The Double Bowline

those reasons alone it is essential to know for emergency situations.

Swami Belt

Very occasionally you might see a climber from the 1970s climbing in a swami belt, which consists of four or five turns of wide webbing around the waist, secured with a ring bend. Like the bowline-on-a-coil, the swami has been entirely supplanted by the modern harness, and its only viable use is in a genuine pinch. Since a "pinch" will invariably arise sometime in your climbing career, you'll need to know how to tie a swami belt.

The wraps should be snug but not constricting. It takes some practice to tie the ring bend while keeping the swami snug. A loose swami belt is hazardous as it can (but will not always) creep up your torso, inhibiting breathing and doing the pick-axe number on the ribs. The basic swami was originally constructed from 1-inch webbing, but as soon as 2-inch webbing was available (circa 1974), everyone switched over to the wider, stronger, and more comfortable webbing. Tie the ring bend with a generous tail—plenty of extra webbing beyond the knot. Once tied, slide the knot around your back, occasionally inspecting it for peace of mind. Falling on a swami or simple bowline-on-a-coil is not necessarily as uncomfortable as it may sound; with the tightening rope the swami pulls up snugly underneath the rib cage. Hanging for very long on a simple

cannot, by definition, be used if there is a need to rappel or anchor to the cliff independently of the rope. Particularly as falling became an accepted side of the sport, and with the advent of tubular webbing and sewn harnesses, the bowline-on-a-coil became obsolete and is almost never seen. Still, it is absolutely secure and works dependably in a pinch. For

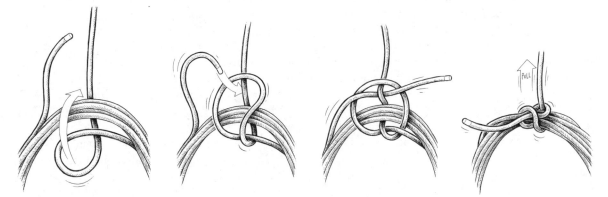

The Bowline-on-a-coil. Finish up with a half-hitch check knot as illustrated above.

swami is distinctly uncomfortable—even danger-ous—and is a poor and perilous substitute for the comfort and safety of a sewn harness.

The swami belt has no place in today's climbing world as anything but a stopgap device. Modern har-nesses are superior in every way, save strength (sev-eral wraps of 2-inch tubular webbing is good to beyond 20,000 pounds!). As an emergency measure, however, a swami is viable. I climbed more than twenty big walls with nothing more than a swami. If the angle is steep or overhanging, you'll need to fashion a pair of makeshift leg loops out of 1-inch-wide runners. You can only free hang from a swami for about twenty minutes, max, before passing out.

Harnesses

Anyone who plans to climb more than once or twice should invest in a quality, properly fitting sewn harness. A harness features a waist strap and leg loops that are sewn into one unit. The harness has come into its own only in the last twenty years. Though they've been around for thirty-plus years (and sev-eral models, even longer), early designs were often of such questionable quality that a popular instruction manual published a dozen years ago barely men-tioned them. The first batch were cumbersome, un-comfortable, and shoddily made, and they were absolutely hell on genitalia during a fall. Others tended to leave you hanging sideways, even upside down, after a fall. Present-day harnesses are feather-weight, stronger than necessary, and fit so well it's hard to remember you even have one on. There are hundreds to choose from, and with a little shopping it's easy to find the right one. Most manufacturers make several models—for alpine climbing, general rock climbing, and sport climbing; it is the latter two styles that are often the lightest and most comfort-able.

A good harness should be easy to put on. Dur-ing all-around use, it should be comfortable and not feature unnecessary buckles, joints, or pressure points that can abrade the climber like a burr under the saddle. A good fit is critical to the performance of a harness, but it might be impossible if your physique is even a little off the norm (although manufacturers

Sewn harness

currently make harnesses specifically for men, women, and kids). You might have to try on several to get the right one. A harness is a very personal, specialized piece of gear, so general craftsmanship should reflect this.

Gear racking loops are necessary, but if possible, avoid adjustable harnesses that are often overbuilt and feature superfluous buckles and doodads. Many harnesses have individual methods of threading the rope through them for the best tie-in knot. Like-wise, most harnesses have some safety procedure that, if neglected, render the harness potentially dan-gerous—a double pass-through buckle, for example. Read any instructions carefully, follow them to the letter, and always double-check your harness setup before you leave the ground. There is still another problem. Given the morning coffee, the ready can-teen, and the hiking and exertion, even the world-class climber will at some time yearn for bladder relief; and neither the brash nor the bashful find any glory in just "holding it." This presents little problem for your harnessed male. Most harnesses are pretty

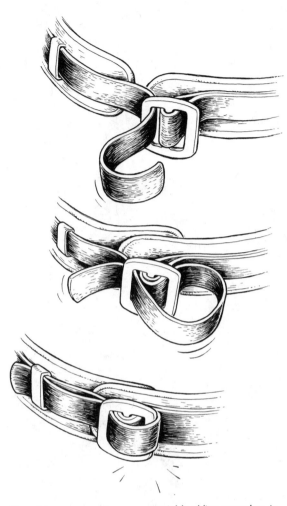

Many harnesses require some special buckling procedure in order for them to be secure, perhaps similar to the double pass-through illustrated here.

free in the front—aside from the tie-in knot—and a male's plumbing is readily deployed and can usually navigate these obstacles, even on a wall. For women, special harnesses are available where the leg loops can drop out while the waist belt stays fastened.

One other type of harness—the chest harness—bears mentioning, but in more than twenty-five years of climbing I have never seen anyone but kids using one, in either sport climbing or rescue work.

In sport climbing, the applications are few, if any, but there's no harm done if you have surplus cash and want to experiment with one. Supposedly, they are useful on exceptionally overhanging artificial routes, where you spend hours, or days, dangling upside down; or for rope soloing (a risky undertaking for experts only). Chest harnesses have usually been avoided, first because they generally are needless, and second because upper body mobility is crucial on difficult free climbs.

Tying One On

There are probably a dozen knots suitable for connecting the end of the rope to the swami or harness, but over the years the figure eight follow-through (Flemish Bend, or double figure eight) has become standard. And for good reason. The figure eight has one of the highest strengths of all climbing knots, it does not have a tendency to come untied, and it is easy to visually inspect. Like the majority of knots used in climbing (there are only about six primary knots, and another ten or so specialty or trick knots), the figure eight follow-through is a "cinch" knot: The tighter you pull, the tighter the knot becomes. Like all knots, the figure eight follow-through must be double-checked before relying on it.

Carabiners

Also known as biners (bean-ers), a carabiner is an aluminum alloy snap link used to connect various pieces of the climbing chain. They come in three basic designs: oval, D, and asymmetrical D. The D and asymmetrical D have the advantage of greater strength, they open easier when weighted (important in artificial climbing), and the rope flows easier through them. Many climbers always position any D or asymmetrical D carabiner so the gate opens down and away from the rock. That way the rope feeds through the bigger end. The oval can be positioned with gate up or down, but it's easier to clip the rope in if the gate opens down. Ovals are becoming less and less prominent, but they are still superior for racking wired tapers and for aid climbing. Many popular brands of quickdraws are sold as composite

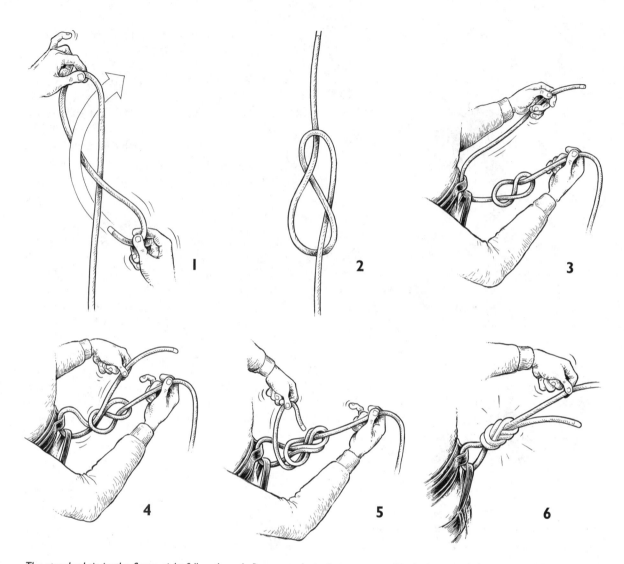

The standard tie-in: the figure eight follow-through. Be sure to loop the rope around both the waist belt or swami and the sling that bridges between the leg loops.

units, with two biners and a connecting draw. Another recent innovation is a biner that has dispensed with the solid gate and replaced it with a stiff, wire-like gate. This technology was fleeced from industry and has proven a boon as a lightweight, easy to clip alternative to the standard, solid gate models. Sometimes during a fall or when the gate is quickly loaded and unloaded, the gate on a standard biner can "flutter" and possibly open (very rare), and these new wire gate biners supposedly eliminate this remote possibility.

Each biner features a spring-loaded gate that opens inward, accepting rope or runner, and that snaps closed when the pressure is released from the gate. All carabiners are designed to be weighted along the major axis—lengthwise—and in this manner they are exceptionally strong, some with upwards of 5,000 pounds breaking strength. The strength of carabiners is usually marked somewhere on the gate, generally in kilo Newtons (kN). One kN is about equal to a big firefighter, roughly 220 pounds. Under no circumstances should the biner ever be set up so there is pressure pulling straight out on the gate, as the biner is then only as strong as the pin upon which the gate rotates—usually under 500 pounds. The load should always be along the long axis of the biner. Until the climbing explosion in the mid-1970s, it was common to find poorly machined biners in climbing stores, and you had to use discretion in buying anything but the name-brand biners. Commercial competition is now so fierce that a shoddy biner has little chance of making it to the shelves, but inspect them before buying just the same. The gate should have fluid action, should pivot strongly on the axis pin, and should mesh perfectly with the mouth of the biner. The finish should be smooth and burr free, and the inside radius of the carabiner must not be too small or it will severely stress the rope. The strength should be at least 4,400 pounds (20kN) with the gate closed, and 1,540 pounds (7kN) with the gate open.

Though durable, biners do wear out. Whenever the gate is bent askew, the spring action becomes soft or stiff, or the body becomes noticeably gouged, pitch it. Dropping a carabiner even 10 feet can result in invisible fatigue cracks that greatly diminish the strength. Most biners are made of aircraft quality, 7000 series aluminum alloy, with a useful life span exceeding ten years. But effects from normal work hardening can shorten the life span. Metal fatigue is a much-bandied word that is usually misinterpreted. Metal does not get tired. The term metal fatigue refers to cracks in the material that develop over time with repeated loading of the carabiner. If the biner is cracked, you obviously pitch it. Corrosion is the arch foe of aluminum and manifests in a white powdery dust. Climbers active on sea cliffs should take special note of this. If there's ever any doubt that the biner is defective, pitch it. If you don't, you'll in-

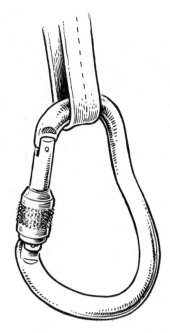

Locking carabiner

evitably find yourself at a crux with only one biner left—the dubious one. You'll clip that old, corroded, creaking biner into the anchor and cry a river because you were too cheap or stupid not to have retired a piece of gear when its time was up.

It's not unheard of for a carabiner to mysteriously come open at the worst possible time. Whenever this is even a remote possibility, use two carabiners and turn them so the gates are opposing—so they can only open in opposite directions. A special "locking" carabiner was designed to safeguard against unwanted opening. It features a threaded or spring-loaded sleeve that fits over the mouth of the biner and prohibits it from opening. Locking biners are standard gear with everyone these days. Always use a locking carabiner for attaching your belay/rappel device to your harness. It's also a sound idea to clip into key anchors with two locking biners, or two carabiners with gates opposed. Though many climbers don't bother doing so, they should. The rule of thumb with every climbing

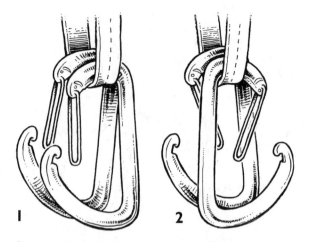

Secure carabiners against unwanted opening:

1. the wrong way   2. gates in opposition

at the hinge, blown clean with an air hose, works wonders for gate action. This also works well with the lock ring, or sleeve, on locking biners. Don't use oil."

Anchors

The anchor is the fail-safe spot to which we attach ourselves; it is the single most important part of the climbing protection system. Normally this is to secure the climber to the cliff, but not always. Commencing a climb, we may choose to "tie off" (anchor to) a tree or block on the ground. Anchors furnished by the terrain are called natural anchors, be they trees, chockstones, horns, or whatever. Artificial anchors are provided by specially designed climbing hardware that exploits cracks and hollows in the rock. When the rock is bereft of both natural anchors and cracks, a climber may drill a hole in the rock and place a bolt—a permanent anchor.

Anchors (for example, a sling wrapped around a tree) that can withstand force from any angle are called multidirectional anchors. Anchors such as runners over horns or flakes are only good for downward pull, and these are called directional anchors.

Natural Anchors

Runners are vital in exploiting natural protection and can be looped around, over, or through anything that can provide a solid anchor: knobs, spikes, flakes, blocks, chockstones, trees, car bumpers (common at "drive-up" sport climbing cliffs), or other fixed objects. Sometimes it is handy to have a double runner (12 feet, carried in a double loop over your shoulder; or better yet, tripled, knotted, and racked on a gear sling/harness), though many climbers choose to simply tie or loop two normal length runners together. Runners simply looped over protuberances can be marginal—fine for downward pull, but susceptible to slipping or being lifted off from lateral pull or rope drag. Whenever possible, tie the knob (or horn, spike, etc.) off by forming a slipknot in the runner and cinching it snug. With flakes, pull the runner down behind the flake to where it is lodged

system is "redundancy," that is, always engineering a backup into the system whenever possible.

Also available is the "bent gate" biner. The gate is bowed in and, when depressed, gives a wider gate opening than other biners. This can be a real advantage when you're desperate and eye-to-eye with fixed protection. With a bent gate you can slap the rope into the bowed gate; a little pressure and a jerk and the biner is clipped. Unfortunately, because the rope clips in so easily, it also unclips easily; so bent gate carabiners can be dangerous, particularly if the rope is running across the gate. (More on carabiners and quickdraws in the next chapter.) The rule is: Bent gate biners should only be used on the rope end of quickdraws.

Your biners will get dirty with use and the action will get "sticky," meaning the gate will open and close with difficulty. Once a year I pour a gallon of white gas (or other solvent) into a bucket and toss in my biners. An hour or so stewing in this solution and a little swirling around (with a stick) for good measure, and fluid gate action is restored.

Black Diamond Equipment has offered this advice on carabiner maintenance: "If gates are a bit sticky, cross pressure on the gate (while open) can straighten it slightly. A small amount of dry silicone

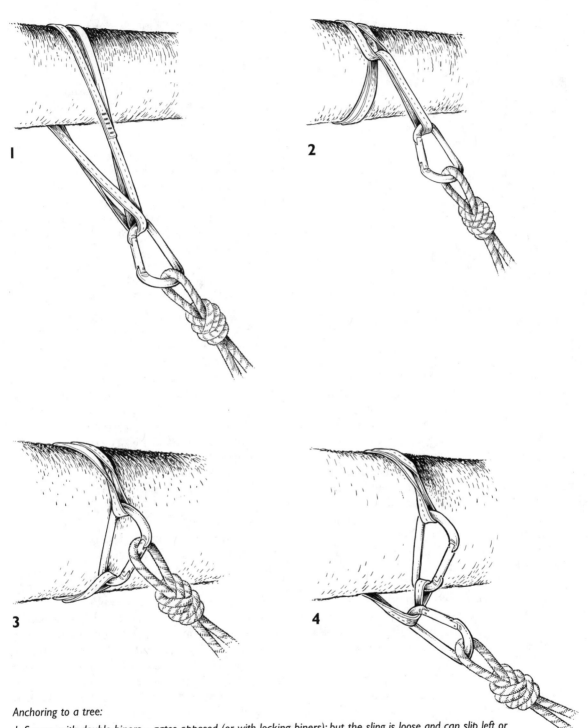

Anchoring to a tree:

1. Secure, with double biners—gates opposed (or with locking biners); but the sling is loose and can slip left or right when weighted. Not advised. 2. Best, especially when used with doubled locking biners. 3. Dangerous. This stresses the relatively weak gate of the carabiner. 4. Better, but the sling is overly stressed.

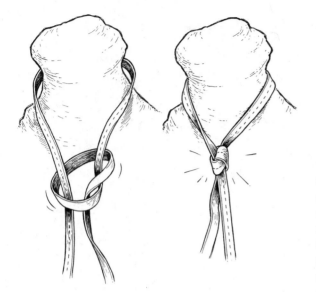

Slinging a horn with a slipknot on a runner

between the flake and the wall. If all else fails, clip a piece of gear onto the bottom of the runner. A little extra weight can keep a runner from simply sliding off. Whatever the setup—and the variations are countless—whenever you tie slings around natural anchors, watch out for sharp edges that can cut the sling(s). With trees, inspect for sap (very common).

Common sense and sober judgment are necessary in determining if a natural anchor is good, or something less. For most climbers, a little experience makes this question pretty cut and dried. You usually know if a chockstone is loose or whether a sling will slip off a knob—but not always. You wouldn't bother to place an anchor if you didn't need one, so always test the rock or tree or whatever if there are any doubts as to its strength. With potentially loose chockstones or flakes, test them gingerly, lest you pull them off on yourself or someone below.

Nuts

Also known as chocks, nuts are the first type of artificial anchor we will discuss. They are metal wedges of various sizes and designs, strung with cable, that fit into constrictions or cavities in the rock. Except for the more difficult artificial climbs, nuts have all but replaced pitons as the means of securing anchors in the rock. Prior to 1970, pitons were the standard way to obtain anchors. Pitons were originally made of soft iron, and because removal could ruin them, they were usually left "fixed" in the crack. American ingenuity came up with almost indestructible chrome-moly steel pitons around 1958. With these there evolved the American ethic of always removing your pitons, leaving the crack "clean" for the next party by not leaving a string of fixed pitons to aid and mark the way for later ascents. This provided for high adventure and, for those later ascents, a feeling similar to the pioneers who first climbed the route. But owing to the nigh imperishable steel, the new pitons brutalized the rock. Repeated placement and removal ruined more than one climb, leaving huge and unsightly "piton scars"—literally holes blasted into the rock—and nuts came to replace pitons none too soon. To the climber, there is aesthetic allure to a perfect crack rifling into the sky. That we can now climb these without ravishing their form is a testament to how far climbing has evolved. Nuts cause no damage to the stone, and many climbers find that "clean climbing" is a much more artistic and satisfying way to climb than hammering their way to the summit or chasing a line of bolts up a face.

Tradition says that the modern chock evolved from the British technique of tying off natural chockstones in the cracks. This led to placing chockstones in the cracks and stringing runners over them. Next came machine nuts (found along the railroad tracks below the British crags) through which rope was slung. Sometime in the 1960s someone began making nuts particularly for rock climbing. The first nuts were crude and had limited applications, but once the wide use of nuts caught on in the early 1970s, the designs steadily improved to where now, in most cases, nuts can provide better anchors than driven pitons ever could.

When weighted, a nut will lodge in the narrowing slot in which it is placed. Obviously, a nut is placed with a certain direction of pull in mind, usu-

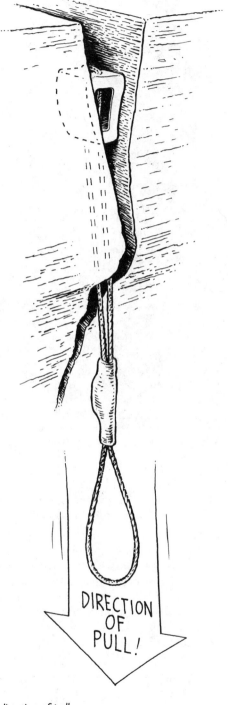

DIRECTION OF PULL!

The direction of pull

ally straight down. In some instances, a nut is placed so the direction of pull is straight out, or even straight up (explained later). Whatever the placement, the loop of sling or cable issuing from the nut can be considered an arrow that when extended from the nut, clearly shows where the direction of pull should be.

Nuts are placed in a wide variety of cracks and hollows, so they come in many shapes and sizes. Still, nuts are basically variations of two themes: tapers (or stoppers) and hexentrics (or hexes). Both are designed to slot into constrictions, or bottlenecks, in the crack. Placing a sound nut is relatively easy with a little practice, but keep these points in mind: (1) try to select the nut that best matches the taper of the crack; (2) set the nut so maximum surface area is on the rock (you don't want the nut lodged on just a few crystals); (3) remember that usually—but not always—a bigger nut is more secure than a smaller one, if you have a choice; (4) make sure the rock is solid where you set the nut—a great placement in rock still yields poor quality protection; (5) place the nut no deeper than is necessary to meet the above criteria. To do otherwise only makes removal difficult; it does not make the nut more secure. More tricks used in placing nuts will be further reviewed in Chapter 5: The Art of Leading. For now, we will examine the different types of nuts.

Tapers

These are made by dozens of different manufacturers, each giving a little different look to the basic timeless design. The first tapers were much wider than they were thick. Now, virtually all tapers have adopted a boxier shape, better for several reasons, especially endwise placement. They vary from thumbnail-sized micros strung with what appears to be piano wire, to weighty, inch-and-a-half bombers strung with special Spectra cord that pound for pound is stronger than steel. Originally, all but the smallest tapers were strung with rope. Now, swaged cable has replaced rope. The cable gives us several advantages. It is generally stronger than rope of corresponding size. The stiff cable allows easier placement. Where a taper strung with rope will droop when

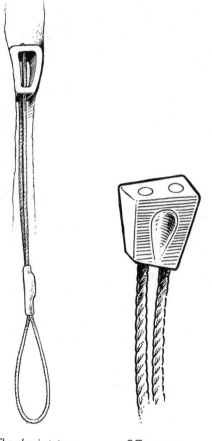

The classic taper   Offset taper

Medium-size taper sunk in a bottleneck Kevin Powell photo

held, the wired nut is like a knife and can be slotted with one hand; and the stiff cable allows a few inches of extra reach, which can sometimes make an important difference.

Variations on the taper follow four basic patterns: the straight taper, the curved taper, the offset taper, and the micro brass or micro steel taper.

The straight taper is the original design. Even the smallest ones are stronger than you would think. The wider, or "face," sides are flat and taper down at the same angle. These are most useful in a crack where the sides taper uniformly and where the slot best matches the taper of the nut. A good match means a good fit, and again, a good fit means most of the surface area of the nut is on the rock. A com-

mon error is to try to place the biggest taper the crack will accept. Much more important is finding the placement that seats solidly in the crack. The obvious bottleneck leaves little to chance; the nut locks in as if the crack was made for it, and the lip of the crack pinches off to prevent an outward pull from dislodging the nut. But when the crack is flared, convoluted, or shallow, it often takes some fiddling to find the best placement—or any placement. All but the smallest tapers can be placed endwise as well, so try whatever works best. The better tapers feature slightly beveled edges that make them easier to both place and remove. The rounded edges also increase purchase in marginal edge-contact placements. The two ends of the wire cable are secured with a swage

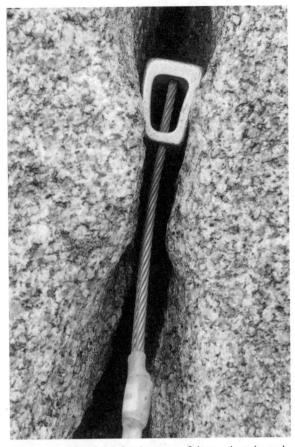

The curve of the chock fits the curve of the crack and equals a bomber placement.

The taper set endwise in a constriction

Kevin Powell photos

(a piece of metal compressed around the cable), over which a rubber shrink-tube swage cover is secured, creating a very secure loop. Most manufacturers will in some manner color code the sizes in its line. With practice, you will learn what color signifies what size nut and can then grab the right one quickly—a grace when the going's grim.

The curved taper has virtually replaced the straight taper in the medium to large range. One side is concave, the other convex. The theory is that most tapers are placed where the sides of the crack vary slightly. When placed and yanked on, the curved taper does a quasi-camming action on the convex side until it rotates into the best spot. The top of the concave side is milled flat, which with the camming action on the other side results in a three-point foundation once seated. They work especially well when the constriction is gently curved. This sounds confusing, even to me, but once you place a curved taper, all will be clear. The curved taper can also be placed endwise, both ends forming a straight taper as thick as the next widest nut; so you have the best of both worlds. The curve of the taper varies with each manufacturer. When the curving is less pronounced, they are generally easier to remove.

A useful variation to the taper is the offset, available only in small sizes and tapered on all sides, forming an asymmetrical trapezoid. I didn't understand that either. Basically, one edge is thicker than the other—or "offset." (Better get one and look at it.)

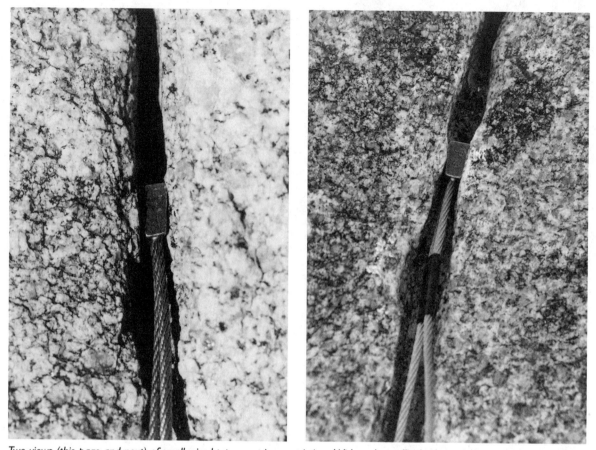

Two views (this page and next) of small wired tapers set in constrictions. With such small tolerances the taper of the nut must perfectly correspond with the taper of the crack. Kevin Powell photos

These offsets are perfect for flaring cracks that narrow in the back, in which a straight or curved taper will find scant purchase. Be warned, however, that offsets are less forgiving in marginal placements, and unless you've got most of the surface area firmly locked, offsets can "pop" quicker than you can say "Watch me." Originally offsets were viewed as a specialty item for use on big artificial routes, but many free climbers carry a few for those "oddball" placements, where nothing else works quite as well. A novice would do well to experiment with these chocks before trusting one in a critical situation. Their use is limited and specific, and even experts

need to fiddle with these units to understand when they work well, or at all.

Micro tapers are made in remarkably small sizes, and most often resemble a straight taper in profile. The super-thin but strong cable on these tiny nuts is either silver-soldered or cast with the nut, resulting in cable strengths that exceed those of the body of the nut. Some are made of hard brass; some, stainless steel; others are cast from "investment cast" brass. In a fall, the harder brass and stainless steel tend to break the surrounding rock away if the rock is poor. The investment cast brass is somewhat malleable, so it is less likely to break the rock and seats well owing to

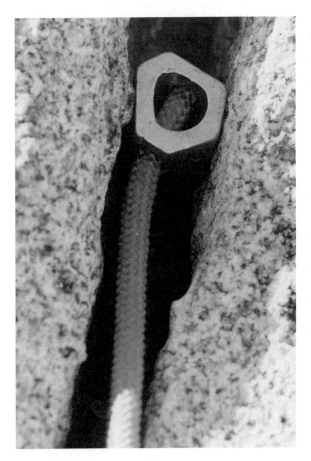

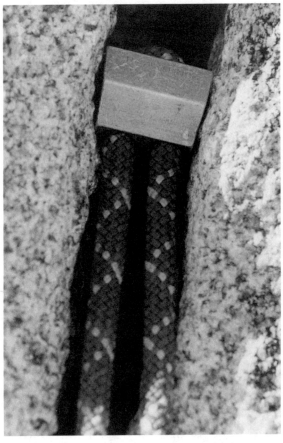

increased friction and bite. When the rock is diamond-hard, the malleable brass taper may deform and shear through the placement, so there's a trade-off involved. Most practiced climbers carry both kinds and vary use according to need.

It is important to understand the extremely small tolerances involved when using any micro nut. A fraction of an inch can make the difference between a good placement and a useless one. This type of protection requires an experienced eye and hand to properly set. A good rule of thumb is to not trust any small nut till you are experienced with using the larger articles. It is not uncommon for a beginner to trust a micro taper and for it to blow out. Typically the novice will blame the nut, and typically his own judgment, or the lack of it, caused the problem.

Wild Country, a manufacturer of these tiny tapers, offers the following advice: "The limiting factor with small nuts is not their lower strength, but rather their small surface area, which concentrates the impact of a fall so intensely that when they fail, it is likely because they rip out, not through broken wires." Be aware, though, that with long use, the cable usually frays beneath the head of the nut.

There are other modifications on the taper that you'll see as well. The faces of some of the smaller tapers have been gouged out to form a teardrop cut-away, or a scoop. This supposedly adds purchase when the nut is placed between a cluster of crystals. Other tapers have been filed this way and that, are banana-shaped, squat, tall, titanium, plastic, or even wooden. But they all work by being slotted into a constriction and weighted in the direction of the cable or cord.

Hexentrics

Six-sided and barrel-shaped, hexentrics—or simply "hexes"—are good for wide cracks, bottlenecks, and the crack that is more suited to a round (as opposed to tapered) nut. The sides are shaped so they can be wedged in three different attitudes, camming fairly well even in parallel-sided cracks. Placed endwise, both ends are tapered, and the hex is slotted like a big taper. Since Chouinard Equipment (now Black Diamond Equipment) introduced them in 1971, they have steadily evolved. The newest batch features angled sidewalls for better endwise placements.

Since the introduction of spring-loaded camming devices (SLCDs), hexes, long the only viable nut for wide cracks, have almost disappeared. But for the true bottleneck placement, a bomber hex is still the strongest nut in town. Not one has ever broken in use. They are relatively inexpensive and many times can find better purchase than any high-tech SLCDs. Consequently, most climbers carry a selection on their rack. They come in ten sizes.

Tri-Cams

Many climbers have considered this odd-looking nut just a piece of esoterica, but some climbers swear by them. The design creates a tripod with two parallel camming rails flat against one side of the crack or pocket and the fulcrum point on the other. They're uniquely good in horizontal placements, providing both cam and wedging action. Tri-cams also work well in desert sandstone, with the point digging into the soft rock. In certain shallow pocket placements, they have no peer. They come in eleven sizes.

Stringing Your Nuts

All but the smallest hexes and tapers are made to accept a length of rope rather than a swaged cable. This is particularly useful in hexentrics because it allows

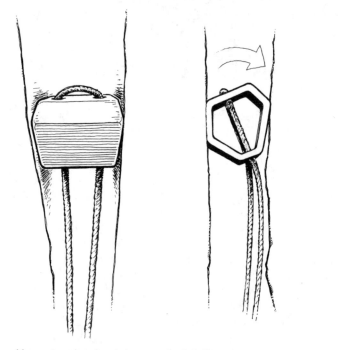

Hexentrics, placed endwise as a chock (left), and as a cam (right)

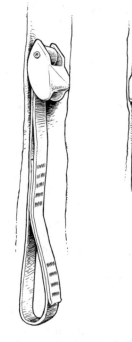

A Tri-cam in camming position (left), and a Tri-cam placed as a chock (right)

A Tri-cam. A downward pull rocks the cam and increases purchase on the opposite contact point. Kevin Powell photo

Use the double or triple fisherman's knot to secure the cord because it is a knot that is relatively permanent. (Note: The manufacturer recommends use of the triple fisherman's knot for Spectra cord.) Keep the knot near the carabiner end of the loop so that it does not interfere with the nut placement and, by its stiffness, tends to keep the loop open to accept a biner readily.

Removing Nuts

Removing, or "cleaning," nuts is sometimes nasty work, especially if they've been fallen on. The best strategy in cleaning any nut is to first examine the placement with an eye toward simply reversing the path by which the nut was placed. Sometimes, just a tap with a carabiner can jar a set nut free. If the nut cannot be wiggled loose and lifted out, a moderate upward jerk will often free it.

If the nut is buried deep in a crack, you may have to really yard on it. Be warned that this can bend any cable and, if done repeatedly, can not only ruin the nut's symmetry but weaken the cable; you can actually break the cable on the smaller tapers. Always keep an eye peeled for frays in the cable, especially around the swage and above the holes in the top of the nut. The broken strands not only diminish strength, but these "wild hairs" can prick the fingers hatefully. When this occurs, just pitch them.

An invaluable aid to tapping out well-lodged nuts, cleaning tools are made in a dozen different forms, all thin and blade-shaped. A little experimentation will show just how to pry and tap out stubborn nuts. If all else fails, set the cleaning tool against the nut and tap it with a rock, large chock, or other object to set the nut free. Make sure to attach a keeper sling to your cleaning tool: ⅛-inch diameter nylon accessory cord will do. With visions of a shiv buried in their belly, some climbers are loath to carry what is essentially a blunt knife, fearing a fall might somehow result in a puncture from the cleaning tool. Though I've never once heard of this happening, more than a few climbers are not looking to be first. Whatever, tapers are often left on climbs when a cleaning tool would more often than not have gotten the nut free.

an unrestricted camming action of the nut. Originally, both tapers and hexentrics were strung with various dimensions of nylon rope. Once Spectra cord hit the market, everyone shifted to it because it proved to be much stronger than nylon of the same size and it wore well. Presently, most nuts machined to accept cord have holes drilled for the standard 5.5 mm Spectra line. Gemini, a blend of Spectra and Kevlar, allows light and durable use of the otherwise slippery Spectra. Both fiber blends are available in 5.5 mm for chock cord and in flat stock for runners and quickdraws.

Bill Basores tip-toes out a monzonite intrusion on I Can't Believe It's A Girdle, *Joshua Tree, California.* Kevin Powell photo

Spring-Loaded Camming Devices

In 1967, Greg Lowe invented the first camming device for protecting rock climbs. Greg's version was a bust, but it got the concept out there. Finally, in 1978, Ray Jardine improved upon the concept and started marketing "Friends," and climbing has never been the same.

Friends work so well that when they first came out, many past rock masters thought they were a means of cheating. Climbs that for twenty years were feared owing to poor protection were now reduced to mere physical endeavors. Friends had taken the horror right out of them, for you could place a Friend whenever and whatever you wanted, and the placement was generally bomber. No longer did a climber cast off on a rugged lead hoping he could get in good nuts, and hoping the nuts were somewhere near the crux. Now you could throw in a Friend whenever the going got tough. And they were easy to place. Gone forever were the days when a climber was greasing out of an overhanging crack, trying to wiggle a hex in where the crack just wouldn't have it and there was no going on without it.

The great benefit of spring-loaded camming devices (SLCDs) is that the crack need not constrict to afford a viable placement. In fact, SLCDs usually work well in parallel-sided cracks, a place where all other nuts are either marginal or useless. Since Friends first hit the market, they have been copied by everyone with a machine shop; now there are Camalots, TCUs, Quad Cams, Aliens, Big Dudes, and many others. Some, like TCUs (three-cam

Marginal SLCD. Outside cam on right side barely contacts the rock.

Tight but secure SLCD

No good—cams are fully deployed.

Too tight because the cams are cranked down to minimum width—removal might be difficult.

Perfect (above and right). Cam at midrange and contacting flat surfaces inside the crack. Kevin Powell photos

SLCD in a typical parallel-sided placement

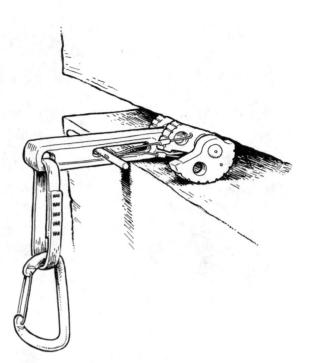

Incorrect use of a rigid-stem Friend in a horizontal placement risks shearing the stem

units), are designed specifically for thin cracks. They have three rather than four cams, and their lower profile allows a better range of protection in narrow cracks and pockets, but the lack of a fourth cam sacrifices some strength and stability. Camalots feature a double axis for the cams, resulting in a wider range of application than other SLCDs of the same size. Flexible Friends supplant the rigid stem with a cable stem, giving it a lower profile for thin cracks and making it far better for horizontal placements. Still, SLCDs all work on the same principle.

Wild Country, the manufacturer of Friends, has offered the following advice regarding SLCDs, but the advice is so sound that it applies to all protection. Parenthetical additions are mine. "The security of climbing protection has always depended on the experience and knowledge of the climber placing it. Climbing hardware is only a tool, and knowledge about how the tool works properly is important to achieving its greatest performance. With this knowl-

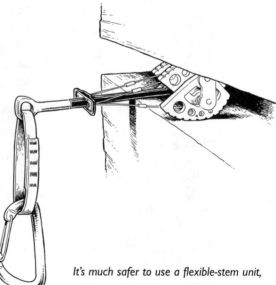

It's much safer to use a flexible-stem unit, which can bend downward loading.

edge, if you have to make a risky gear placement, you'll do so out of intelligence and not out of ignorance. Per SLCDs: Always align stem and cams in the direction of loading (i.e., direction of pull). Don't offset the cams—they have little holding power that way. Realign the cams evenly. Avoid a "tipped" placement, where the cams are placed wide open and rocking on the cam tips. In such a position there is little room for further expansion, and stability is poor. Always use a sling long enough to ensure you won't move the SLCD by climbing past it. (All SLCDs have the tendency to either "walk" in or out of the crack when even nominal rope drag is pulling on them. A sling connected to the end of the SLCD alleviates the problem.) Don't allow the cams to invert—inverted cams won't hold. Don't stuff a too large SLCD into an undersized placement; it may make removal difficult. (It may make removal impossible. Ideally, the cams should be 0 to 50 percent deployed, with the device placed in the most uniformly parallel section of the crack. You must reduce the cam ratio to pull out the SLCD. If you force the SLCD into an undersized placement, you've torqued the cams to their minimum displacement. Since they are spring-loaded, the cams are never passive, so you can't simply slide the SLCD out, and you have no way of reducing the profile any further because it's already at its minimum. So you've just lost an expensive piece of gear.) Never place a rigid stem SLCD so that the stem is not aligned with the direction of pull; especially avoid placements where the stem is loaded over an edge, where a fall can either bend or break the unit. Referring to placements when the stem is not in the direction of pull: Bottoming cracks should be avoided as they make cleaning (removal) difficult and may hinder stem alignment during a fall. Flexible Friends will work in such positions, but stems aligned in the direction of pull are always more secure. (And what happens when you encounter a flared or bottoming crack and you can't avoid it? You try to place a taper or a hex. If impossible, you place a SLCD with a flexible shaft and hope it doesn't rip out.) Always regard flexible stems as less predictable than rigid stems. ("Predictable" here means the rigid stem SLCDs rip

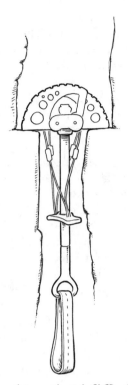

The twin-axle Camalots are the only SLCDs that can be used as a passive chock, though a passive nut is almost always a better option.

out less frequently when fallen on.) Four camming surfaces are generally more secure than three. (Sometimes the crack is too shallow to "sink" the SLCD, so one or more cams are hanging out of the crack. Such placements are very suspect.)

These remarks apply to most SLCDs. Black Diamond Camalots and Metolius 4-Cam Units can be placed in their fully open, or "umbrella," configuration, essentially placed like a hex. A hex will generally be much better here, but these cams have this capability. Most other SLCDs do not, but check with your local retailer because manufacturers are constantly improving their hardware. Though up-to-date, the information here should be augmented by reading magazine reviews and technical essays, as well as the promotional material put out by the various manufacturers.

Small SLCDs are much less forgiving on placement size than the larger ones. This is the same principle we discussed earlier with tapers. The smaller sizes are far trickier to use than the larger units, owing to the small tolerances involved. A fraction of an inch can make the difference between a solid SLCD placement and a poor, or even useless, one. Placing SLCDs is part science, part art. Learn to place the larger sizes first. Trust the smaller ones only after you know which placements are sound. Also, remember that the smaller units are considerably weaker than the larger ones.

Per placements: A truly parallel-sided crack is not the ideal placement for any SLCD. A doubly constricting pocket provides the best placement, where the curves of the pocket roughly correspond with the curves of the unit's lobes. Here, the unit is "keyed" into place much as a taper slots into a constriction.

The working strength of all SLCDs has only a marginal relation to the number on the card that the unit came with. Actual holding strength depends on rock quality, direction of pull, size and shape of the crack, type of impact, and a host of other factors. Knowing how to place SLCDs properly takes experience. Believing the notion that SLCDs provide instant and foolproof protection is the surest and most dangerous way to discover the fallacy of this notion.

As with all forms of protection, get an SLCD and start placing it in every conceivable configuration, and discover for yourself what does and does not work. As you get the hang of placing these units, you will know at a glance which ones are likely reliable and which ones are probably questionable.

Sliding Nuts

There is a last, specialized genre of protection that combines aspects of the taper and the SLCD, generically called sliding nuts. All sliding nuts include some form of inverted taper that is fixed to a cable. A second taper, inverted the other way, slides up and down the face of the first taper, controlled by a spring-loaded cable. Owing to the sliding taper, the device has a variable range and can conform to the exact dimensions of the placement. In rather fast-paced evolution, the first of these units, Sliders, led to Quickies, Rock 'n Rollers, LoweBalls, Cobras, and a slew of Korean knockoffs that cost half as much and worked hardly at all. Though sliding nuts are specialized tackle to be sure and are used less than 5 percent of the time under typical climbing circumstances, almost all of them work like magic in narrow, shallow, parallel-sided fissures. While all sliding nuts are tricky to place, they are even trickier to remove. The chief problem is that once seated, yanked, and perhaps fallen on, the opposing wedges become lodged so tightly they're nearly impossible to clean, as there's no way other than wiggling them to retract the wedges. Like micro nuts and the smaller SLCDs, their use, especially in critical situations, is best left to experienced hands.

All climbing equipment seems suspect at the outset, when in fact your experience and judgment are the most suspicious part of the equation. Not to labor the point, but all of these descriptions can only point you in a direction that hopefully stacks the

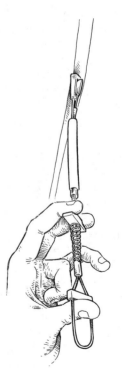

LoweBall in use

safety odds in your favor until you can discover for yourself how and why the equipment and techniques work in actual practice. A million words and as many photos are both poor substitutes for grabbing a handful of nuts and going to a crag to practice placing them. Find several cracks at ground level and experiment to find out how the basic principles apply, how to spot the best placements, and what nut best fits where. Clip a runner into them, step on them, pull on them, and discover just how good, or bad, they are. And don't expect expertise in an afternoon. Better than thirty years have gone into refining the modern nut, and statistically, an experienced climber not given to rashness has little chance of hurting himself. But there is no sport on the face of the earth less forgiving to those who make a mistake or oversight in regard to safety. You can get killed in a second by ignoring any aspect of proper climbing. So when it comes time to test your own judgment on whether a nut is good—whether you should trust your life to it—do so only after you feel confident you can make the right decision. And the only way for a novice to gain this confidence is to practice nutcraft where it doesn't count—near the ground.

Wide Crack Anchors

Wide cracks—those over 4 or 5 inches—have traditionally proved difficult to provide anchorage. Large "tube" chocks that appeared in the early 1970s replaced the huge pitons that hitherto had provided a semblance of security. The tubes required a slight constriction to work, however, and with the introduction of Friends, backyard machine shops soon produced monster Friends. Now commercially available as Big Dudes and other quirky names, these SLCDs, while heavy, bulky, and certainly expensive, still provide good security in the wider cracks. Also available for wide cracks is the BigBro, a tube that works best in parallel-sided cracks and is incredibly strong, compact, and less costly. A push button releases the spring-loaded inner sleeve. The tube is bridged across to both sides of the crack, and a threaded ring is spun to lock it all to size. A sling on one end provides the means to clip in. Placing a

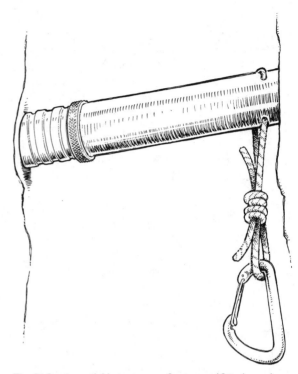

The BigBro is available in sizes to fit up to a 12-inch crack.

good BigBro takes practice, even for an expert. Practice on a ground-level crack before you start experimenting on lead.

With gear such as Big Dudes, which are truly specialty items often fashioned out of someone's garage, the "manufacturers" come and go with the wind. The generic product, however, will no doubt be made by others, using other brand names. So some of the names here might be gone in a month, but the product, in some form, will likely live on since they are required in certain instances.

Pitons

Pitons ("pins" or "pegs") are steel devices, usually spike-shaped, that are hammered into cracks to secure anchors. The shapes are many, but every modern piton has an eye through which a carabiner is clipped. A recreational climber today might frequent a popular sport climbing area for five years and never hear the ring of a piton being driven. Chocks, SLCDs, and bolts have made pitons unnecessary in almost all cases; but for big artificial climbs, and now and again in free climbing, pitons still have their place. Regardless, the ranks of climbers experienced in placing pitons is shrinking, and the number of accidents as a result of misplaced trust in fixed piton anchors shows the need for developing pitoning skills.

As mentioned, prior to World War II, pitons were made of malleable soft iron so they could conform to the crack. Even one placement would maul their shape, and they were usually left in situ, or "fixed," since removal would destroy them. The most common soft steel piton today's climber will run across is the ring-angle, a pin of channel design with a welded ring. Obviously these are very old, and in addition to being of questionable security, the welded ring design may fail at relatively low loads. There really is no practical way to test such pitons. It's best to assume them to be worthless.

In 1946, a Swiss expatriate named John Salathe hand-tooled pegs from Model-T axle stock for the first ascent of Lost Arrow Spire in Yosemite Valley. Tradition says these Salathe pins were the first ever made from hard steel. In the 1950s, Chuck Wilts invented the "knife-blade," a wafer-thin peg he fashioned from chrome molybdenum ("chrome-moly") steel. Like Salathe's, these hard steel pins could withstand repeated placement and removal, enabling climbers to scale multi-day climbs and carry a limited selection, rather than lugging a duffel bag full of soft iron. In the late 1950s, Yvon Chouinard began manufacturing chrome-moly pitons in his mom's backyard. He quickly expanded and by the early 1960s any climber could purchase state-of-the-art chrome-moly pitons. That the first ascent of Yosemite's mightiest walls corresponded with the availability of good pitons was no fluke. While every other facet of climbing technology has steadily evolved, pitons have changed little in the last forty years—either in design or construction. Chouinard had it down by 1962.

Various European manufacturers still market pitons, but in the United States, what was Chouinard Equipment—now Black Diamond—has totally locked this limited market and is the only company making them on any kind of scale. Black Diamond Equipment makes pitons in four different shapes. Each model is either stamped or forged of alloy steel, and for better or worse, all are far more enduring than the hardest granite or limestone.

Again, pitons are rarely used in sport climbing. The one exception is climbers making first ascents. It is rare even for them to use pegs, but in the case of a hole or a thin, parallel-sided crack, sometimes only a piton can secure the desired protection, although in most cases nowadays, leading climbers just place bolts where they can't get in good chock protection (dreadfully, sometimes even where they can). To preserve the rock and avoid future climbers having to place the pin, it is always left fixed. Never remove a piton from an established free climb. It's there for a reason. To adequately judge the security of a fixed piton, however, you must have experience in placing them, and a hammer. Most piton hammers have a forged steel head attached to a wooden handle. Steel- and aluminum-handled piton hammers are also available. The vibrations from hammering travel up your arm; over the course of a big wall (several days), they can deaden your arm; over the course of a career, they can cause pesky elbow and wrist problems (a condition that essentially retired Yosemite legend Royal Robbins). A wooden handle absorbs the vibrations better than a metal handle. Hammers weigh in around twenty-four ounces and last for many years.

Choose the piton that best corresponds to the shape of the crack. Insert the piton by hand. Ideally about 75 percent of its length should enter before you start hammering. Drive it to the hilt. As you hammer it home, a rising ring—like a scale on a xylophone—usually means a sound piton. When you have the choice between placements in a horizontal and vertical crack, the horizontal peg is often better. In such horizontal placements the eye of the piton should always be positioned down. When placing pitons straight up, use the longest pin that will fit. These placements are often better than you would think.

To remove the pin, knock the piton back and forth along the axis of the crack as far as it will go until it's loose, then snatch it as it comes free. If the pin is stubborn and requires extensive hammering to remove, clip a sling into the eye so if it comes out while hammering, you won't drop it. If it's loose, yet still won't come out, try prying with the hammer pick through the eye.

Since the unnecessary use of pitons is frowned upon in virtually every climbing area, how does one practice their use? Basic pitoning is a pretty straightforward technique, but you should try your hand at it before heading onto a climb where you expect to place them. Most climbing areas have rock outcrops that, owing to poor rock or whatever, no one climbs on. Often such cliffs are some distance from the central climbing area, which is all the better. Any scrappy crag will do, as long as it has some cracks in it. Find some privacy and experiment, but never place pins on established clean routes.

Bolts

When there are no cracks for traditional nuts or pitons, a climber can retreat, ignore the need for an anchor and simply "go for it," or drill a hole into the blank stone and hammer in a bolt—a permanent anchor.

The use of bolts has been one of the most controversial issues in the climbing game. Slowly but surely most climbers have begun to accept a proliferation of bolts, especially at the sport climbing areas. Most climbers, however, have the intuitive understanding that artistic climbing is to follow a weakness up a given cliff. You work with what nature has provided. There is something inherently distasteful about changing the medium to fit our need, and bolting does just that. Bolting has been called "the murder of the impossible" because with the bolt, you can climb anything, anywhere. We can hammer one in the underside of a glass-smooth ceiling if we want to. But should we? We clear the land because we need a place to hang our hat. But we don't need to climb. We choose to. So what do we do when we come across an otherwise unclimbable section of rock? It has always been a question when

the rock, in its natural state, is either unclimbable or too dangerous to try, whether it's okay to permanently alter it—by placing a bolt—so that we can climb it. Well, that depends. . . .

Say there is a 2,000-foot crack that blanks out for 30 feet. Surely it is okay to drill a few bolts for the blank stretch if it means putting together a 2,000-foot dandy. But what if the blank section is 100 feet and requires eight bolts? What if the blank section is 1,000 feet and requires eighty bolts? And what if all 2,000 feet are blank? What if the 2,000-foot wall is featured with plentiful holds but few cracks and would tender a face climb of the first order if only we took the time to install the requisite bolts—say 200? Bolting is compromising the rock—there's no way around that. So where do we draw the line? Should we draw the line?

This is a philosophical question that the beginner need not face but should be aware of from the start. The question is reserved for those who make first ascents—the first people to establish a climbing route. These pioneers experience the same excitement of discovery that has motivated climbers since the first climber looked overhead and cast off for glory. As today's pacesetters look ever harder for new lines, they increasingly face the bolting question. This is not the venue to pass judgment on the pros and cons of bolting. Climbing's allure is that everyone is left to decide for himself. There are no governing bodies, thank God. The flip side is that when a climber places a bolt, he impacts the world of all climbers for all time.

The bolt has been an integral part of American climbing for more than fifty years. Many of America's best climbs have dozens of bolts. Most face climbs wouldn't exist, or would be suicidal, without bolt anchors. As you get immersed in climbing, you will quickly learn how bolts are "at once a blessing and a curse," as Yosemite legend Royal Robbins said. By and large, in today's world the bolt controversy is dead, and the modern sport climber is usually looking for more bolts, not decrying those already in place. For now, let's see just what they are and how they work.

First is the hole. Holes were traditionally drilled

by hammering on a drill bit held by a rolled steel sleeve/holder. By hammering the holder and twisting it at the same time, the hole was accomplished, taking up to half an hour for a 1½-inch-deep hole drilled in hard granite—even longer in dense limestone. For years this tedious drilling deterred excessive bolting. The introduction of lightweight battery- and gasoline-powered drills changed all that, with thirty seconds for a hole. Later climbers were back to hand drilling when many government bodies banned automated drilling on national lands.

For decades, the ¼-inch diameter bolt was standard. As more and more of these sheared off unexpectedly, ⅜- and ½-inch bolts have come to replace the old ¼-inchers. The bolt is nail-like, and there are several types. The contraction bolt has a split flange that is squeezed together as it's driven in the narrow hole. The expansion bolt expands a surrounding sleeve (either as it is driven in or after it is set) by wrenching down the head. Some of the best bolt anchors simply combine a threaded bolt with epoxy that is stronger than the rock.

Carabiners can be clipped to the bolt hanger, a strip of bent metal that is usually secured by a nut screwed onto the bolt. Other bolts are like normal machine bolts, and the hanger is already affixed when the bolt is driven home. Most of the new ⅜- and ½-inch bolts have a minimum strength of 4,000 pounds; the older, ¼-inch bolts hold significantly less.

A beginner should not worry about the mechanics of placing a bolt. You never place bolts on existing routes, so you'll never need that "skill" until you're an expert doing first ascents; and many experts never do first ascents. For general sport climbing you need only know how to judge the condition of a bolt on an existing route. There is no absolutely reliable way to test bolts in situ, but plenty of reasons to want to. Here are some suggestions.

Always consider a ¼-inch bolt suspect. They are no longer placed as anchors (and haven't been for more than 20 years), though they are commonly found on existing routes, and any you come across are bound to be old.

Make sure the hanger is flush to the wall, not a "spinner," where the hanger spins around. This means the hole was drilled too shallow for the bolt stud. And don't try to "fix" the spinner by hammering on it. Had that been possible the first party would have sunk it. Further hammering will only damage the shank and the head. Again, never hit an existing bolt with a hammer.

Modern (meaning made in the last few years), commercially made hangers are fashioned from stainless steel, good for more than 4,000 pounds. Older, commercially made hangers were never that strong, however, and are considered questionable as a general rule. Beware of homemade hangers. Most are fashioned from inferior aluminum or steel angle stock, prone to work hardening, eventual brittleness, and failure. Chances are the climber who made the hanger doesn't even know the alloy used or the strength of the hanger.

If the bolt is a "screw-head," make sure the nut is snug and the threads are in good shape. If the threads are denuded or stripped, the nut has little resistance and can pop off under surprisingly low impact force. If the bolt is a "button-head" or looks like a machine bolt, again see if it's snugly set and free of fatigue cracks.

If the bolt is bent or looks to be set in an oblique hole, beware! Rust is another thing to look for. Discoloration is natural enough, but a lot of rust denotes a "coffin nail," and you know what those are used for.

Whenever you use bolts, first inspect the hanger for cracks. A lot of the older SMC (Seattle Mountaineering Corp.) hangers are developing cracks that you won't notice unless you look for them. Also, most of the bolts out there are much stronger when stressed in the sheer direction, so try and only pull on them along the rock (not directly out). Many are very weak when loaded perpendicular to the rock (directly out). While this is sound advice, it is also nearly impossible (or at least impractical) when climbing difficult sport climbs, where simply clipping the bolts is sometimes the harshest part of the route. Our consolation here is that the vast majority (though not all) of sport climbs feature good bolts placed in controlled circumstances (installed by someone hanging on a toprope or standing in aid slings).

Well nigh crucified, Doug Englekirk Rambos on at Hueco Tanks, Texas. Bill Hatcher photo

Likewise, bolts on popular climbs at popular sport climbing areas have repeatedly been tested by falling climbers, so whatever is there tends to be good (but there are absolutely no guarantees). Also, when a bolt is bad, the word gets out quickly, and normally the bad bolt is soon replaced.

Use common sense. If the bolt looks funky, don't trust it. And always back up a bolt with a nut if possible. A perfect bolt is nearly impossible to pull out, even from an astronomical fall. But be careful: There are a lot of bad bolts out there.

How Safe Are Those Fixed Anchors?

Besides bolts, many popular climbs have fixed nuts and/or pitons. Gear is expensive. So the gear usually was not left on purpose, but because someone couldn't remove it. But not always. Fatigue, terror, and inexperience often keep a person from really trying to clean a stubborn nut. So never trust fixed gear outright. With nuts, first check the placement. Is it good? If so, has the nut been mauled by greedy hammers? Has the cable been torn by people trying to force it out? This is usually the case. If it checks out, it's probably okay, but back it up anyway.

Inspect all fixed pitons closely. A piton that Herman Munster couldn't clean with a nine-pound sledge becomes, after the winter freeze and thaw, loose as a tent stake in peat. Check that it's firmly placed. To test a fixed piton well, a piton hammer is a necessity; a couple of good blows along the axis of the crack will give a good indication of how tightly it has been placed. Follow up with blows to set the pin. Keeping in mind that few climbers test fixed pitons, it's advisable to either carry a hammer, test the pin (inadequately) with blows from the heaviest nut you have, or treat the fixed pin as worthless; it often is. Often the eye is cracked, and if you can't back it up, it's a judgment call. Sometimes larger fixed angles will be more secure if treated like a chockstone and wrapped with a sling. If you know a route features a lot of fixed pitons, carrying a hammer and testing the pitons is the only way to intelligently ensure your security.

A triangular sling configuration, sometimes called the American Triangle, is commonly seen when two fixed anchors are side by side—two bolts on a smooth wall, two pitons driven into a horizontal crack, etc. A sling is fed through the two anchors, which form two points of the triangle. The third point of the triangle is where the rope or biner passes through the sling, at the bottom of the setup. There probably is not a cliff in America that doesn't sport this configuration, most likely as a popular, fixed rappel point (cold shuts have largely replaced this configuration but not altogether). Considering that the physics are all wrong with this setup—it actually increases the load on each anchor—it's a wonder more of these rigs don't fail. As with other fixed anchors, you may well find an abundance of slings threaded through the anchor, climbers not realizing that it's not so much the slings that present the danger, rather the triangular rigging that so stresses the anchor.

Obviously, when the anchors are truly bombproof, it doesn't much matter how you tie them off—providing the slings are good and the knots properly tied. But anything shy of big new bolts should not be subjected to such inward loading as caused by a triangle. Even the stoutest fixed pins will work loose after a while, and to use the American Triangle to connect passive anchors is to invite disaster.

The solution is easy. Tie the anchors off individually and rappel or belay from two or more slings, or equalize the force on them with the sliding knot and back it up. Remember, the sliding knot (explained shortly) yields no redundancy.

Fixed SLCDs are rare but not unheard of. The cheapest ones are $40, so everyone and his brother has probably tried to clean it. Make sure the sling or cable is in good shape before trusting it. Fixed slings should never be trusted blindly; hidden damage may spell calamity for anyone who does not instead examine what the sling is attached to and rerig the anchor accordingly. Most climbers try to clean fixed slings just to get that trash off the cliff.

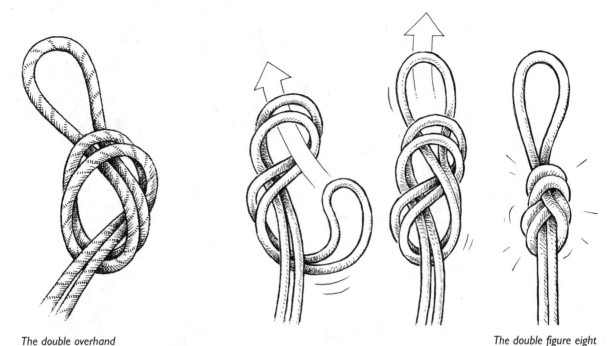

The double overhand   *The double figure eight*

Tying into the Anchor

You must first uncoil, or "flake out," the rope. Find the end, then feed out the line in a neat stack, making sure not to bury (hide) the ends. You now have a bottom and top of the pile, and to avoid tangles, you always draw the rope from the top. The rope bag, now in standard use, features two short loops into which the respective ends of the line are tied. Usually, the white or black loop marks the bottom of the pile, with the top ("live" or "business" end) tied to a colored loop. Now you're at the bottom of the cliff, harnessed, booted up, tied in to the rope, and chomping at the bit. Beginners should always use an anchor when belaying. Later, when you know the ropes, you might dispense with the ground anchor, but never if the belay site is at all exposed or if the leader significantly outweighs the belayer. Here, you will always want a solid ground anchor. Look for a natural anchor—a stout tree or a large block. You could use the rope to tie these off, but you'll go with slings. Better to get tree sap on a $2.00 piece of webbing than the rope. And the anchor is often weighted, pulled on, and jerked about, so you'll let

the sling take any abuse. The rope is plenty strong for this, but why scuff it up if you don't have to? Understand, however, that the climber should always be more concerned about rope/sheath damage from sharp edges and rough rock than the possibility of getting sap on the line.

Once you have arranged a natural anchor, you must tie into it. Since you are already tied into the end of the rope, you must use a knot for the "middle" of the rope (meaning any place other than the ends). For this purpose, either of two knots, the double overhand or the double figure eight, provides the strength and ease of tying to make their use exclusive of any other for the main tie-in to the anchor. The double overhand is the simplest knot imaginable, but once weighted can be a bearcat to untie. The double figure eight is better; it's strong and easy to untie.

A tie-in knot that is quick and easy to tie, is easy to adjust for length once tied, and unties easily is naturally a knot welcomed by climbers. The clove hitch is such a knot. It is particularly useful in constructing multi-nut anchors. The trade-off for all this utility is less strength than other knots. Clove hitches

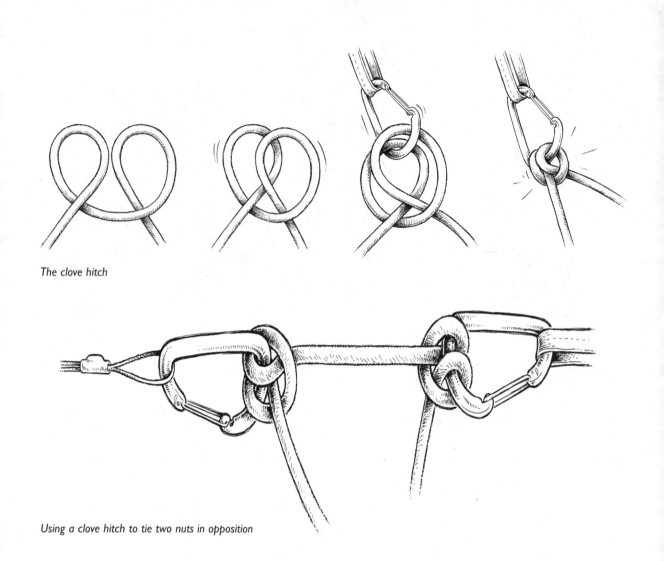

The clove hitch

Using a clove hitch to tie two nuts in opposition

reportedly slip at around 1,000 pounds of load. This slipping can actually improve equalization of the load between the anchors and help absorb energy from a leader fall, but it may not be good for the rope. Clove hitches also have a tendency to work loose. Be sure they are kept snug (by pulling equally tight on both strands) at the bottom of the carabiner, away from the gate. The reliability of a clove hitch can be improved by using a locking carabiner. Tying the clove hitch is something of an art and requires some practice to master. Practice with a short piece of rope. Keep it nearby the TV or in the shower and fiddle with it till you know the nuances.

There are several other things to consider whenever using the clove hitch. The load strand of the rope coming from the clove hitch should be aligned near the spine of the carabiner and away from the gate, or you sacrifice nearly one-third of the carabiner's strength. The clove hitch should not be used as the sole tie-in knot; the wise climber uses a figure eight somewhere in the anchor system. I have never seen a properly tied clove hitch failing in any climbing situation, though I've heard of it happening. Likewise, carabiner failure is almost unheard of as well. Still, you need to be apprised of the possibilities.

Knot now in hand, be certain never to tie off an anchor with only one non-locking carabiner. That is relying too much on a piece of equipment that can easily hide flaws. Besides which, the gate might get torqued open by a bight of rope. A slim chance, granted, but you won't be taking any chances, so you use two carabiners, gates opposed, or better yet, two locking carabiners (with the gates locked, of course). It cannot be overstated: The importance of redundancy with every link of the climbing chain is fundamental to all safe and sane climbing.

If there is no substantial natural anchor—a tree, block, or large bush—you must construct an artificial anchor using nuts. The first rule with anchors is never use only one piece of gear. Never. Most experienced climbers don't consider an anchor secure until they have set a minimum of three good nuts. Again: redundancy.

Multi-nut Anchors

Constructing a multi-nut anchor will at first take some time and trouble, but a trained eye and the knack for finding propitious nut slots—both a result of experience—quickly make this routine. Climbers are called on to do this many times each outing (at a "trad" or traditional climbing area, whereas at a sport climbing venue, nuts are rarely used), so the training comes quickly. When setting an anchor system, always consider the following details.

- Find a spot that provides convenient anchor placements. Take a moment to plan the entire system. Analyze the situation and prepare the anchors for any possible direction of pull. Also make sure the spot is safe from rockfall, dropped gear, a falling climber, etc. Keep the system simple, so it is quick to set and easy to double-check and keep tabs on. Use the minimal amount of gear to safely and efficiently do the job.
- As mentioned, remember that any anchor is only as strong as the rock it is set in.
- Make sure the anchor system is SRENE: solid, redundant, equalized, and allows no extension.

(This acronym is somewhat modified from one used by the American Mountain Guides Association.)

This all can sound overly technical and complicated, but in fact all of these concepts are based on common sense and simple mechanical laws that are usually self-evident once you gain experience. Still, let us look closer at the fundamental concepts behind SRENE.

SRENE
Solid
Redundant
Equalized
No Extension

Solid means just that. The individual anchors and the system as a whole must be bombproof, able to stop a rogue elephant, without question.

Redundancy generally means placing three or four solid anchors (more if the anchors are less than ideal). Never use only one nut. Never. Most experienced climbers don't consider an anchor secure until they have set a minimum of three solid pieces of gear. Two bombproof anchors is the absolute minimum. In emergencies, climbers occasionally will use a single bolt, bush, or boulder for an anchor, but secure backup anchors will greatly reduce the chance of a catastrophe. Redundancy should exist through the entire anchor system: All anchors, slings, and carabiners should be backed up. Redundancy also can include setting anchors in more than one crack system to avoid relying on a single rock feature.

Equalization means distributing the load equally between the various anchors in the system, which increases the overall strength of the system and reduces the chance of a single anchor pulling out under stress. Understand that the anticipated direction of pull is critically linked to equalization. Generally, a system that is equalized for one direction of pull is not equalized when loaded in another direction. More on this later.

No Extension means that if one of the anchors in the system should fail, the system will not suddenly become slack and drop the climber a short distance, shock-loading the remaining anchors.

The first step is to locate where you want to belay—what physical location is best for tending the line, what affords the best stance, what allows use of the remaining gear on your rack. And as just mentioned, make sure the spot is safe from falling objects. If adequate anchor placements aren't available, consider moving the station higher or lower if possible. Often, you won't have a choice. There will only be a small shelf, or one crack. In that case, you look for the best, most obvious big nut you can arrange. Most belay anchors are built around a couple of atomic bombproof nuts—a primary anchor. If there are more than two such groupings, go with the ones that are more handily located, ideally about chest level, where you can remain standing, can hang the rack, and can keep an eye on the whole works. Sometimes, you'll have to rig the anchor at your feet, off to one side, or wherever the good placements are, then tie yourself off with slack enough to get back in position to belay (always tying off taut and in line with the direction of pull). Whatever the situation dictates, the first priority is to sink those primary, bombproof nuts. If you're at a dicey stance, you might want to clip into these pieces before you finish rigging the belay anchor.

The second step is to shore up the primary placements with secondary anchors. Set one nut to oppose the primary placements and create a multi-directional matrix, then set at least two more pieces in the downward direction to back up the primary bomber. Remember that you want an efficient anchor, not simply one that will bear the most impact. That means the nuts should ideally be straightforward to place and remove and as centrally located as possible—a nice, tight grouping as opposed to a dazzling web of nuts crisscrossing the station. Once the primary placements are set, try to rig the secondary anchors in close proximity, but not so close that they are cramped or virtually on top of each other. If the rock is less than perfect quality, you may want to spread the anchors out to preserve redundancy. Don't put all your eggs in one pail. Be sure that the one closest to you (first to be loaded in the event of an upward pull) is multidirectional.

Personally, I like to place a minimum of four pieces, three in the downward direction and one upward, opposing the primary anchor—no matter how inviolate the placements seem individually. Sometimes, three are enough, and sometimes that's all you'll get. Anything less is a crap shoot.

Lastly, you must connect the various components of the system so they function as one unit. In many cases, this is the most critical, and complicated, part of the whole procedure. Several possibilities exist for connecting the anchors. A viable and quick method is to tie tightly to a bombproof multidirectional anchor set near your waist, then tie in to two more bombproof downward anchors placed above the first, with the belayer's body in line between the anchors and the anticipated direction of pull. This is simple but very difficult to equalize, and should only be used when every placement is truly bombproof. It's a good idea to tie into the most bombproof anchor with a figure eight knot, while clove hitches should suffice for the remaining anchors. It takes some practice to learn just how to feather the clove hitches so the whole rig is more or less under equal tension. This popular rope tie-in is usually the quickest method, requiring the least amount of extra gear, and in years past, it was used ten-to-one over all other setups. Newer methods have since replaced this standard setup, however.

Equalizing the Anchor

Once you have set the nuts, equalizing the system provides the greatest strength from the anchors. Equalizing the anchors is especially important if the anchors are anything less than bombproof; all the force is divided and distributed evenly between the various placements.

To distribute the force, use a self-equalizing "sliding knot" and clip into the sling. Make sure you put the proper twist in the sling so you're still connected into the sling if one of the anchors fails. And once the anchor is all set up, apply some tension in the direction of pull and scrutinize it like an engineer. Often you will want to make some small finishing adjustments to get the system just as you want

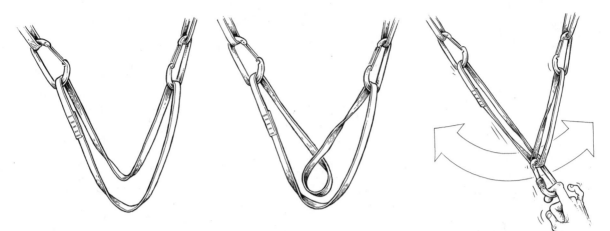

Self-equalizing sliding knot. Remember to double up the tie-in carabiner!

it. All components of the anchor should have all the slack removed, usually accomplished by cinching up the clove hitches.

Always use independent slings of the correct length from each piece if you know the direction of loading, and remember that the direction of pull is critically linked to equalization. More elaborate methods of equalizing an anchor are possible; these listed are the most common modes.

SLCDs are very useful in rigging anchors because you can jockey the SLCD around to an ideal location, rather than hoping for bottlenecks or constrictions in the right place.

Use of a cordelette greatly facilitates equalizing the load between two, three, or four anchors. A cordelette is a 16-foot section of 6 mm Spectra tied into a loop. It can be clipped through all the anchor pieces and tied off with an overhand knot to create a single tie-in point. The biggest shortcoming to the system is that it doesn't maintain perfect equalization if the loading direction changes. It does, however, nicely form separate, redundant, and equalized loops that offer no extension if one of the anchors fails. For this reason, and because they can greatly simplify a complex rigging task, cordelettes have become standard tackle with most climbers.

Horizontal Cracks

Depending on the cliff, we're left to rig anchors in horizontal cracks at least some of the time. Part of the system is built on opposing placements, where the direction of pull is toward the middle, but often the best single nut is the one set for a direct, outward pull. With a taper or hex, you find a slot, wiggle the nut in, and move it horizontally to where the lip of the crack is narrower than the depths. When the anchor is pulled straight out, the rock would have to break away for the nut to fail. Of course, SLCDs have simplified this process, for you only need a reasonable crack to arrange the anchor as you see fit. Remember that with all SLCDs, the alignment of the unit is crucial; and anytime the stem is running over an edge—which should be avoided if at all possible—the unit must have a flexible stem.

Angle of the Dangle

We can secure ourselves to an anchor matrix with various rigging systems, including using slings and cordelettes, tying in directly with the rope, or using combinations of slings, cordelettes, and the climbing rope. When the anchors are vertically oriented—meaning that the individual placements are, say, all placed in a vertical crack—the main considerations are to rig the system so it complies with SRENE

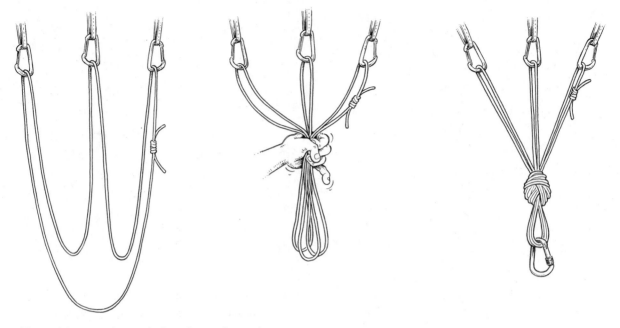

The cordelette equalizes multiple anchors with a single tie-in point.

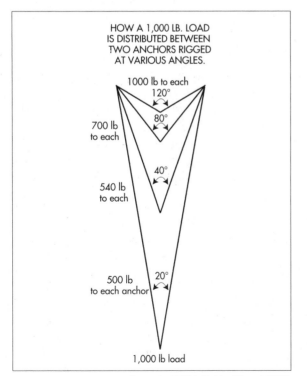

HOW A 1,000 LB. LOAD
IS DISTRIBUTED BETWEEN
TWO ANCHORS RIGGED
AT VARIOUS ANGLES.

1000 lb to each
120°

700 lb
to each
80°

540 lb
to each
40°

500 lb
to each anchor
20°

1,000 lb load

(from the AMGA Guides Manual 1992)

standards. When some or all of the individual placements of an anchor are set in a horizontal crack, we must take another factor into consideration.

Every anchor set in a horizontal crack will necessarily form a triangular shape, easily visualized by picturing the letter V. The points of the triangle are formed by the farthest left-hand placement (A), the farthest right-hand placement (B), and the point at which you secure the rigging to the climbing rope—the anchor point (C). The critical thing to grasp here is that the bigger the angle formed by this V, the greater the force placed on the A and B placements. Again, as the angle of the V increases, the forces on the A and B placements increase. The phenomenon is known as "load multiplication," and it's sobering to see how quickly the force increases as the angle of the V increases.

The rule of thumb: Whenever connecting horizontal placements with a sling or cordelette, strive to keep the angle of the V at the anchor point around thirty to sixty degrees. Some guides insist you can push this angle up to ninety degrees, but this is pushing things too far for my skin. To decrease the angle of the V, extend the anchor point below the placements with slings. Remember, the greater the angle of the V, the greater the forces on the placements. Play it safe: Keep the angle of the V below sixty degrees.

A Few More Thoughts on Anchors

The anchor is the foundation of safe climbing. A poor anchor is like jogging on the freeway—you won't last long. There is no mystery to rigging a sound one. If there is ever any doubt, double up the anchor. While three nuts are often adequate, it's not uncommon to see an anchor with four, even five nuts, all equalized. When the crack is thin, forcing the use of smaller protection, place more rather than fewer. Trusting an anchor rigged completely from small units is petrifying duty, and should only happen in extreme emergencies, never out of choice. SLCDs have proven their utility, but many climbers avoid rigging anchors completely from mechanical devices, particularly for toprope situations, where the weighting and unweighting can cause the SLCD to walk around. There's nothing like a bomber "passive" (nonmechanical) nut buried in a bottleneck. Come hell or high water, that nut's going nowhere. There are situations in climbing where you may take a calculated risk, but never with the anchor.

The limitations of attempting to cover every fundamental in one book is never so evident than with anchors, a subject that deserves 500 pages alone. We have two consolations: First, once you understand the basics, building your own anchors and watching how others build theirs—both of which are easy to do at any "trad" crag—will teach you faster and perhaps better than any manual can. Second, while I'm hamstrung for space in this manual, there are two other inexpensive books that deal strictly with anchors, also in the How to Rock Climb Series: *Climbing Anchors,* and *More Climbing Anchors.* These or similar texts, plus anything else you can read on the subject (particularly in climbing magazines), should be required for all beginners. The art of fashioning anchors is a lifetime study and continues to evolve with each passing year and as new equipment is introduced.

The Belay

Belaying—the technique of managing the rope to safeguard a climber against a fall—is the most important responsibility climbers routinely face. We will look carefully at each aspect of the belaying system, but first, here's a brief overview.

The belayer passes the rope through a belay device and clips it into a locking carabiner attached to his harness. He feeds out or takes in rope as needed to keep the climber safe. The belayer locks the rope off if the climber falls, and might lower the climber back to the ground at the end of the climb. A belayer keeps excess slack out of the rope, but doesn't allow the rope to pull down on the leader. He also doesn't "hoist" a toproped climber up the route. The responsible belayer double-checks the leader's and his own harness buckles, the anchor setup, belay device, locking biner, and tie-in knots before either leaves the ground (much as a pilot will quickly go over a checklist). The belayer is responsible for the safety of the person climbing. He must be proficient, and he must stay focused on the climber. The belayer should situate himself in a secure stance so he can't trip over his own feet, say, and pull the leader off. Finally, he should stack the rope to feed nicely, preferably not in the dirt, before the climber sets off.

When belaying a leader, the belayer feeds out rope through the belay device, or "belays" (belay devices will be discussed more fully later). Both his anchor and location are generically called "the belay," or "belay station." You climb in stages called "pitches," which usually refers to the distance between belay stations, something less than a rope length. A pitch is rarely a whole rope length, since you often stop short at a ledge, a good stance, or a crack that offers a convenient place to belay. A bombproof anchor is far more important than stretching out a lead simply to make it longer. If you pass obvious belay stances, you often end up wasting time constructing an anchor in a poor crack or at an awkward locale.

Belaying is the technique of not only paying out the rope, but holding it fast should your partner fall. The entire protection system of rock climbing

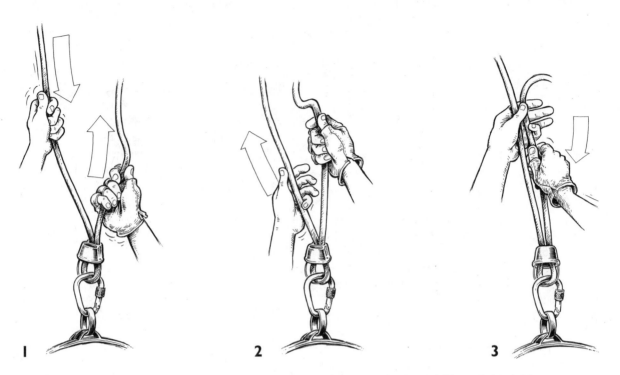

BELAYING Taking rope in: 1. Both hands grasping tightly, the rope is fed through the device. 2. The guide hand slides up. 3. Clasps both ends of the rope above the other hand to allow the brake hand to slide down, and the series begins again.

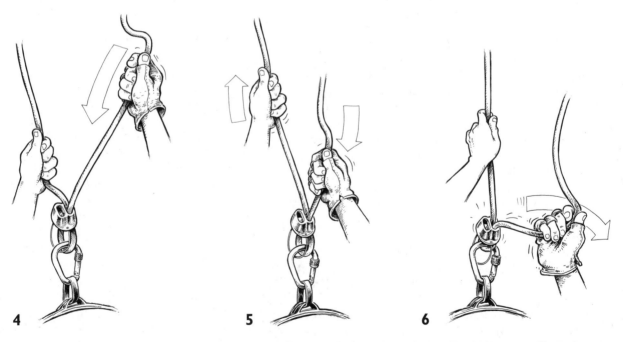

BELAYING Letting rope out: 4, 5. Both hands grasping tightly, the rope is fed through the device. 6. The braking action: The brake hand bends the rope across the belay device.

depends on the certainty of both the belay anchor and the belayer to do their job—to stop the climber should she fall, and to remain fastened to the cliff. It is very rare that both the belay and anchor should fail, and it's into the beyond if they do. That is why extreme vigilance is always paid to both the anchor and belay.

The mechanics of belaying are basic; consequently, some climbers pay less than perfect attention to the task. Don't fall into this dangerous trap, for a belayer literally holds his partner's life in his hands. A cavalier attitude toward the importance of the belay or the anchors will get someone killed in a hurry. The process is fundamental, and the technique is simple and reliable. Still, 40 percent of all fatal climbing accidents in Yosemite are due to mistakes and failures in the belay chain. Consequently, the importance of a sound belay system cannot be overstated.

There are two ends of the rope: your end, which you are tied into and which is tied off to the anchor, and the "live," or "business" end, which goes to the person climbing. The rope is fed through a belay device and locking carabiner attached to your waist. The live end going to the climber is handled by the "guide" hand. The "brake" hand holds the rope on the other side of the belay device. When the climber is leading away from you, the guide hand feeds the rope out, pulling it through the belay device; when the climber is ascending up to you, the guide hand pulls in the slack as the climber ascends. As the rope is reeled in, it passes through the belay device to the brake hand, which is also pulling in slack. The brake hand pulls the rope away, and the guide hand pulls it toward you; always keep the rope snug through the device.

Belaying a climber leading away from you is fairly simple: The guide hand shuffles out the rope in little tugs, the paid-out rope moving smoothly through the belay device and the brake hand on the other side. Taking the rope up, or belaying a climber "in," is a little tricky at first, and involves a three-part sequence. The guide hand is extended away from the waist. It clasps the rope and pulls it in. Simultaneously, the brake hand is pulling out, clasping the rope

and pulling it away from your body as it passes through your belay device. That's the first stroke: The guide hand pulls in, the brake hand pulls out. At the end of that stroke, the guide hand is at the belay device, and the brake hand is extended out from the device.

Part two requires the brake hand to momentarily hold fast while the guide hand slides back out along the live end. When the arm is fully extended, the guide hand—still holding the rope on that side—reaches across and grabs the brake hand rope above the brake hand.

Part three involves the brake hand sliding back to the belay device and the process is repeated: Guide hand pulls in, brake hand slides back. This procedure sounds complicated but is very simple to perform. It is the best way to belay. Always observe the absolute rule: *The brake hand never leaves the rope.* Not only does it never leave the rope, your fingers are always curled around it, ready to clench hard when necessary.

A fall is checked by bending the ropes across the belay device with your brake hand, which collapses the belay device onto the locking carabiner and locks the rope fast. When you try to belay the rope in, never letting your brake hand leave the clenched position, you'll see there is only one way to do so— the way just described.

The ability to stop a falling climber depends on several factors. You must not be caught unaware. Your attention must remain focused on the climber whose life you are entrusted with. When a climber falls, your brake hand must quickly bend the rope across the belay device (extending the brake hand at a forty-five-degree angle away from the device), causing the friction to increase and the rope to automatically lock up. Properly performed, most falls can be held with little effort. In time, this reaction will become instinctive. To efficiently arrest a fall, you must be properly braced, anticipating both the impact force and the direction of pull caused by the falling climber. But all of this is of little value if you are not properly anchored. To say it again: The anchor is the backbone of the safety system. It, beyond anything, must be secure!

On sport routes and toproped climbs, the belayer often lowers the climber back to the ground at the end of the route. A retreating leader may also need to be lowered to the ground, or to the belay. To lower a climber, first lock the rope off by bending it across the belay device. Next, lean back, or "sit into," the rope to give the climber tension. Place both hands on the brake side of the rope and slowly but fluidly lower the climber to the ground. When the climber reaches the ground, slowly ease her onto her feet. (For a more detailed discussion of lowering, see Chapter 7: Sport Climbing.)

While this description provides the basics and is a good review for a novice, far and away the best and most efficient venue to learn belaying fundamentals is in a climbing gym with an instructor watching your every move and backing you up to avert mishaps. The controlled environment and chance to practice in a toprope situation minimize the learning risks to almost zero (they are never zero). Because the gym climbs are short, you'll tend to climb many more routes inside than you would outdoors, so you'll find yourself belaying quite a bit in the gym. And practice makes perfect. After belaying a few hundred times, which you can accomplish in less than a month in most any gym, the process becomes very natural, and you'll know the mistakes to avoid.

When you start a climb, remember to make sure the site is safe and, if at all possible, protected from rockfall, dropped gear, a falling climber, etc. Ideally, the belayer should be located close to, if not right at, the base of the rock and should always be tied taut to the belay anchor. If there is any slack between belayer and anchor, a long fall can jerk the belayer off his feet and thrash him around until he comes taut to the anchor. The rope, meanwhile, can be ripped from his hands, resulting in disaster. Every fall generates force in one direction—the direction of pull. Always station yourself in a direct line between the direction of pull and the anchor. If you don't, the force of the fall may drag you there anyway, and you might forfeit the belay—and the leader's life—during the flight. Remember ABC: Anchor-Belayer-Climber.

To clarify, consider these examples. You're tied off to a tree 10 feet away from the cliff, but you're belaying several feet to the side of the start of the climb. If the leader falls, you can plot the ideal direction of pull as a straight line from the tree to her first anchor. If you're not also in line with that pull—because you are some ways off to the side—the impact will, perforce, drag you in line. If you are in line but have tied the anchor off with a lot of slack, you will probably be dragged toward (or even up) the cliff until the rope becomes taut to the anchor. In both instances the leader has fallen that much farther. The belay is of little value while you are bouncing over the ground, and it's perilous to get banged against the cliff, for the sudden force can jar your brake hand off the rope. If you're set up correctly, catching a fall is an effortless and routine event.

If you must arrange your anchor on the cliff, try to rig it directly below the start of the climb (remembering our credo about the site safe from rockfall, dropped gear, a falling climber, etc.). This puts the direction of pull straight up, which is far less awkward than having to compensate for a belay coming in from the side and forcing the belayer into an oblique angle. The location of the belay stance is of key importance when you are belaying from the ground and are anchored to protection that is placed in the cliff (as opposed to, say, being anchored to a tree some ways back from the cliffside). When you are belaying on the ground and are anchored to the rock, always tie off short to anchor, with no slack, which keeps you from being lifted off the ground. Since a fall will draw you toward the cliff, many belayers like to keep one leg braced against the wall, acting as a shock absorber in the event of a fall. If you're belaying safely on the ground, and your partner does not significantly outweigh you, you may want to forego the anchor so you can get out of the way of potential rockfall or dropped gear.

Belay Devices

Many types of belay devices are currently available. Most work by creating friction on the rope so the belayer can easily hold the force generated in a fall. A belay using a device has commonly been called a "static" belay, as the rope is locked tight in the device in the event of a fall (several of the devices actually let a few inches of the rope slip through them before they lock). Since most belay devices are normally clipped to the front of a harness, the term "static belay" is an overstatement. The rope is indeed locked fast in the device when stopping a fall, but you'd have to be a twenty-ton Roman statue to keep your torso from moving with the pull. The main value of a belay device is that it requires very little strength to hold even the longest possible fall, and there's little chance of it ever failing or the belayer suffering abrasions or rope burns—if the whole system is properly rigged. When the disparity of weight is substantial between belayer and leader, belay devices really shine over the outmoded hip belay (to be explained later). For several years I did most of my climbing with Lynn Hill, who I outweighed by more than a hundred pounds. I fell countless times, and she always caught me effortlessly and never got a scratch.

The first belay device was the Sticht plate, invented by a German engineer in the early 1970s. The plate is a four-ounce aluminum disk with one or two channel holes machined through it. A bight of rope is passed through one of the channels and clipped through a locking carabiner attached to your harness. (Two regular biners with the gates opposed will also work, though not as conveniently). The plate has a keeper loop that, when clipped into the carabiner, keeps the plate from floating out away from the waist. Since the plate will sometimes lock up when you don't want it to, some plates have a spring on the back to prohibit this. Using two carabiners to attach the rope to your harness also helps prevent the plate from locking up, and provides smoother belaying and rappelling.

Sticht plates come in all manner of sizes and dimensions for use with 9, 10, and 11 mm rope, and other configurations for double ropes. A plate with two 11 mm slots is probably the most versatile for belaying and rappelling. There are also micro versions of the Sticht plate, which work exactly like the Sticht, are as strong, and weigh less than one ounce; however, they are often too small for 11 mm ropes

Ian Green reaches for hand hams on Scarface (5.11c) in Indian Creek Canyon, Utah. Stewart M. Green photo

and usually overheat quickly. Though once popular, the Sticht plate is rarely seen these days.

The Lowe Tuber, Black Diamond Air Traffic Controller (ATC), Trango Pyramid (plus a host of European versions of the same device) are cone- or pyramid-shaped tubes that are light, feed rope a bit more smoothly than a flat plate, and have more

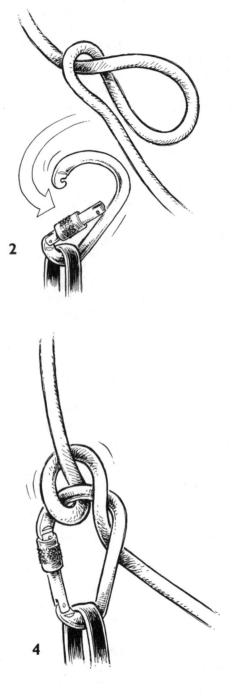

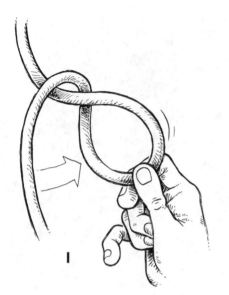

THE MUNTER HITCH:
1. Twist rope.   2. Twist again.   3. Clip doubled rope in   4. and pull up and out.

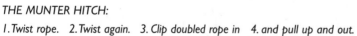

surface area for heat dissipation. A bight of rope passes in and around a locking carabiner and back out the tube. During a fall, the tube, like the Sticht plate, locks the rope off at the biner. The amount of working friction depends on what end of the tube you have against the locking biner, as well as the angle of the brake rope. For belaying with 9 mm or smaller ropes, the small end of the device should be toward the carabiner. With larger ropes the device will feed rope more smoothly with the large end of the tube toward the carabiner. For rappelling, the small end should be toward the carabiner, unless the rock angle is low and you're using two large diameter ropes, in which case the large end should be toward the carabiner. Like the Sticht plate, a keeper loop holds the Tuber, ATC, Pyramid, or other device close to the biner. This style of belay device has become standardized gear in most gyms and, consequently, is the most popular unit on the cliffside as well.

Some climbers belay with a figure eight rappel device. It is acceptable to belay a toproped climber with the rope arranged in the figure eight as you would for rappelling, but this setup does not provide enough friction for belaying a leader. The smaller hole on most figure eights is designed for a bight of rope to be passed through and clipped into a locking carabiner, like you would rig a belay plate. This is the only safe way to belay a leader with a figure eight. It is not advised, however.

Someone was bound to create a device that automatically locks up the rope in the event of a fall, whether your brake hand is on the rope or not. The Petzl Gri Gri and the Salewa Antz are two such products that have been in common usage for over a decade. Both devices come with extensive instructions about their safe usage, and both require practice by even an expert climber to become proficient with them. These self-locking belay devices are excellent when you're being belayed by a novice. They're also great for sport climbing, when the climber is spending a lot of time hanging on the rope to work out moves. Both devices must be properly rigged, however, or the climber can hit the deck if he falls. For a majority of advanced climbers, the Gri Gri is the device of choice.

Long used by stevedores to tether onerous loads on the docks, the Munter hitch is a handy alternative to devices because it only requires a large-mouthed, locking biner attached to your harness. Knowing the Munter hitch could prove to be essential if you ever drop your belay device. When Swiss climber Werner Munter introduced this hitch to climbing—claiming the invention—the UIAA conducted extensive tests and gave it the thumbs up; it has steadily caught on ever since. During a fall, the brake hand goes out, and the hitch locks on itself. Always use a carabiner with a large opening—an oversized pear-shaped biner with a locking gate—for the Munter hitch. The mouth on a regular, or even a D, carabiner is not wide enough to keep the hitch from binding when you switch from taking in to feeding out rope, or vice versa. Most climbers who have tried the Munter hitch have found it to work quite well. The action is good, the setup instantaneous, and you don't have to carry a device, even if it only weighs an ounce. The drawback is that the rope often gets excessively kinked, so the technique can *never* be recommended over the more functional cone- or pyramid-shaped devices. A word of caution: Because the rope is continually running through the biner, the action can unscrew the sleeve on a locking biner, so crank the sleeve tight before belaying and keep an eye on it. For these reasons, a belay device is recommended over the Munter hitch by virtually everyone. Another word of caution: Belay devices perform only as well as you know how to use them, and a good belay is safe only if you observe the rules we've laid down. The belay anchor must be inviolate; always tie in taut to the belay anchor; get in line with, and anticipate, the direction of pull; maintain a good brace or stance; stay alert; and never take your brake hand off the rope—the absolute rule—lest your belay prove lethal to your partner and, perhaps, to yourself.

Hip Belay

With the advent of modern-day belay devices, the hip belay has become obsolete. However, it is essential to know how to belay with little or no equipment in case you accidentally drop your gear. The hip belay is also the quickest belay to set up for short

THE HIP BELAY

1 and 2. Both hands grasping tightly, the rope is fed around the back. 2. The guide hand clasps both ends of the rope above the other hand to allow the brake hand to slide down, and the series begins again. Kevin Powell photos

THE HIP BELAY (continued)
For taking rope in:
3. The guide (left) hand clasps both ends of the rope above the brake (right) hand, then the brake hand is slid back (never releasing the rope) to draw in more rope. Then the prodecure is repeated.

4. To stop a fall, the brake (right) hand wraps the rope around the waist.
Kevin Powell photos

Praying the holds are sound and the runner stays put, Gigi Bonilla-Goldfarb creeps cautiously up a sheer and pebbly wall at the Needles, South Dakota. Bill Hatcher photo

stretches of belaying on fourth class terrain. It was the primary belay method for decades and works quite well when performed correctly. A belay device substantially increases the margin of safety, however.

Hip belaying is similar to belaying with a device, with your body substituting for the device. As before, you have two ends of rope: your end and the live end, which goes to the climber. The rope is wrapped around your waist and grasped firmly in each hand. The live end is handled by the guide hand, and the brake hand holds the rope on your other side. Feed the rope out with your guide hand, pulling it around your waist and through the brake hand on your other side. Take the rope in, using the same three-step sequence that you do with a belay device. The guide hand pulls in while the brake hand pulls out. The guide hand extends and grabs both sides of the rope. Finally, the brake hand slides back, and the guide hand drops the brake rope. Again, the absolute rule is to keep the brake hand on the rope.

When using the hip belay, there is a remote chance that the rope can be lifted over your back—if the guide hand is somehow jerked loose from the rope. A "guiding" biner solves this. Clip a biner into your harness near the guide hand. The live end is then taken up or paid out through the biner, and even if the guide hand comes loose, the line still goes around the back to the brake hand. You will quickly learn that the guide hand is no more than a guide and does little to stop the fall. It's the friction around the waist and the brake hand coming across the opposite hip that accomplish the brake.

When the pull is straight up, many climbers pass the rope under their butt instead of around their waist. Even with the guide biner, the upward pull will often draw the rope up your back, which is quite sensitive and fairly lean. So your bottom—

with the rope running under it—is a better and more secure cushion when belaying for the upward pull. In any event, always wear a shirt, and keep it tucked in unless you want some "galley slave" scars.

On paper, the hip belay sounds both strenuous and painful, and it's easy to envision a long fall sawing you in half or striping you with bone-deep rope burns. Neither should happen. Much of the impact force is absorbed by the rope, which stretches quite a bit; by the equipment the rope is running through; by the belay anchor; and, finally, by the belayer. And the friction afforded by your back or bottom, plus the natural dampening effect of your body is such that—if the system is rigged and executed correctly—a grandma could hold a baker's apprentice on the biggest fall he could take.

Beginners frequently develop a penchant for belaying one way, always using the same brake hand. Situations arise that will require you to belay with one hand or the other, so practice belaying both ways from the start.

The hip belay has been described as a "dynamic" belay in several recent articles and manuals, and this is a misnomer. Years ago, when the old hemp ropes would snap under high impacts, several authorities suggested letting a little rope intentionally slip through the hands to ease the shock on the hemp—a true "dynamic" belay. I'd wager this was never accomplished, though, because once the rope gets to speed, hands haven't been made that can simply crimp it to a stop. The recent reinvention of the term "dynamic belay" simply refers to inherent give in the system and in no way harks back to the diabolical suggestion of letting some line smoke through your mitts in a misguided attempt to ease a fall.

CHAPTER 5

The Art of Leading

Most veterans admit that climbing doesn't really start until you cast off on the lead. You can boulder around enchanted forests and follow a leader up the world's greatest rock climbs, but the moment you're the first on the rope, it's suddenly real in an altogether different way. Everything is magnified because now you're playing for keeps. The decisions are all yours—as are the rewards and the consequences. Whether that first lead is up a razor-cut crack at the base of El Capitan or on some filthy slab in a scrap heap quarry, the feeling of command and the special demands are always the same. It's no longer just an exhilarating physical challenge but a creative problem-solving design requiring many intangibles with the penalty of injury, or even death, for a major oversight.

Because leading is a procedure involving equipment and an applied system, we can nail down certain objective realities, at least in a generic sense. But the deeper we go, the grayer it all becomes. It's like discussing a fine painting or a classic wine: If you talk long enough, you'll eventually cast off into windy abstractions regardless of your expertise. Every climb, like every canvas and every wine, is a little different, and very little applies to one and all. Every climber is ultimately self-taught. We can open the way a bit, suggesting what fine leading is about, and not about, and ever stressing safety, but more than that must not be expected from an instruction manual. A professional guide can take you a bit further in preparing for those first leads, but when you do take the sharp end, it's just you and the rock.

The First Lead

Ideally, you will have taken a climbing course and had the fundamentals drummed into you by a competent instructor. You will have spent time placing nuts and rigging/equalizing anchors, so when you grab the lead, you don't have nagging doubts about your ability to do the basic things safely. You will have complemented your practical experience by reading this manual, or one like it. And you will have served at least a brief apprenticeship following an experienced leader up a host of climbs, becoming familiar with the nuances that a book, or even the best personal instruction, cannot impart. And ideally I would be a sultan on a South Pacific Island with no duties save to count my trunkful of black pearls. We don't live in an ideal world, and many first-time leaders have little experience. Some have no experience. Others can't be bothered with instruction and don't want to follow anyone, anywhere. They'll lead from day one and thank you very much for your advice. I don't suggest this latter tactic. It's a quick way to get hurt. You don't want to learn leading through trial and error. A first-time leader should know the whole procedure well before stepping out as boss. But either way, you'll have to decide what it is you want to lead.

Guidebooks

Picture a cliff, a quarter-mile long and 300 feet high. Folks first started climbing there in 1950, and the cliff has become a favorite for rock climbers. Since the first climber discovered the first way up the cliff,

Amos and Coco #11:
Out on the Sharp End

Amos and Coco drove up to Pico Raquilita after Coco's last yoga class on Friday night. After six months of yoga and a diet long on roughage, tubers, and kiwis and short on Jolt and Fatburgers, Amos had trimmed down to 200 pounds and was "limber as a pipe cleaner," according to his personal appraisal ("More like bamboo," said Coco). Coco, now a brown belt in aikido, had maintained her strength training and presently sported the physique of a fitness model minus the torpedo implants and Vegas make-up job. In both physique and character, the pair had transformed themselves.

All the way up the winding mountain road to Pico Raquilita, as Coco gunned Amos's fire-breathing truck up the switchbacks, Amos read from the guidebook and the pair discussed possible routes for their first lead. Following the advice of instructor Jules Pinkus, whose word was indubitable, they were looking for a well-established and well-protected "trade route" well within their abilities. Both had accomplished the 5.9 grade in the gym and at Mt. Gorgeous, the local practice cliff, so a route in the 5.6 or 5.7 range seemed appropriate. There were at least fifty such routes at Pico Raquilita, and choosing a specific one was impossible inside the truck. But they narrowed their choice down to a handful.

That night, sacked out in their sleeping bags beneath a continent of stars, Amos pictured himself on the "sharp end," erect and heroic as Gaston Rébuffat in *Starlight and Storm*, gliding up an alpine wall set against an azure sky. Then he glanced over at Coco, her face frosted in blue moonlight. Amos smiled and wiggled a little closer to her bag; she rolled over and told him to go to sleep. Amos had vowed to keep things Platonic with his partner, but just now he felt like murdering Plato and everyone in the Republic. Then he realized all those Greeks were dead and gone, but that didn't help the fire-fighter at all.

Next morning, the pair woke early and Amos just about ran up the trail, Coco a short ways behind. They settled at the Wall of Cracks, which featured some half dozen, one-pitch crack routes, each ending at a big ledge with a slew of huge trees. The guidebook gave *The Hatchet* five stars, and Amos thought the 5.7 hand crack was perfect for their first lead. Amos harnessed up, got a rack together, flaked out the rope, rigged a stout anchor off a pine tree near the base, balanced his vital energies—and sent Coco up. Coco didn't much admire the route's name, but *The Hatchet* looked classic and safe—a polished hand crack from bottom to top—so she cast off.

After 10 feet she felt about 10,000 volts coursing through her taut loins. Few circumstances in life present an experience of so thoroughly being the author of your own fate, a fact Coco soon realized out on the "sharp end." She recalled the words of that indomitable mountaineer, Jules Pinkus, who said that when you get scared or excited, you have only your training to fall back on. And Coco's training had been extensive. She'd placed countless nuts when it didn't count and gained the confidence that when it did count, like now, she knew a bomber nut from something less. She slotted a nut and jammed for glory, while Amos, nervous as a rattler, kept begging her to slot another nut. "Shut your pie hole and just let me climb," she said. And climb she did, glibly moving up the wavering crack, gaining the ledge and a big tree. She'd always heard the phrase that we are creators of our own lives, but nothing could replace the concrete experience of that idea. She felt 10 feet tall as Amos followed her lead.

They rappelled off and Amos dashed up a nearby chimney, relishing the charged mixture of fear and freedom he felt ratcheting up the bombay slot, placing protection whenever he saw fit. Over the day, exchanging leads, the pair dusted off another dozen short climbs.

"Sky's the limit," said Amos. Coco suggested that on the next day, they boot up the difficulty beyond the 5.6 and 5.7 routes they'd dashed up since her breakout effort on *The Hatchet*. "Providing you're ready for that," she joked. "Sugarplum," said Amos, "I was born ready."

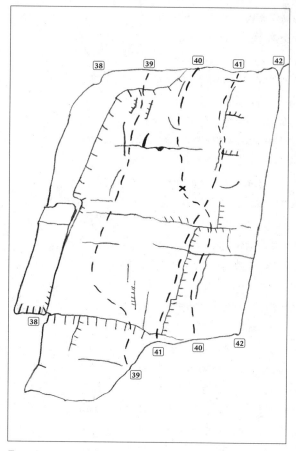

Typical guidebook topo   Topo by D. Fasulo

Most guidebooks have several master photos, or topographic drawings, with lines superimposed to show the various routes, or at least prominent features allowing you to find specific climbs by reference. A guidebook is indispensable—to experts who want to know where the hardest routes are, to beginners who yearn for easy ground, and to everyone in between. It allows us to pick a route that best suits our taste and expertise. Many guidebooks have a quality rating, or at least a list of recommended routes, so a visiting climber can spend a few days and know he's tasted some of the best the crag has to offer. A guidebook is particularly important for the beginning leader, who can use all the guidance he can get.

The early guidebooks used photos and written descriptions. In the mid-1970s the written description was replaced by the "topo," or topographic guide. A topo is simply a minimal blueprint of the climb—really just a detailed line drawing—featuring prominent features, belay locations, (usually) any fixed anchors, the type of climbing (liebacking, etc.), and the difficulty, all rendered in a facile set of symbols. This graphic representation of cliffs and their climbs is the most precise and convenient means of route description, easily understood and capable of crossing language barriers (though inexactly). Every topo guide has a key at the beginning to clarify the symbols, though most are as obvious as a road sign of a cow crossing the road.

Topos are normally more detailed than prose but are still in truncated form, so it takes some experience to learn how to read them at a glance. Though rare, some guidebooks still use prose descriptions, so become familiar with both formats. Many times the guidebook is bulky, so climbers often photocopy the topos and carry a page instead of a book.

Choose a route well within your abilities for that first lead. Most every cliff has a classic easy route that hundreds of people have broken in on. Whatever you choose, be certain the protection is sound, that you are at least somewhat adept in the techniques involved, and that the route is straightforward, requiring no unusual shenanigans or special skills. A

exploration has been steady until now there are more than 300 different ways—or "routes"—up the wall. How do we know this? Since 1950, each route was recorded and later published in a guidebook. A guidebook lists first ascents—the names and dates of the first people to climb a given route. At a modern sport climbing area, most of the routes were probably established from the late 1980s up to the present, but the method of rating, naming, and recording the routes remains the same as in the "old" days.

Each route is named and rated by the first ascenders, and by the time a route makes it into print, it's usually had enough ascents that the rating is at least somewhat objective, arrived at by consensus.

direct, easy climb—that's what you want. If the first lead proves too easy, no one's stopping you from hopping right back onto something a little stiffer. Getting in over your head on your first lead is a horrible and potentially dangerous experience that may color, if not end, your climbing career. Take it slow. Cut loose only when you know what's happening. Present-day climbers are apt to first lead a bolted sport climb requiring the leader to place no gear save the biners/quickdraws needed to clip the bolts.

The Rack

The collection of gear the climber takes up the climb is called the rack. There are two considerations: what gear to take and how to take, or "rack," it.

Once you have decided on a climb, the guidebook should tell you the requisite equipment needed for safe passage. If it doesn't, you're left to eyeball the route and estimate what's needed. A "standard" rack may be the catchall rack that works for 80 percent of the routes at 80 percent of the areas (not counting the clip-and-go sport routes). This consists of a complete set of "wires" (cabled micro tapers to tapers of about an inch across), a progressively sized selection of SLCDs to about 2 or 3 inches, five or six shoulder-length runners, ten or so quickdraws, carabiners for each nut carried (and a few extra as well), and a nut tool to remove stuck nuts. In any case, climbers routinely ask around to get the lowdown: What's the best rack? Is there any hidden placement and where is it? Does a certain nut work best at the crux? Although such advice is often very valuable, you can waste considerable time getting it—and it's sometimes contradictory because everyone does things a little differently. Also, the suggested rack is often a little "thin," so use your own judgment. The suggested rack normally refers only to sizes encountered, not specific nuts by brand names. Learn to translate this relative to the gear you own. And remember: It's better to take more than you need rather than less.

There are two methods to rack gear, or "hardware": You can clip it on a gear sling worn over the shoulder (largely outdated these days) or on gear loops on the side of your harness. Either method

works, but on steep and overhanging climbs, gear on a shoulder sling will follow gravity and slip around your back, making quick access difficult and putting more of the weight on your hands. Gear racked on a harness hangs directly over both hips, and depending on your free hand, you may discover the desired nut on the opposite hip, requiring an awkward reach and some fumbling to even unclip it. Also, on wide cracks, especially "off-width," any gear racked on your harness will inevitably get hung up and grind on both the rock and your hips, making progress extremely awkward. So while racking gear on a shoulder sling is a method rarely if ever used on a sport climb, the practice comes into its own when conditions (wide cracks, etc.) dictate.

Whatever method you choose, gear should be racked systematically according to size, in an order you have memorized for ready access. Rack small nuts up front, progressively bigger going back. SLCDs and medium to large hexes are racked individually—one biner for each nut. Clip the carabiner in so the gate is facing the body and opens from the top. This way the thumb will naturally go to the gate and you can lift the nut straight off, rather than having to twist it about, opening the gate with your fingers. Wired nuts are racked in bunches, from micro nuts on up, perhaps six on one biner. How they are clipped onto your rack depends on how you want them. Some climbers unclip the appropriate bunch, fit the nut of choice, unclip it from the bunch, and return the remainder to the rack. (The danger here is that you might drop the entire bunch.) Others know at first glance what nut they want and remove it individually from the sling or harness. (If you're wrong, it's better to have had the whole bunch in hand for an easy second try.) If you move wires individually, rack the carabiner gate out, so you can lift the nut out, instead of back and under. If you remove the whole bunch, rack the biner so the gate faces your body. Free biners should be racked together, either in front of or behind the nuts. (Additional equipment will be explained later.)

There are other ways to do things, but perhaps more important than aping the most common routines is to discover what works best for you

Climbing Signals

"ON BELAY?" The question the climber asks before he proceeds.

"BELAY ON" The response the belayer tells the climber when his belay is set and ready.

"CLIMBING" What the climber says to the belayer indicating the climber is starting to climb.

"CLIMB" The belayer's response that he's ready to belay the rope, proceeding to do so as the climber advances.

"SLACK" A command to the belayer to let out some rope, give slack.

"UP ROPE" A command to the belayer to take in the rope, pull up the slack.

"TENSION" or "TAKE" A command to the belayer to hold the climber on tension by holding the belay fast.

"LOWER" A command to the belayer that the climber is ready to be lowered.

"WATCH ME" commands the belayer to pay close attention, expect or be prepared for a fall.

"FALLING!" The climber is falling—a statement of fact.

"BELAY OFF" The climber's signal to the belayer that he has anchored himself and that the belayer's responsibility to belay should end.

"OFF BELAY!" The belayer's response to the climber that the belay has ended.

"ROCK!" Akin to yelling "Fore" on a golf course. Rocks are coming down; take cover.

"ROPE!" A rope is coming down; watch for it.

(likely what we've described) and to generally do things the same way each time. Standardizing your modus operandi means you will become familiar with one method as your customary practice. That way your hand will automatically know where to reach for a free biner or the wired nuts because they're always racked in the same way and at the same place. When you vary your racking methods according to whim, you must discover where things are with every climb. Not good. Stick to one method and get efficient with that method. At moderate climbing levels efficiency is a virtue but not a necessity; when you start pushing your envelope, if you have to fumble around trying to locate gear, your common refrain might well become "Falling!"

Starting Out

You've picked a route and you know where it goes. You're racked up, tied in, and breathing fire, but who's that tending your line? A cousin sprung from reform school to whom you explained the fundamentals on the hike in? No, sir! You must have full confidence that your belayer will catch you if you fall. If you can, get an experienced climber to belay you for that first lead. He can give valuable coaching from below and can critique your lead once done. Moreover, you will know he can belay and can catch any fall you might take, which frees your mind to concentrate on the lead.

A standardized protocol of communication removes any doubt as to what the leader and the belayer are doing, are expected to do, are asked to do, and are warned to do. (See list of climbing signals.) When you anticipate being unable to hear each other because of wind or river noise, for example, work out your own protocol in rope tugs before the leader starts the pitch. Maybe three sharp tugs from the leader would mean you can take him off belay, and two sharp tugs from the leader would mean you can climb. In such difficult situations it is the responsibility of the belayer to be particularly sensitive to the rope so the leader has the proper amount of slack or tension.

Before you start up, study the rock above and spot any key holds, obvious features, or nut placements. Climb up mentally, imagining the required techniques. On easy climbs, the sequence is usually no mystery—just a matter of execution—so picture yourself doing the moves, then go after it.

The first section above the ground is crucial because if you fall there, you hit the deck. So climb no higher than you feel comfortable jumping off from, then set your first nut. (All gear placed to protect the leader is called "protection," or simply "pro.") Make certain that the first pro is especially good and, if at all possible, multidirectional. And make certain your belayer knows you're clipped in. The belay is worthless to the first pro because you aren't clipped into anything. Now you're plugged in, and the system is operative. If the pro seems questionable, double it up—place two or even three nuts until you know something will stop your fall. At the outset, the leader must always calculate how far he has to fall to hit the ground, a ledge, or other feature on the route, and he should always have some pro in to preclude this. Up higher, once you have several nuts in—providing they're good—"decking out" is no longer a concern. But "rope drag" is.

Protection: The Direction of Pull

As a leader, you must continually assess the direction the rope will pull on all the protection below you should you fall. Until you can, you won't be a safe leader. Though it sounds confusing, the concept is easy.

Rarely does a climb follow a perfectly straight line. Even cracks curve and snake around, so to some extent the rope has to bend about according to the contour of the crack your pro is in. To ably predict the direction of pull, a leader must be conscious of the various forces on the entire system. When you fall, the rope becomes tight, and the transmission of force pulls all the protection toward the middle, toward an imaginary straight line between leader and belayer. Pro not placed directly in that line is subject to considerable sideways and upward pull, and can easily be wrenched free if you have not compensated for the oblique force. So when the route zigzags around, there are certain things we can do.

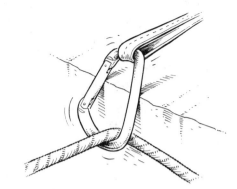

Stressing a carabiner sideways over an edge is dangerous.

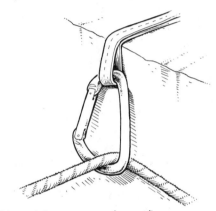

It's much better to use a longer sling.

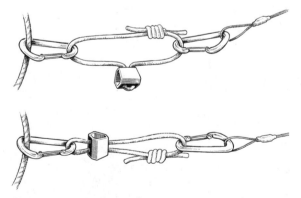

Top: Incorrect use of a nut sling as a runner
Bottom: A much stronger way

Using slings to allow the rope to run freely and keep the protection properly aligned

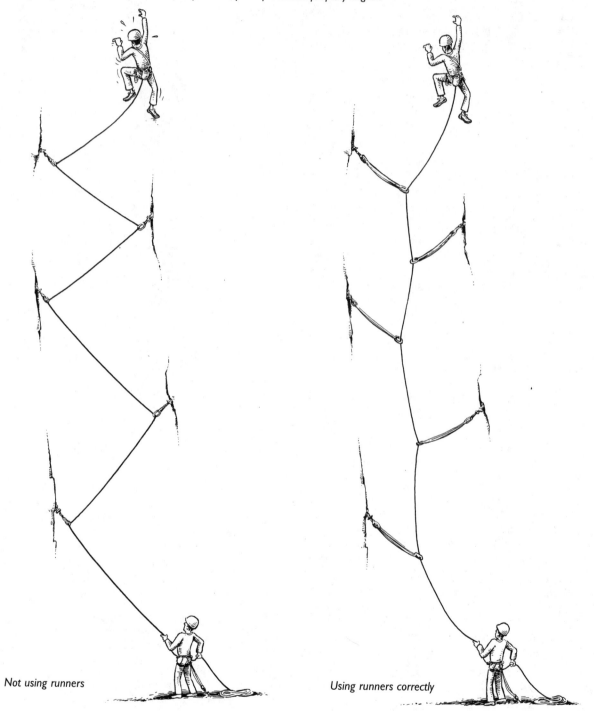

Not using runners

Using runners correctly

You always want the rope to follow as straight a line as possible, even if all your protection is from bolts (which cannot be wrenched free from sideways forces). The more crooks the rope makes, the greater the friction (the "rope drag"), which is somewhat like the belayer holding you back. An experienced leader imagines a plumb line between the belayer and the end of the first pitch, and arranges protection so the rope follows that line as closely as possible. When protection is by necessity placed to the side of the plumb line, we attach runners to the pro that, in effect, extend the protection toward the imaginary midline. The drawback with runners is that they increase the distance of a potential fall to twice the length of the runner. For this reason, and because the runner is like a free tether and can move rather than being just a fixed point, it is very rare that someone will attach a runner bigger than the normal length worn over the shoulder. If the runner is well off to the side and a fall will still transmit lateral force on the nut, either set the nut with a firm downward jerk or place an oppositional nut beneath it to form a multidirectional protection (some SLCD placements also work as multidirectionals).

The theory is simple: You are not just trailing a rope but dragging it through your protection. Runners keep that drag at a minimum and the nuts in place.

When clipping into fixed protection or cabled nuts, even if they're placed in a direct line, it has long become standard practice to use quickdraws. Quickdraws are small, sewn runners fashioned from either 1-inch or %6-inch tubular webbing that harbor two carabiners, one for the pro, one for the rope. Quickdraws are short, so they don't appreciably increase the potential fall, and they really facilitate the rope running smoothly. Moreover, cabled nuts are stiff and, when clipped off with single biners, can be lifted from the crack by rope drag. Quickdraws prevent this. Some climbers prefer to rack their shoulder slings as quickdraws by tripling the loops; this allows you to easily extend the quickdraws to a full-sized runner as required. Standard quickdraws, however, are lighter and much less bulky.

Use of a multidirectional anchor to prevent the rope from lifting the protection from the crack

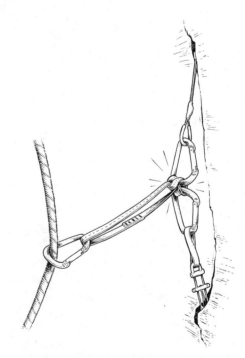

Close-up of a multidirectional anchor

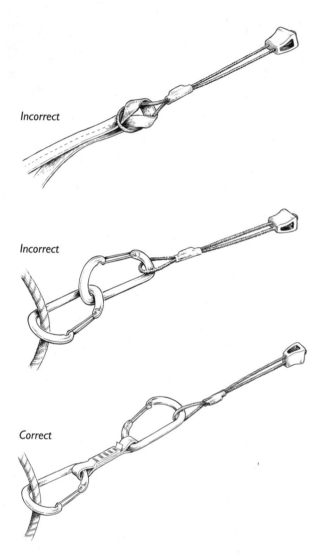

Incorrect

Incorrect

Correct

Clipping into wired nuts:

Top: Never thread sling material directly into a wire; with a solid fall the wire will slice right on through!

Middle: Never clip into an anchor that has any stiffness to it (like a wire) with two carabiners; a twist in the rope can pull the nut free or force the biners to unclip themselves.

Bottom: Correct use of the quickdraw, with rope-end biner gate down and out to easily accept the rope

If you're climbing directly above the last protection point, you'll want the rope running between your legs. If you're angling left or right off your last pro, try to avoid having the rope run directly between your legs—it's better to trail it over a leg; in the event of a fall, there is less danger of the tightening rope flipping you over backwards and increasing the chance of head injury. This rarely happens, but it's not unheard of.

When to Place Protection

There is no hard-and-fast rule concerning when to place protection or when to simply carry on. Experienced climbers place pro when they need it. To the beginning leader the experience is all new and he might not know when he needs pro; he is likely to think he always needs it. You definitely want sound protection at the start of a pitch and before any hard, or "crux," section. Anticipate the crux; place protection when you can, not counting on the hope that you can slot something 15 feet higher at the hard move. Whenever you encounter an obvious bottleneck or are resting on a big hold, slot a nut—even when the climbing is easy. If the climbing feels manageable and you feel vigorous, go 10 or 15 feet between nuts and feel the thrill and freedom of the lead. But always be aware of ledges or features you may hit should you fall, and protect yourself accordingly. Avoid the temptation to "run the rope out," going long distances between protection, even if the climbing is clearly moderate. Once you are a good judge of both your own prowess and the terrain encountered, do whatever you like. But the beginning leader will rarely want to go more than about 15 feet between nuts, if that far. That's only eight nuts for a 135-foot pitch, which isn't excessive by any count.

If one hand is holding you to the rock, clipping in can be trying. The universal method is to reach down below your tie-in, pull up a loop, and hold it in your teeth; reach down for more slack and clip in. Sounds odd, but there's not a leader alive who doesn't do this. Sometimes fixed protection is found in awkward positions and can be very grueling even to clip. Climbers sometimes rig quickdraws with one end clipped to a shoulder sling and the other slipped through the lead rope. At a desperate clip, just unclip from the gear sling and clip the fixed pro, and your rope is clipped in as well. If you discover the fixed pro is good enough, you're set. If it's bad, you're no worse off.

Hanging from two fingers, feet smeared on the merest wrinkles, Tom Richardson yanks up slack and bites a mouthful before clipping a bolt (pictured just above him with a quickdraw attached). Jim Thornburg photo

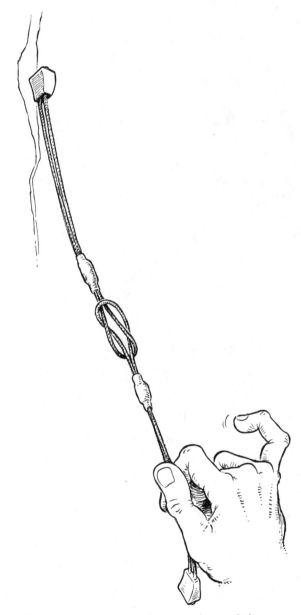

Using two wires woven together to reach a good placement

As mentioned, bent gate carabiners, though great to clip a rope into, should only be used for that purpose. Never use them to clip into a bolt, fixed pin, or wired nut. Even quickdraws can bind and open the gate all too easily. Watch them.

Route Finding

Part of learning to be a good leader is knowing what makes a bad one—knowing how climbers defeat themselves—and avoiding these needless mistakes. Good climbing requires you to use available holds the easiest way; good route finding requires you to keep to the easiest holds. Follow the line of least resistance, not wandering onto more difficult rock on

Spread 'em, partner!
Judy Carmine stems
up an open book.
Jim Thornburg photo

the flanks. Route finding is part instinct and part experience (which you might not be long on). Study the topo and compare it against what you see. Locate salient features such as bushes or roofs, and know where the hard parts are in relation to them. The topo should tell you this information—for example, that the section above the mulberry bush is hard, that the crux is after the crack peters out. Get yourself prepared before you start by memorizing all the given information.

If you feel you have wandered off route, look for the signs of climbing: chalk and boot marks, fixed protection, and broken flakes or holds. On popular routes, the texture and color of the rock is often different, smoother and lighter than the bordering stone because hundreds of shoes have paddled over every hold, probably for many years. With crack climbs, the route is often obvious. Face climbs are more nebulous.

Cruxes: The Hard Parts

Even easy climbs have "cruxes," sections harder than the rest. You will recognize them because the holds will suddenly run out; the crack will thin, widen, or get shallow; or the angle will bulge. Don't climb mechanically, but with all your savvy. Recognize the crux before you are on it. Set a good nut, or several nuts. Study the holds or crack and plot a likely strategy; but once you have committed yourself to it, improvise if your theory is wrong and forces you into sketchy movements. And climb aggressively. Use whatever works best and easiest, which sometimes might be an improbable sequence. If a fall seems possible, or likely, make certain your pro is solid, and observe what, if anything, you will hit if you come off. If everything checks out, alert your belayer and go after it. No leader wants to fall, and you don't start up something without some hope of succeeding. The fact that success is not a given defines the challenge in climbing. But the fear of falling prohibits your best effort, and if everything checks out the fears are probably groundless. Falling has become an integral part of modern climbing. Good protection and realistic judgment keep the sport sane.

Falling

Sixty years ago the incontrovertible rule was that the leader must never fall. The equipment was unreliable, and there was always the chance—though remote—of the rope breaking. Present-day gear is remarkably sound, and while no one yearns to fall, controlled falling has become standard practice for virtually all active sport climbers. Many leading climbers don't feel they have pushed themselves until they have logged some "air time." Indeed, you can never discover your limits unless you exceed them. Climbers routinely do, and the smart ones rarely get a scratch, even from 20-foot falls. This relaxed attitude is not due entirely to the gear, however. Climbers have become expert in calculating the risks and potential consequences, and people have learned how to fall.

There are two principal issues involved when you commit yourself to a potential fall: Is the protection adequate to hold the longest possible fall, and

Yippie-Kiyai! Paul Piana airing it out on the Wild Iris Wall.
Bill Hatcher photo

what will you hit should you fall? The belay is never in question because unless you're a lunatic, you don't climb with someone who can't hold your fall, however long or short it may be. If the pro is sound and the rock steep and smooth, it's fairly common to see a climber spend a whole afternoon falling off a difficult route. However, if the protection is dubious and there's something to hit, it's very rare to see a

Amos and Coco #12:
"Sweet Baby Jesus!"

"Falling!" Amos yelled, then plunged down the slab and came onto the rope after 10 feet. "Biscuit!" he grumbled. He quickly got situated on a foothold and unweighted from the rope. Then he gazed up at the bolt that had caught him, the fifth of eight protection bolts on a 100-foot steep face climb called *Wall Street*, which the guidebook rated 5.9.

Paradoxically, while the fall had frightened him, he gained the confidence that only comes to a climber who has taken that first fall—and lives to take another. Until then, a leader really doesn't know from direct experience that the system works as advertised. After that first fall—providing it's uneventful, something that is never a given—he is freed up to really go after it. If all things check out—the pro is good and there is nothing to hit if he pings off—he might as well pull till he either makes it, or pops. And Amos made it on his next try, clawing over the crux and knowing if he came off a second time, he'd be good as gold and would simply have at it again. Coco followed and also slipped off at the fifth bolt, but quickly gathered herself, revised her sequence, and climbed to victory.

After the two rappelled off, Amos mentioned that, in his limited experience, *Wall Street* seemed rather tough for the 5.9 grade. "*Wall Street's* actually an easy 5.9," another climber put in. "But *Wall Street's* over there," he added, motioning to a line of bolts 30 feet to their left. "What you guys just did is called *Jimminy Grip It*, and it's rated 5.10b."

As is often the case, when climbers don't know the rating of a particular climb, they are not intimidated by big numbers and can often pull off what their minds think they cannot. In fact, *Wall Street* was easier than routes both climbers had done in the gym and at Mt. Gorgeous, but proving as much takes the affair out of the realm of fantasy and into experience, to which there is no substitute. It also hurled the duo past the first great technical threshold—the legendary 5.10 grade.

"You hear that, cream horn!" Amos shouted at Coco. "Sweet Baby Jesus!" he exclaimed. "Hell, if we didn't just bag us a genuine 5.10!" "I say we bag another one," said Coco. "And it's my turn to lead." "Now you're talking my lingo," said Amos, who immediately struck a variety of bizarre postures, trying to balance those vital energies. Coco looked at him like he was a perfect fool, laughed and said, "What am I going to do with you?" "Whatever you want," said Amos. "And you will anyhow since you women always make the important decisions." Coco was caught off guard by Amos's insight. Amos stopped the clowning and looked her in the eye. "I only look stupid, you know." "You look fine, Tarzan," she said, and she kissed him on the forehead.

climber carry on unless he is virtually certain he will not fall—and no one can know this with 100 percent certainty. It's not the act of falling but the consequences that are the issue.

Climbing and protecting are separate skills, each of which keeps you alive, so for any lead—especially the first—don't challenge yourself in both at the same time. The beginning leader should avoid falling at all costs, but the possibility will arise, and both his and the expert's concerns are the same: the security of the pro and what he might hit if he loses it.

Falling is an art. When you fall, you need to maintain body control, stay facing the rock, and avoid tumbling. On a slab, you slide down on your feet, both hands pressing off the slab, keeping your chest and head far away from the surface. Keep your legs bent and spread apart, catlike. The rope stretches considerably, so the jolt is less than expected. I once caught a partner on a 50-footer on a steep slab, which did nothing but wear his shoes out prematurely. He stayed relaxed and just slid down on his feet, balancing with his hands—like a high-angle slide. I saw another person take the same fall, freeze up, and start tumbling. He needlessly broke a wrist.

On vertical climbs, you don't slide, but plummet—and very quickly. Remember to keep your legs a little extended and bent so at impact they absorb the force like shock absorbers. Don't freeze up

or go limp. That only invites injury. The screaming, rag-doll fall is worse still. The flailing arms will invariably smack something rock hard.

When you have traversed away from protection, a fall will swing you, pendulum fashion. The catlike stance is your only hope to avoid tumbling. Be prepared for your weight coming onto the rope, which otherwise can wrench you askew, even spin you like a top. Remember, pendulum falls are dangerous no matter your posture or agility. Slamming into a corner from 20 feet to the side is almost the same as falling 20 feet straight down and smacking a ledge on your side.

Even a long fall happens so fast that you don't have time to think. All the yarns about a person's life flashing before his eyes are pure bunk. You only have time to react, then it's over. Often it's the shorter, 8- to 10-foot falls that are the "wrenchers," where little rope is out, and the rope stretches less than on a longer fall. Remember, any fall on a small amount of rope will be a wrencher since so little rope is out, thus restricting the dynamic qualities (the stretch) of the line. But whatever the length of the fall, avoid freezing up, stay relaxed, and face the wall, legs and arms bent; and you'll usually not be hurt if your calculations were right.

Even as little as twenty years ago, falling was avoided at almost all costs. As bolt-protected sport climbs and indoor gyms came into vogue, falling became a minor annoyance experienced by all. The danger here is that sport climbers have taken a casual attitude toward falling into the "trad" milieu, where you have to place all your own protection, which rarely is as sound as a string of bolts on a sport climb. Learning to predict the consequences of a fall is part experience, part common sense and judgment. But understand from the start that all falls are not equal to short gym falls or skidders on a sport route bolted from bottom to top.

After a fall of more than 20 feet, the rope suffers appreciable fiber elongation and structural deformation, most of which is recovered in time. After a longish fall (20 feet or more), lower down and wait at least ten minutes for the rope to recover some of its stretch. The knot will absorb up to 30 percent of the impact force, so after lowering down, tie into your anchor with a sling and loosen the knot.

Often you will know you're going to fall before you do: You're bunched up and you can't move, your fingers or toes are buttering off the holds, or your strength is ebbing fast. Warn your belayer, and don't panic. Fall as gracefully as you can—not to impress anyone, but to keep your form. The person who falls out of control may have popped unexpectedly but more likely panicked once airborne—a sure recipe for trouble. Don't underestimate even the smallest fall. A fall can break bones and even kill you if it goes wrong, so calculating and reacting to the consequences is extremely important. This is something a manual can only suggest.

Loose Rock

Most climbs of any length have at least some loose or rotten rock (a.k.a., "choss") and the two are quite different, though the dangers are real in both cases. Loose rock doesn't necessarily mean the rock quality is poor. A flake, chockstone, block, or hold might be diamond-hard but still ready to go if you so much as breathe on it. Common sense is your best guide here. Delicately test suspect holds (if you have to use them) by tapping them with the heel of your hand or kicking them with your foot. The sound can tell you a lot. Try to avoid them if at all possible. Arrange your protection so the rope can't knock the rocks off, which is the most common way that rocks get dislodged by climbers. If there is a chance of rocks coming off, warn your belayer.

Rotten rock, crumbly and decomposing, is a nightmare. Every hold, every flake, and every nut is suspect because you don't know what will hold and what won't. It's all instinct and judgment. Stay clear of such routes until you have the experience to know you shouldn't climb them anyway. If you dislodge rocks onto the rope, inspect the whole rope at the first opportunity. A bounding stone can chop a new rope in a heartbeat.

Protecting the Second

The leader is responsible for the second's well-being as well as his own. He's got to do more than just warn the belayer of rockfall or tell him he's about to fall. He must protect the second with the same acumen as he protects himself. This is most essential on traverses, where the leader moves sideways off a piece of protection. Note that when the leader reaches a traverse, he slots a nut that protects his lateral movement. When the second follows, he cleans that nut, so if he falls off, he'll swing all the way to the next nut. The direction of pull is of principal concern here. For instance, when a leader moves directly right off a belay, slots a nut, keeps moving right, and falls off, he impacts the anchor with the direction of pull toward the belay (left). When the second follows the pitch and falls before gaining the first nut, the direction of pull will not be left (toward the former belay), rather it will impact the nut toward the right, the exact opposite of the leader. For this reason it's essential that for traverses, all protection should strive to be multidirectional.

When the rope runs dead horizontal, it's very hard to keep from tumbling if you fall, so a leader should always protect at regular intervals—for his and his partner's safety.

Leading on the Face

Aside from what's already been said, it's a slippery task trying to explain the alchemy of leading a difficult face climb. But the following should help.

*It is the leader's responsibility to ensure that the second does not have to follow a crux traverse without protection—usually simply a matter of putting in pro **after** the crux.*

A good face climber is a master of strategy. The first step is to break the climb down into sections between obvious footholds or rest stops. That way you can concentrate on one section at a time and climb a succession of short climbs, rather than one long and ghastly one. Before a crux section, arrange pro you are certain is sound so you can concentrate on the moves, not the consequences. Get on a foothold and scrutinize the face. Spot the best holds and break the section down to body lengths. Keep reducing each section down to the last visible hold. Then construct a mental sequence and visualize yourself climbing it. If it's too strenuous to pause very long, size up the holds and cast off. On strenuous leads, you have to be aggressive and really go after it, but never abandon your form. Look at the baseball player who goes with a grand slam swing. Instead of trying to stroke the ball, he tries to murder it. He's overanxious, and usually returns to the pine hailed by boos. Savvy, alertness, and controlled aggression are all vague terms that apply to leading a hard face.

Learning to downclimb is particularly important to the face climber. If you know you can reverse a section, then you minimize the potential danger and fear. Successful leaders will often venture out several times to gain the confidence to eventually go for it, getting more familiar with each effort and further reducing the hard section to the last, crux move.

Severe face climbs and steep sport routes, however, are virtually impossible to reverse, and in any event you'll eventually have to go for it. But climbing up and down—if and when possible—can often help a leader settle in and muster the needed resolve.

Leading Crack Climbs

We have discussed the necessary techniques for climbing cracks—but the fact is that often the hardest part of leading a crack is not the climbing, but arranging the protection. When the climbing is strenuous, the leader often finds himself hanging from a questionable jam and desperately trying to place a nut. Here are a few tricks to remember.

On thin to medium-sized cracks, don't plug up the best jams with protection. An experienced leader will often opt for a smaller nut that fits into constrictions between the bigger, better jams.

You will normally place protection above your hands. Sometimes, if the only good nut slots are where your fingers are, you will place a nut below your hands, slotting it just after you have removed your fingers. Try to set these nuts quickly, as often you are hanging on in a crunched-up position with a bent arm, which is more strenuous than the straight-arm hang.

Be conscious that your feet don't get entangled in the rope. If your foot gets caught under both the rope and the nut, an upward step can lift the nut from the crack.

When the crack is parallel-sided and strenuous,

go with SLCDs, which are much faster to place and usually better.

Utilize all rest opportunities, and get a good nut in while you're there. Arrange sound protection before any crux section of liebacking or jamming, and if it's safe, power over the section without stopping. Hanging on in the middle of a crux section to arrange added protection is rarely a sage tactic and can result in a fall you wouldn't have taken if you'd powered on. Conversely, if the protection is sketchy and your strength is dwindling fast, you'd best think hard about casting off. The lead is no place to push on if you're soon to be out of control. Better to lower off and regroup.

Husband your energy. Don't use brute strength unless you need to—and sometimes you will, especially on precipitous sport climbs. Stay relaxed and try to get into a rhythm, a groove. Never thrash. Understand, of course, that we all occasionally do desperate things on the lead. The secret is to know when you're desperate and not make this mode of ascent your personal style. Everyone has desperate moments, and boldness can sometimes deliver us (and other times make us run up our insurance premium). The key here is "sometimes." No one can climb precariously for long and not pay the devil for it.

Setting the Belay

Once you have completed the first lead, you must rig an anchor to belay the second climber up. The anchor, of course, must be atomic bomb-proof unless you wish to risk getting ripped off the wall if the second falls, a scenario that is fatal every time. There are countless different possible belay constructs, all dictated by what the climb affords. As mentioned, always stop at an obvious ledge or belay spot. Try to rig the anchor directly above the line of ascent so you can belay in line with the direction of pull. If you're on a ledge, tie yourself off with enough slack so you can belay at the lip of the ledge. This facilitates easy rope handling and communication, and keeps the rope from running over a potentially sharp edge. You'll usually choose to sit, facing out and down, but you can stand if you have a good brace. Just make certain you are tied off taut to the belay. If

not, a fall will drag you straight over the lip. Not good.

If the belay is on a small ledge or stance, you'll belay facing the anchor. Tie in with enough slack so you can lean back.

Rig the rope so it comes up, runs through the anchor, then back to you. Belaying through the anchor puts the load directly on the hardware, so (for the hundredth time) the anchor must be stout. Also, the force of a fall will draw you directly toward the wall, so remain braced.

Belaying through the anchor is not a requirement. Climbers do so because it is usually safer and always more comfortable. The anchor, rather than your waist, takes the bulk of the force during a fall. If for some reason you cannot get an anchor set to your utmost satisfaction—which does happen—you should probably belay right off your waist and hope you're on a good stance. If the second climber falls, the force is not extreme, and if you're properly braced and ready, your torso can absorb the force, sometimes with no help from the anchor at all.

Some climbers (though not many) argue that you should never belay through the anchor because it loads the system unnecessarily. They would rather the torso absorb at least some of the force, saving the anchor for a backup. But for me and thousands of others, the anchor is not a backup but the whole shooting match, and all the talk about saving or guarding the anchor is balderdash. Anyone who has climbed a big wall knows that if your anchor isn't good enough to belay through, it's not an anchor at all, but a lethal liability. The so-called "direct belay," which is endorsed and advocated by most guide services, clips the belay device not into the harness but directly into the belay anchor. And if the guides don't know what to do, who does?

Hang Man

Sometimes there are no belay ledges, stances, or even good footholds. Here you must construct a "sling," or "hanging" belay. Many hanging belays feature permanent anchors—bolts, pitons, or both. If you have to construct an artificial anchor, observe the rules we've gone over. Once the anchor is equalized, tie yourself off with enough slack so you can hang at, but not below, the hardware—and not so far out that you can't easily reach the anchor if need be. You normally belay through, or directly off ("direct" belay), the anchor on a hanging belay.

Always pay close attention to the rope. As you belay it in, keep it organized and stack it neatly. Don't let it loop down onto the rock below unless it can't get in the second's way and there are absolutely no knobs or flakes for it to snag on or cracks for it to drop into. Never allow the slack to slip into a deep crevice or behind a narrow flake. If there's anything for it to snag on, it will. If need be, loop the slack over your lap (lap coiling) or through a sling, thus keeping it out of potential snares. This is essential with sea cliff climbing.

If you climb long enough, you'll probably lose a rope due to a hang-up, even if you're paying close attention. Strong winds, common on north faces, can blow the unattended rope exactly where you don't want it.

Changing Leads

Once the second has followed the pitch, having cleaned all the protection you put in, the first thing he does upon gaining the belay is tie himself into the anchor—before he is taken off belay. He should always tie into more than one biner. Next, pull out the topo. Eyeball the hell out of the next lead and re-rack the gear accordingly. Don't take off with an unorganized rack; you won't want to fumble for the right gear in an awkward position above. Relax. Don't take off until you have gone through the ceremony of figuring out as much as you can from below. Discuss questions and strategy with your partner. All this can take only a few minutes once you get the hang of it.

Though your anchor is bombproof, there's no need to prove it is, so get a few nuts in immediately off the belay. Falling directly onto the belay is a worst-case scenario. The belay devices will do their job, but the force can sprain backs and slam the belayer into the wall hard enough to knock him cold. Even a short fall onto the belay transmits forces in excess of a thousand pounds to both the belayer and

the anchor—and there is always the chance you might land on the belayer, somehow jarring his brake hand free, in which case you'll plummet to the end of the rope or to the ground, whichever comes first . . . and last. So even if the climbing is simple, get some pro in straightaway. To do otherwise is to violate a rule as fundamental as never removing your brake hand from the belay rope. *Again, whenever leaving a belay, the leader's first order of business is to set protection to safeguard against falling directly onto the belay anchor.*

If you are not "swinging" leads (the second intends to follow every pitch), you face several options—depending on the nature of the belay station. If you're on a good ledge, you can both tie into the anchor with slings looped through your harnesses. The leader unties from the anchor and ties the second in as he was tied in. That gives the leader a free rope, and he's set to go. On small stances or hanging belays, this can be an enormous hassle, and some climbers choose to simply change ends—untying the knots and swapping ends. Though this is a scenario you'll see, I would never suggest untying from the rope under any circumstances. To avoid this situation, rig another anchor SRENE with one good, redundant clip-in point. Then you only have to flip the rope over (or restack it) and go.

If you are a party of three, it is easiest for the third climber to climb past on a second rope that is trailed by the second climber. At the belay the third is tied off, and the free end is trailed again on the following lead. If the third climber wishes to lead a pitch, he is simply put on belay and clipped through the anchor, then off he goes. If for some reason he wants to go second, you are looking at some weird rope shenanigans, untying and switching knots, which is more hassle than it's worth but possible using the aforesaid techniques. If the route wanders, it is the second's job to clip the third's rope through key nuts to check any drastic sideways falls. The third climber must then remove the pro his rope has been clipped through.

Double Rope Technique

In years past, though far less frequently today, most Europeans and many British climbers led on two

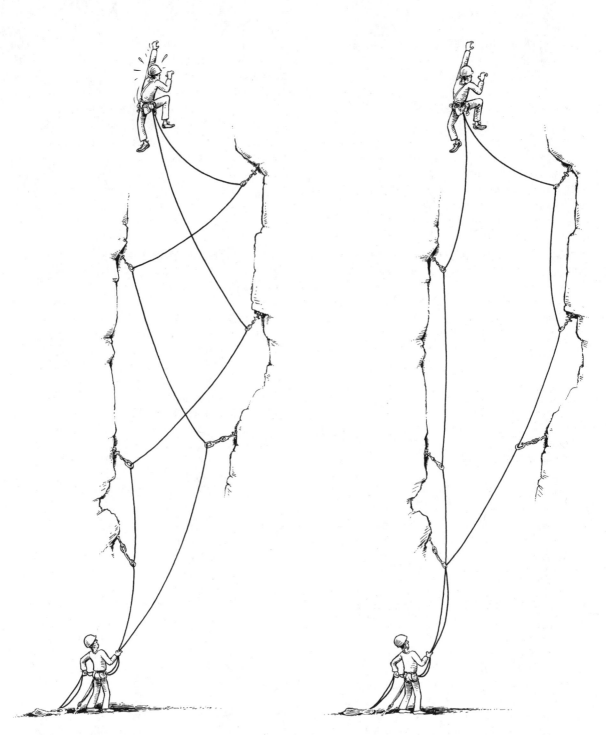

Poor (left) and proper (right) use of double rope technique

Protecting the second on a traverse with double ropes by belaying from both sides. The far anchor, remaining fixed, need only be as good as a sling through a fixed pin to secure the relatively gentle force of the falling second.

9 mm ropes. For several reasons, the technique has never fully caught on in America. Managing a single lead rope is easier. There is less weight for the leader to drag behind him, and the belayer's task is easier as well. Since American climbs tend to follow straight lines, the single 10.5 mm rope has remained the standard. The following list explains the advantages of using double ropes.

1. When a route wanders, a single rope will zigzag extravagantly through the protection, and a hundred runners can't eliminate the rope drag. By using two different-colored, 9 mm ropes, you can clip one line through protection on the left and one on the right, each rope running somewhat parallel and straight—or at least avoiding the drastic jags of a single rope.

2. When the climber leading on a single rope pulls up a loop to clip in, he's adding distance to a potential fall at twice the length of the pulled-up loop. With double ropes, if the top pro should fail, or if the climber falls just before clipping in, the extra loop is not added to the fall since the other line is clipped in below and he will come onto it first.

3. When the protection is poor, you can stack or duplicate placements, distributing the force of a fall between two nuts and two ropes, reducing impact on both.

4. On horizontal traverses, a single rope must go sideways with the line of protection. With double ropes, providing that the leader was able to climb above the traverse before belaying, one of the ropes can be left unclipped from the traverse protection so the rope runs up and across to the belayer, instead of dead horizontal—much better if the second should fall.

5. Perhaps the most important advantage is for those who climb regularly on sharp-edged rock like limestone, quartzite, or gneiss, where it is possible that a single rope could be cut during a fall. I've only heard once of a fall that resulted in a severed rope, but for those climbers frequenting areas where it is even conceivable, double ropes are a solution.

6. Lastly, the second rope is immediately available for descent without trailing an extraneous second rope.

As the leader places pro, he will forewarn the belayer which rope he is going to clip in, saying "Slack on the yellow," for example. And herein lies the single biggest disadvantage with double ropes: their eminent potential for snarling and snagging—not only on rock features, but on themselves. A hip belay with double ropes is tricky business, requiring the lines to be fed out or drawn in alternately. With the belay devices, it's often hard to keep both lines running smoothly and ordered in a tidy pile. The lines can likewise become crossed in or behind the

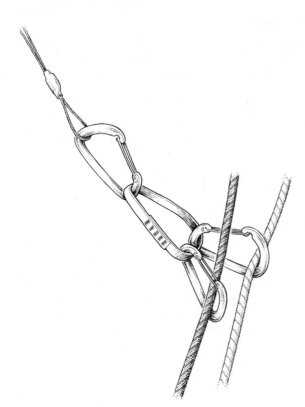

Whenever two ropes are run through one anchor they should be clipped into separate carabiners.

device. These problems are manageable with experience, so make sure you have some before belaying on double lines.

Twin Ropes

Another technique involves leading on two 8.8 mm ropes by using them as one rope, clipping both lines into the protection, though through separate biners. Aside from reducing the chance of total rope failure through cutting over an edge and the ability to make full-length rappels, there seems little else to recommend using twin ropes, a technique that is rarely seen in American rock climbing. A single strand of 8.8 mm rope does not pass the regular UIAA test. It does pass the "half-rope" test, which substitutes a 50-kilogram dropped weight for one weighing 80 kilograms. Because it can hold seven such falls, climbers

have started using the 8.8 mm lines for double rope technique as well. With either twin or double ropes, it is safe practice to clip the first couple of anchors off the belay with both ropes to safeguard against the high impact force of the leader falling close to the belay. With the thinner twin ropes, this practice should be continued until well into the lead to provide plenty of rope to absorb any fall.

Again, twin rope technique and using 8.8 mm ropes as double ropes are as yet unestablished practices in America (and are likely to remain so), and are used only by experts in specialized situations. Time will render the verdict. For the novice, it's best to stick with the older, less complicated methods.

Retreat and Self-Rescue

No climber has a 100 percent success ratio. Unexpected dangers, sore hands, hornets, apathy, no water, rainstorms—the causes are many that may force a team off the cliff. There are two considerations when retreating: getting down unscathed and doing so without leaving all your gear behind.

The most common practice is simply to lower the leader down to the belay. Oftentimes, if the leader doesn't fancy the pitch, the second will try his hand before the team throws the towel in altogether. If the decision is made to retreat, you will lower down, removing all the protection between the lowering point and the belay. This means that if what you are lowering off of should fail, you will fall a very long way, so make certain it is bombproof. A good rule is to never lower off one nut. Back it up and equalize it if necessary. And don't try to save a biner by running the rope through a runner threaded through the lowering anchor. The generated friction on weighted nylon can saw right through it. Better to lose a piece of gear than your life. Dozens of climbers have thought otherwise, and their headstones tell the tale.

If you (as leader) have more than half the rope out, you cannot return to the belay straight off because the rope won't reach. (Clearly, if you're 90 feet above the belay, you need 180 feet of rope to lower back to it, one reason that 200-foot ropes are now available.) One choice is to downclimb to a point

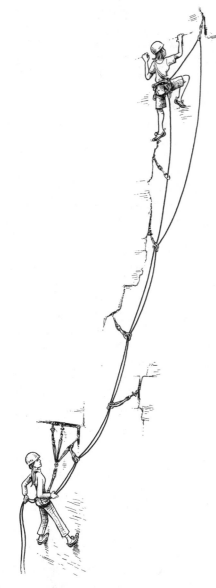

Twin rope technique

the rope off. You don't want it getting away from you, which would leave you marooned. Once you've pulled it through the top anchor, tie back in, take up the slack, and lower back down.

If the leader is hurt or unconscious, you as belayer should try to lower him down, hopefully to a ledge. If there is not enough rope, you have little option but to tie him off, a procedure that may require innovation and the use of a prusik or Bachmann knot (discussed in the next chapter) in order to free yourself from the belay; then retreat for help (provided you have another rope)—and yell for it. And fast. An injured climber should not be left dangling. It constricts circulation and inhibits breathing, and his head will invariably be drooping in an abnormal attitude. Such a scenario is a true emergency and should be treated as one. A rescue team will have to climb up to him, establish an anchor, and lower him off on another free rope, or come down from the top, whichever is easier. Such a procedure requires at least one other climber and two more ropes. So you'll need help, no matter who you are. The chief concern is to get the injured climber down quickly. It's usually much faster to simply leave all the gear behind, retrieving it when someone's health is not at stake. The drawback with this advice is that it's very advanced for a beginning book. Furthermore, everything depends so much on the situation that even this advice cannot be given as a hard and fast rule. One major problem: Dragging a trauma victim down a rock can potentially compound injuries. And yet to do nothing might also cost the injured climber his life. It's the classic "stuck between a rock and a hard spot," and there's no pat answer as to what's best.

If you are on exceptionally steep rock and are left dangling from the wall after a fall, it is hoped you have foreseen the possibility. The belayer is left to tie you off. Wise leaders take another rope to pull back in with or lead on double ropes for the same purpose. If you are on a single rope, you can often initiate enough swing—by flopping about in space—to pendulum back to the wall. If you can't you're in a fine mess, and extracting yourself is quite involved. Hopefully there is some lesser-angled rock below

where you have sufficient rope to lower off. The other choice is to lower down past the halfway point, taking pro out as you descend. Then do the following: Arrange an anchor that is bombproof and tie off to it with slings threaded through your harness. Before you untie and pull the rope through, tie

that you can lower to. If not, these are your options. Try to hand–over–hand the rope back to the last nut, having the belayer reel the slack in once you've clasped the nut. This is nearly impossible, but it has been done. You can use a prusik or Bachmann knot setup to climb back up to the last nut (explained in Chapter 6: Getting Down), or you can wait for a rescue. Someone will have to climb up to you, toss you a rope, and pull you back into the wall. If there is any possibility of these scenarios happening, trail another rope so you can get back to the cliff. Anyone who doesn't almost deserves the consequent hassles. In the end, however, a second rope is not necessarily the best option: The ability to climb the rope is.

There is another method of retreat, involving rappelling off an anchor, that we will discuss in the next chapter.

By predicting the possibilities, you can avoid the consequences. You can never predict a rainstorm or case of the "willies," so expect at some time to "bail off" a climb. Just never bail off one nut or lower down with your rope running through slings.

The Fear of Leading

Justified fear is a shrewd advisor, but groundless fear is self-defeating and can exhaust you. If you are terrified, quickly take stock of your situation (a reality test). Is the belay good? It better be. That's a given. Is the protection adequate? If so, you might be confusing exhilaration with fear—which is common to beginners. Get on a foothold and settle down. Relax. If you know you're safe yet still feel like fouling your britches, write it off to the jitters. If you eventually learn that you just can't adjust to the vertical environment, you might be in the wrong sport.

Climbing's not for everyone. And yet I've never yet seen someone with a fear of heights—and I've seen many such people—who could not eventually overcome their fear. The secret is to skip all the gruff talk and consider the climber (or yourself, if you're trying to work through this) as a child, without being condescending or patronizing. Humiliating someone with a phobia only sharpens their fear. Go slow and use great patience. Overcoming phobias is the process of reprogramming subconscious beliefs, projected terror feelings, and mental pictures of dis-

aster. These are very strong and very real for the person experiencing them, for they are inevitably tied up with some forgotten trauma which the person is rarely aware of and typically will swear they are not the victim of. A fear of heights is normal. Teeth-chattering terror at the very thought of getting 10 feet off the ground is not innate to man, however. Such terror is likely hooked up with some past event. Trowling through the past is not a particularly effective method of dealing with phobias of any kind. Slow (read: SLOW) immersion into the present fear is the best way I've seen for someone to integrate their paralyzing fear of heights. Remember that when these fears take hold, the person is terrified about what "might" happen, not what is actually happening, so their condition can be viewed as a trance state that takes them out of the present moment. Grounding them in the present, in concrete ways (engaging the senses), is a proven method.

To overcome height phobias, start on low-angled slabs, getting only a few feet off the ground. Encourage the person to talk, or if it's you who is struggling, vocalize all your thoughts and feelings, no matter how absurd. What you're after is the feeling (from direct experience) that what is actually happening is altogether different than what your mind is saying is happening or will happen.

Calm Yourself

Relaxation is essential in any exacting work. While telling someone to just relax is simple enough, beginning leaders often say, "Here I am, 100 feet up a vertical cliff, trembling on a little foothold with my rope clipped through a few pieces of wire. How am I supposed to relax?!" First, avoid things that cause panic. Never rush. Concentrate on relaxed, fluid breathing. Loss of concentration leads to poor self-control and frantic climbing. Try to climb in a measured, self-contained manner. You're not in a race. Be realistic about the difficulties and hazards. If you're nervous, ask yourself why. Assess the problems; take a reality test. If the risks are imagined, you can usually talk yourself down. If they are real, you must retain self-control. If you don't, you short-circuit any rational response, and you might get hurt as a direct result of being afraid to get hurt.

Amos and Coco #13:
Amos Moves Like Water; Coco Rolls Up Her Sleeves

In the several months following their first leading adventures at Pico Raquilita, Amos and Coco ticked off a slew of traditional, or "trad," routes, slowly building their skill and confidence till they could bag most any climb up to the low end of 5.10. Since the vast majority of established routes were minimal 5.10 or below, there was no end of routes to choose from. Coco was naturally brilliant on the face climbs, on which Amos sometimes struggled. Amos, on the other hand, was turning into a crack machine, a venue on which Coco needed work. To make ground on their weaknesses, every outing the pair would climb a mixture of cracks and faces. In a few months Amos was moving like water over the face climbs, and Coco was rolling up her sleeves to get at the cracks. Their previous weaknesses were slowly turning into favored techniques.

They both especially liked climbing old classic routes, marveling over how the old pioneers, some fifty or even sixty years before, had managed these climbs in tennis shoes and with soft iron pitons, steel carabiners, and manila ropes. Every time Amos bagged a classic, he felt a haunting blend of awe and nostalgia, knowing that he was enjoying the same experience as the pioneers, whose grainy archive pictures were featured in the guidebook. There was something grand about the whole enterprise, like a rookie ballplayer taking his first cuts in Yankee Stadium, "The House that Ruth Built." The Babe Ruths of climbing included such names as Robert Underhill, Jim Smith, Dick Jones, Glen Dawson, John Mendenhall, Chuck Wilts, Warren Harding, Royal Robbins, Jerry Gallwas, Mike Sherrick, Don Wilson, Frank Hoover, and many others. It was on routes these and other pioneers had first established that Amos and Coco really learned the ropes.

As they progressed, Amos and Coco naturally started climbing more multi-pitch routes, and new horizons opened up for the pair. But there always seemed more to learn. As soon as they developed basic route finding skills, they faced yet other challenges, like rigging hanging belays from tapers (always an exciting drill), rappelling off at mid-route when the rain came pounding down, and a host of other things. As their skill and experience increased, so did their ambition to visit other areas and tackle the classic routes they read about in the magazines. To review all they had learned, and to get an objective appraisal of where they were technique-wise before heading off for parts unknown, the pair negotiated with that stalwart mountaineer, Jules Pinkus, for a day of guided climbing.

The Psychology of Success

Climbers have long recognized the link between mental attitude and physical performance, and there's a lot of talk bandied about concerning visualization, imaging, tantric breathing, et al. These disciplines can greatly enhance your performance, but remember that they're all ineffective if you can't unleash the tiger in your heart—and that's something that's difficult to teach. Likewise, your mental attitude reflects your physical capabilities, and there are times that, even with the heart of a tiger, you still can't chin yourself on a burnished limestone wart, and there's no sense in telling yourself you can. The value of the mental exercises is to amplify your actual capabilities and to keep your mind from thwarting your full potential.

The important breakthroughs in climbing have not occurred because someone came along with stronger fingers and better boots. They occurred because someone had a new idea about what was possible, believed in herself, and had the fortitude to see it through. It all started with an idea, a belief.

The starting point to successful climbing is a positive attitude, an honest belief that you are going to give it your best shot and that you have a chance at succeeding if all goes well. You cannot talk yourself into doing something you don't really want to do (or know you don't have a snowball's chance in hell of doing). A positive attitude can bolster your

resolve, but not create it. So on the day of an important climb, on the drive up to the cliff, while hiking to the base, you start programming your mind, telling yourself that you can do what you set out to do if you believe it. You establish your commitment and nip fear in the bud.

The next phase is to reduce your thoughts to the task at hand, eliminating extraneous ideas, emotions, small talk, and distractions. Switch off the boom box and focus on the climb. Get relaxed. Focus and concentrate. The mind is capable of doing many things at once but only one well. Don't split your attention or derail it with things that won't further your immediate aim.

Before and during the climb, visualize yourself doing the moves, climbing smoothly and in complete control. The word "imaging" is popular just now, but it's the same old thing—and still very effective—the basketball player visualizing the ball piercing the hoop with the game-winning shot, the climber seeing himself liebacking over the crux bulge. A climber might study the crux and preview several different sequences in his mind before the most probable one clicks a mental light on.

Throughout the whole process you are verbally telling yourself—silently and out loud—that you will succeed. This is no more than self-hypnosis or autosuggestion and can have remarkable impact on the receptive mind. When effectively done, you are programming the subconscious, where many of your reservations originate.

The ultimate performer is the one who climbs "unconsciously." Not like a zombie, but with a rational, aware mind that is not continually checking the upward flow with negative thoughts. She is like a distant observer. It's a trance-like state that only recognizes the task at hand. The will is crystallized, the attention needled down to a tiny section of space and time, so when you're climbing, the only thing that can hold you back is a true physical impossibility.

Some climbers are so keen to succeed that they defeat themselves by trying too hard. To these climbers, the mental disciplines are particularly effective, for they can instill the control and discipline that their natural gusto would have otherwise negated. The old notion that "the tiger hunts in absolute peace" best illustrates this rather elusive point.

On an exceptionally difficult crux, all the mental games must conclude before you start. The most difficult climbs require a tenacity and degree of effort almost unheard of in any other sport. The mental games are remarkably effective as a beginning ritual, but once you swing into that double overhanging lieback, or onto that bald and bulging face, there's no time to be talking to yourself or imagining anything. It's all focused effort.

A realistic goal, a strong desire, correct programming through visualization, verbal and nonverbal self-commands, and the focus, control, and tenacity to execute the task—that's what you're after.

Climbing with Style

On the face of it, it is debatable that the fashion in which we go about climbing rocks is of any consequence to anyone. We just want to get up safely, and if we ignore decorum here and there, who cares? But a funny thing happens once we are even moderately skilled. Simply getting up at all costs is not

Cameron Burns maintains a relaxed, upright carriage on Giorgio Neanderthal (5.10c), Joshua Tree, California.

Cameron Burns photo

very satisfying. We slowly realize that the "way" we get up is both the means and the end. Virtually anyone who sticks with climbing comes to this conclusion. To understand current mores, let's look at where they originated.

In the classic *Ropes, Knots, and Slings for Climbers*, Walt Wheelock talks about the "Golden Age" of climbing, centered in and around Zermatt, a century ago. "A rope was only to be used as a belay, not as a climbing aid. One just did not put his weight on the rope if he were a worthy member of the Alpine Club. It could be used to aid a descent and in the case of emergency or for safety, but each climber was expected to climb his own peak."

This "fair play" trend continued until climbers,

Amos and Coco #14:
"Holy Half Dome!"

After meeting in the parking lot at Pico Raquilita, Amos, Coco, and instructor Jules Pinkus glanced through the guidebook, and Jules selected a six-pitch route featuring a wide variety of techniques. Amos and Coco were surprised when, at the base of the cliff, Jules said that he would be following all the pitches. "I sorta figured you'd be hauling us up something," said Amos. "And we'd just have to like it."

After Coco had led the first pitch and Amos the second, and the trio had gained a good ledge, Amos and Coco understood Jules's strategy of letting the pair do all the leading. All the way up Jules gave little suggestions—about cutting down on rope drag, placing gear, setting faster and more efficient belay anchors, and so forth. By observing how the pair climbed, how they led and anchored and followed and generally operated, instructor Pinkus could see where they might do things a little more safely and efficiently, and he showed them how to do so. This was not so much learning new techniques, but rather refining what they were already doing.

At the top of the route, Jules said, "Fact is, you guys have rounded out into solid climbers, like I knew you would. And you're safe and fast. Now it's just a matter of going to different places and getting more experience." "So we check out okay?" Coco asked. "Excellent," said Jules. Amos looked relieved. "You get out on your own," he said, "and even though things are going well, you're basically winging it. You start wondering if you're bungling things and thinking you're mint. It's great to know we're on the square."

"Two things," said Jules, whose opinion was golden in mountaineering circles the world over. "'Trad' climbing is really the way to break in because you learn all the basics. But with 'trad' climbing, because the routes tend to be long, it's harder to see what other folks are doing, and you can learn a lot—about what to do and not do—by observing other climbers. So second, you might start splitting your time between 'trad' areas like this and sport climbing areas. You can do stacks of routes, hone up quickly, and also watch and climb with other folks. That's a sure way to steepen your learning curve and keep things interesting."

"I guess we're sort of sport climbing in the gym," said Amos. "We're there once or twice a week," Coco added. "Coco spanks me on those tweaker routes, but I can hold my own on the steeper stuff," said Amos. "Guess it's time to visit the local sport cliffs. There has got to be ten of them within a few hours of the pad." "You guys do that, and keep 'trad' climbing when you can, and in a year or so, you'll be ready for the big time," said Jules. "Big time?" asked Coco. "Big walls," said Pinkus. "You reckon?!" asked Amos. Jules nodded, "I had you guys pegged as big wall climbers since that intermediate seminar."

"Holy Half Dome!" Amos said, glancing at Coco. "Just think of it, pop tart!" "Don't get him started, Jules," Coco said. "One of his yoga teachers told him he had promise and the next day he was trying to drag me off to India." "To hell with Hyderabad!" Amos yelled. "We're heading for the High Lonesome!" "Give it a year and a few sport climbs," said Jules, the tireless veteran of fifty big walls. "Give it a rest," said Coco.

But Amos's mind was already soaring up the sheer ramparts of Leaning Tower, Washington Column, Mt. Watkins, and the other great walls of Yosemite. Then Amos glided into his bizarre postures to steady up those vital energies, and Coco knew that, sure as day follows night, she would someday find herself lashed high in the sky with galaxies of air spilling beneath her boots as a big lug named Amos hammered above her, yelling for slack. Little did Amos know that the idea lit her lamp every bit as much as it did the now-pliant firefighter. The most she could do was to steer them into a season's worth of sport climbs before Amos's enthusiasm would carry them both to heights unimaginable, where he'd flex and yammer and strike various preposterous poses—and send Coco up for the lead.

in their search for new and harder routes, began using equipment for direct assistance. First were pendulums and tension traverses, essentially leaning and swinging off the rope to move sideways over blank or unclimbable rock. Soon climbers were constructing ladders of pitons into which they would clip runged rope stirrups, or "etriers," stepping up and slamming home each new piton in turn. This "direct aid" technique allowed passage over rock otherwise impossible using only hands and feet. The eventual refinement of this technique led to the first ascents of what then were the finest pure rock walls in the world—in Yosemite Valley, California. And as the standards rose in aid (or "artificial") climbing, so did those in free climbing.

In the United States and England, free climbing and aid climbing were always considered different and distinctive forms. With aid climbing, you used gear as your means of ascent—anything goes. With free climbing, you never used the gear except to safeguard against a fall, and even the slightest infraction—resting on a piton, stepping on a bolt—meant you were not free climbing but aid climbing. This attitude is based on the concept that artificial and free climbing are distinct pursuits. One is mechanical, the other athletic. No one argued that free climbing was the purer form. And active climbers stuck by the rules, for a game without rules is meaningless. From the beginning (when alpinists shunned assistance from the hemp), climbers were aware that runaway technology (and dependence on it) would dilute the challenge, so the elements of style were upheld to preserve it. Even on routes requiring extensive aid climbing, pioneers would push the free climbing to the limit before breaking out the etriers as a last resort.

The rules of free climbing, unofficial as they were, brought several points to bear. The spirit of adventure and exploration was the very stuff that animated climbing. Furthermore, since you could conceivably hammer your way up any rock wall using aid techniques, free climbing would have to display some element of honesty and fair play—sportsmanship, if you will—lest the two forms become blurred and the distinctions insignificant.

Some big climbs were obviously aid routes and were approached accordingly. But when there was some doubt, climbers harked back to the original alpinists, when the climber was expected to "climb his own peak," not by hanging on the rope or pitons, but through his own physical effort and skill.

On a prospective free route, an honest free climber avoided anything that could reduce the adventure and challenge: He wouldn't descend the climb first, inspecting the rock for available holds, placing protection in the crux sections, chipping footholds, or doing anything else that could make his ascent easier or give him unnatural advantage before he had actually taken the lead. He would start from the ground and deal with obstacles as he encountered them—"on-sight." If he fell off, he would lower back to the belay and try again, rather than hang on the protection before carrying on. If he was a real stickler, he would pull the rope through the protection and lead it from the ground. If it simply couldn't be free climbed, then aid climb it he did—and right on his heels there would be others trying to free it, often succeeding.

Leading climbers stuck fast to the "on-sight" philosophy, though as early as 1960 people were pre-inspecting leads on rappel and placing bolts for ready protection once they decided to lead the climb. But these efforts were generally considered cheating and were avoided by most leading climbers. By 1975, the hardest climbs were so severe that climbers often had to return several times before they could do them legitimately—climbing from belay to belay with no falls and no assistance from the gear. By 1980, the top climbs were still harder, requiring weeks, even months before a "hardman" could make it in one go. To reduce the time spent, climbers started toproping (belaying from above) the climbs before leading them, pre-placing pro to make the eventual lead less strenuous and dangerous, and rehearsing the moves while hanging on gear (hangdogging). In several pitiful instances they even manufactured holds where there were none. Presently, the hardest free routes are sometimes (though rarely) dangerous, but because the climbers have memorized every toe hold, every crystal, every thumb position, they are far less adventures than remarkable examples of rock gymnastics. The ultimate goal of any climber is still to climb the route as though the rope was not there—climbing the route without falls on the first attempt. However, today's hardest routes are so extreme that most climbers find the old rules impractical, if not passé, but you do eventually have to climb the route from bottom to top, no falls, to claim a "free," or "redpoint," ascent. The methods used to get there, the how of it all, are immaterial if they serve the end of the honest free ascent.

So what does this all mean to the novice? Not much. In fact, it means precious little to anyone save the world-class climber who has his whole existence invested in rock climbing and little else. The novice should approach a climb trying to carry out the old norms, not resting on the protection unless he has to, realizing that top climbers bend the rules because their game is really a different thing altogether. And while the old on-sight rules have been somewhat abridged by the cutting edge, even they observe two absolute edicts: Never place new bolts on existing routes and never chisel holds into the rock. These edicts are the only rules that have sure ethical import, because they can directly and permanently affect someone else's experience. A route is public property, and once a route is established, it is no one else's task to change it to their liking. Can you imagine going to the Getty Museum and taking hammer and chisel to a Grecian frieze, removing the odd mole and straightening an aquiline nose, until you had it just as you liked? You'd be ushered out behind the shed where the big fellas would rearrange your features.

As long as you climb with nuts, you are totally free to do as you choose, and nobody is going to care much. Most climbers find that respecting the old rules is more satisfying than making a joke of them. A novice should concern himself with routes that will challenge him but that he can do without hangdogging or pre-inspecting. Unfortunately many climbers, even novices, feel pressure to climb high-number routes, and they sacrifice every trace of style in trying routes beyond their ability. When they finally manage to hang and yard their way up a route,

they're the first to tell everyone they did, neglecting the ticklish details of style. You haven't "done" a route until you've freed it: Don't be ashamed to include the bald truth when reporting your accomplishments so your integrity will never be questioned. Most climbers find it more rewarding to climb several routes within their ability than to spend all day falling up one over their head. If you stick with climbing, you will discover all this for yourself; and if you find yourself hanging on the protection, no need to tell the priest. Just realize you're not climbing as well as you might be.

Free Soloing

By definition, you are free soloing anytime you climb without a rope, regardless of the difficulty. The common usage, however, refers to a climber who is scaling a fifth class climb where a rope and equipment are usually employed. Yet the true free soloer has neither. He has only a pair of shoes, a chalk bag, and the prowess he brings to the cliffside. Since the penalty for a fall is almost certain death on a route of any length, even experts will question the sanity of the campaign. To the person not given to risk-taking, even the most passionate explanation will ring hollow. Remember, free soloing is rarely a reckless practice—rather a very calculated, conscious act. And it's a matter of degree. The chances of a 5.12 climber falling off 5.9 terrain are remote, but still possible. Yet the nervy aficionado will sometimes push the gamble ever closer to his all-out limit till he is virtually doing a high-wire act above infinity, where a moment's lapse in focus, an imprecise toe placement, a fractured rugosity, and the reaper falls. To the novice witnessing this firsthand, it seems the purest madness. Why do it? You should certainly not attempt it to find out why. The few who regularly practice free soloing are inevitably experts who technically know exactly what they are doing and intuitively know exactly why.

What the free soloer craves is either the raw intensity or the joy and freedom that comes from mastery. If he craves notoriety for his feats, he is motivated by sham values and may pay for his vanity. The reasons to free solo must come from the heart and be monitored by an icy, analytical mind. Anything else courts disaster. We all climb, among other reasons, because it is exciting. So when the free soloer ups the ante to include all the marbles, you can imagine how the thrill is magnified. Foolish? Perhaps, but an element of tomfoolery runs through the skein of any climbing. The free soloer has simply pushed things to their ultimate expression. His rewards, in terms of intensity of experience, are the greatest. And so are the penalties.

Amazingly enough, very few free soloing accidents ever occur (though when they do an obituary soon follows). This is a clear testament that the practice is undertaken by experts in a very measured and sober way. Ultimately, free soloing is a distinctively personal affair, and even daily practitioners discourage the practice, as they should. There is certainly no reason for the recreational climber to ever even consider it.

Legendary mountaineer Ed Webster rappels down Red Twin Spire at the Garden of the Gods, Colorado.

Stewart M. Green photo

CHAPTER 6

Getting Down

Most every climb ends in a descent, so climbers must be well-versed in going down. The options for getting down from a climb include walking off, downclimbing, rappelling, and lowering. (Downclimbing and rappelling are covered in this chapter, and lowering is addressed in Chapter 7: Sport Climbing.) There is an inevitable chicken-and-egg syndrome with this chapter, as I'm introducing terms and practices that are probably unknown to you and that I can't fully explain until I paint the broad picture. If at first you feel lost, bear with me. By the end of the chapter, things I merely touched upon in these first paragraphs will become clear.

Every novice climber should understand that basically, rappelling is very simple. Even the most overhanging rappel requires no athletic ability and hardly any strength. When properly set up, gravity and the rigging—your actual rappel setup—do virtually all the work. This is both a blessing and a curse—a blessing because descending (via rappel) the world's most difficult sport climb can be done by a rank beginner and a curse because people sometimes race through the setup, thinking that since rappelling is physically simple, the rigging requires little bother. Believe it: The tools and techniques for descending are fairly straightforward, but the cost of a mistake can be your life. Good judgment, attention to details, awareness of hazards, and diligent double-checking will keep you alive. Until you're confident that you can safely get back down to the ground under a variety of situations, you don't belong on the rocks without a qualified guide.

A disproportionately large percentage of climbing accidents happen descending. The major causes are fatigue, loss of concentration, and neglecting to follow standard safety procedures. First and foremost, always have a plan for the descent before going up on a route. On sport routes, getting down may require only climbing to a double bolt anchor and lowering to the ground (soon described). Descending longer routes can be involved, devious, and dangerous. Innumerable epics have been suffered because a party neglected to do their homework per the descent. Most guidebooks include information on getting down from the routes; fellow climbers may also be a source of route and descent knowledge. If no information is available about the descent, scope the cliff from the ground. Look for places to walk or climb down, or established rappel anchors. If you can't find an obvious descent, it's sometimes best to rappel the route you just climbed, to avoid going irreversibly down into unknown terrain—which happens more times than you might expect. In a popular area you can most likely get rescued. Pull this stunt a little ways off the beaten track, and it's dust to dust.

Climbers must also know how to improvise a descent for those unavoidable retreats. Sport climbers need only know how to retreat from a bolt in the middle of a pitch. Those who do longer routes must be capable of, and prepared for, a multi-pitch retreat. As I've already said, not one single climber has enjoyed a 100 percent success rate on long climbs. In most cases, the more long routes a climber has bagged, the more times he has also found himself descending a route for reasons ranging from falling stones to ebbing desire. He lives to again mount the high crag simply because he knows how to safely retreat.

Walking down should be the first option if the walk-off is easy, though frequently climbers will lower or rappel instead for convenience. Walking down is normally simple business, though not always. Be mindful not to cut down too soon, to avoid getting "cliffed," where after several hours of bushwhacking, for example, you come to the edge of a 1,000-foot vertical wall. Then it's back the way you came, which is sometimes impossible (if you've already made a few rappels) and usually hateful and exhausting. Use good judgment to find the path of least resistance.

Downclimbing

Should rappelling prove unsafe or impractical, you will most likely have to downclimb. Competent downclimbing is essential to descend gullies, slabs, chimneys, or any stretch of rock encountered once the climb is over. Unless the rappel route is very straightforward, most experienced climbers will opt to climb down off a crag if a simple, realistic route is available. And even when the rappel route is a quick and easy task, climbers will still climb off. It's often faster, and their fate is in their own hands, not dependent on equipment. Downclimbing can be as fun and challenging as climbing up. Almost without exception, downclimbing is done without a rope since the terrain is usually fairly easy. If you haven't made the descent before, you probably have little or no knowledge of the terrain below, so be very careful. Hopefully you at least scoped the descent from the ground so you have some idea where you're headed.

The downclimbing route must be free of loose or rotten rock. If it isn't, no one should be in a position to be hit by rockfall. It is generally best to keep the party close together so falling stones cannot build momentum and the first one down can forewarn those behind of particular danger spots. If you do knock a rock off or if you notice anything falling,

yell "Rock!" even if you think there is no one below. If you are in the line of fire, you have two options: Duck and take cover, or glance up and try and dodge. Often there is not time enough to do both. If "Rock!" is yelled from far overhead, it's probably best to take a glance and react accordingly—at least in theory. The idea is to get into a place shielded from the projectile, hopefully under a roof or at least into a deep crack where the chance of getting struck directly are greatly reduced. If you're on an open face, your only hope is to take a look and try and dodge what's coming down. Rope, haul bags, parties above, wind, rodents—all of these things can dislodge rocks. And whenever rocks or anything else has whistled past, always check your partners and then the rope.

Per downclimbing: Don't be afraid to pull out the rope and rappel or belay if things get too hairy. Never solo down anything you don't feel absolutely confident about. Likewise, never coerce your partners to "down-solo" anything they aren't comfortable with. Again, never solo down or coerce your partners to solo down anything you or they don't feel absolutely confident about. Instead, be the first to offer a rope for your partners, or get ready to buy a shovel.

If you're the stronger partner, you should go down first to find the most logical route and to spot your less experienced partners through the dicey stretches (provided you have a good stance). Again, try to stay close together so any dropped rocks can't gain wrecking ball speed before nailing someone, so both climbers have ready assistance if someone gets into trouble, and so the team doesn't get separated.

If you rope up to downclimb, the weaker climber goes first with a toprope, placing protection for the stronger to "down-lead" on (hopefully the "weaker" partner knows how to place good protection). Rappelling is almost always a safer and quicker option than down-leading, though.

On lower-angled downclimbing, face out so you can see where you're going and lean back to the wall with one or both arms as needed for balance. As the angle steepens, you'll reach a point where it becomes easier to turn in and face the rock, peering past your hip or between your legs for directions. A little experience and all the nuances will come clear.

The ability to downclimb safely and fast is a handy and crucial skill. You can outrun approaching storms, avoid unnecessary rappels and, providing you use common sense, have a fun time doing so. If you start down the wrong gully or shoulder, though, it can get nasty. Against my better instincts I thrashed down a manzanita-choked gully east of Basket Dome in Yosemite Valley, and Lord Jim with a chainsaw couldn't have reversed it. Five hours and a thousand weeping punctures later, we finally gained the valley floor, and I've been careful what I head down ever since.

Rappelling

A million postcards feature a colorfully clad climber "roping down" the sheer crag, bounding in arcs, meters off the wall, a waterfall cascading in the background. To the layman, the image embodies everything quixotic about climbing, though there is no climbing involved. Beginning climbers are anxious to try, though this zeal usually falters as they backpedal toward the dreadful lip. Climbing manuals are quick to state how experienced climbers hate rappelling. In reality, most climbers don't really mind rappelling, though they avoid it if possible. There is uncoiling ropes, setting anchors, sometimes leaving gear behind, and the spooky task of absolutely trusting the gear, rarely with any backup. If the rappels are long and involved, including many anchor transfers and a lot of eerie dangling on the gear, even the best climbers will walk a long way to avoid the hassles. But any way you stack it, if you're going to climb, you're likewise going to have to rappel—and a lot.

"Abseil" (European), "rappel" (American), or "roping down"—call it what you want, it all involves using friction to descend a rope.

Statistically, rappelling is climbing's second most dangerous process, close on the heels of leader accidents. A climber's bulk is continuously stressing the equipment, and if any link in the weighted chain should fail, the result is final. Equipment failure, an-

Legs extended and torso upright and in a 45-degree angle to the wall Kevin Powell photo

chors pulling, knots coming untied, and a host of human errors—usually avoidable—have caused many rappelling tragedies. Consequently, assiduous attention must be paid to every aspect of the procedure, starting with choosing the best rappel route.

The Line of Descent

The first question is: Where are you rappelling to? If you're simply heading for the ground and can see that the rope reaches, your task is relatively simple. If you have to make more than a single rappel to reach the ground or your destination, make certain of several things. Are you descending to a ledge, a stance, or what? Do the ropes reach, and if so, what will be the next anchor? Do you have the necessary gear to rig an anchor? Many times rappel routes are established with fixed anchors; other times they are not. Numerous climbs end at a place from which you can walk off. If not, the way down often rappels the route just climbed. You know the topography, the ledges, the anchors. There is no mystery to it.

If you want to descend a virgin stretch of rock that requires numerous rappels, you have no way of knowing if there are adequate ledges and anchors. Even if you have inspected it with a telescope and can spot a big ledge, you still have no idea how good the anchors might be. Unless you carry a huge bolt kit, you are committing yourself to a real crapshoot that could leave you stranded. Forget about such an expedition.

For normal sport climbing, you need to know the place you're heading for, that there is an anchor or the possibility of getting one, that the same is available below—all the way to the ground—and that your rope will reach every rappel point/anchor in turn. Most guidebooks supply this information, but more often than not your judgment about a situation is what will get you down safely. At popular crags, ask around if you have any doubts about the descent. When in total doubt, rappel an established route, preferably the route you've just climbed—if you have to rappel at all.

Because every detail must be correct, it is critical that you double-check every aspect of the "safety chain" before leaning back to rappel. Double-check your harness buckle (and your partner's), the anchor and the rope's attachment to it, the rappel device and locking carabiner(s), and the rope-connecting knot. Just remember BARK—buckle, anchor, rappel device, and knot. Also, don't forget to inspect your gear often to be sure it's in good condition. Especially be sure that your harness, belay loop, slings, and rope are in good shape. Occasionally check your carabiners and belay/rappel devices for wear or notches. Retire any gear as soon as you have any doubts about its condition.

Anchors

A bombproof anchor is the foundation of sane climbing. Every year climbers—if not entire teams—are killed because of failed rappel anchors. Very occasionally these tragedies are due to acts of God—trees inexplicably coming uprooted, or several bolts or pitons popping mysteriously—but more often than not the accidents occurred because someone chose to save equipment and chance it with a suspect anchor. Is the anchor unquestionably sound? It must be. Go with an indisputable natural anchor whenever possible—a towering ponderosa pine, for instance. With an artificial anchor, a minimum of two nuts, bolts, or pitons are obligatory. Three, even four, different points are sometimes called for, depending on the quality of the placements.

Look the rappel anchors over good. Again, at least two bombproof anchors should be established at rappel stations, and they should conform to the SRENE standard: solid, redundant, equalized, and allow no extension. To review: "Solid" refers to the comparative security of the individual nuts, bolts, etc. "Redundant" simply means that you have a number of solid anchors. "Equalized" refers to the process of equally spreading the stress of a rappel over the various component parts of the anchor (explained in detail in Chapter 4: Ropes, Anchors, and Belays). "No Extension" means that if one of the anchors should pull, there is no slack in the system that would allow the rappeller's body weight to suddenly shock-load onto the remaining anchors.

If the anchors are anything less than bomber, back them up if possible and make sure everything is well equalized. Avoid the American Triangle (see Chapter 4), especially if the anchors are suspect. Occasionally, rappel anchors consist of a single tree or set of slings on a rock feature; climbers should back up these anchors whenever possible. Anchor failure will likely kill you and your partner, so don't be cheap with your lives! If you use a tree, it's usually best to run the rope through slings and two biners, gates opposed rather than around the tree; otherwise, you might damage your rope and the tree, or your rope could get stuck.

Amos and Coco #15:
A Rock and a Hard Spot

Climb long enough and you'll have an epic. These are rarely fatal, and most often are more hassle than harm. Especially in wilderness areas, there are many factors beyond a climber's control, factors that sometimes conspire to provide "hell in a handbasket" to roped teams. Amos and Coco found their handbasket on Keller's Peak, in the Sierra Nevada.

The duo had thrived of late, splitting time between popular "trad" areas and the local sport climbing cliffs. But then came a hankering to get away from it all—the folks and chalk marks and familiar haunts—and to get way out there, where they didn't have to share their experience with anyone. So they'd driven most of the night to a trailhead in the High Sierra, and next morning humped four hours to Keller's Peak, a 1,000-foot granite plug with a classic 5.9 crack and ramp system splitting the blinding North Face. By now the pair had climbed hundreds of pitches together, and they moved like a well-oiled machine. Silence and empathic listening slowly had come to replace Amos's bent to yammer on, and Coco's once feathery ways had constellated into focus and steely determination. In short, they'd moved past the mechanical aspects of their own personalities and knew what the heck they were doing when life and limb were at stake—and they relished every minute of it.

Pitch after pitch fell away as the duo swung leads up the peak. At mid-height, the route took a traversing line up and right, following a ramp and chimney system. They heard the first rumbling an hour later, only two pitches from the summit. The sky had clouded over when they weren't looking—in minutes, as so often happens in the mountains—and the rain soon followed.

In another ten minutes a regular watercourse poured down the ramp, and the pair were quickly soaked. The rain hammered on, and there was no way to press on over the slick rock. They'd have to "bail."

Rappelling is potentially dangerous even in perfect conditions. Here, where the rappels went sideways and the anchor stances were small and awkward with no fixed pins or bolts, the dangers were very real. On their way down, the pair left behind whatever was necessary to ensure a bombproof anchor. Costly, but they could buy the gear back later on. They only had one life apiece, and they weren't going to risk it to save an $8.00 hexcentric or even a $50.00 SLCD.

It took hours of snagged ropes, oblique rappels, and frigid waiting for the duo to reach the top of the first pitch. By then they were shivering so hard they could barely rig their rappels. Coco reflected on the words of that prodigious mountaineer, Jules Pinkus, who said that when things got tight, you fall back on your training. "We take however long it takes to keep things safe," Coco said. "Right you are," said Amos through chattering teeth. They almost had it now, but were aware that accidents frequently happen when the end is in sight and folks hurry the process to be done with it. Not this pair.

The last rappel dropped straight down into space, whereas the first lead had traversed to this spot via a lower-angled ramp system to the left. Because the scree slope at the base was irregular, rising here and dipping there, and because they couldn't see if their doubled ropes actually touched the ground, Amos tied a huge "keeper knot" into the rope ends to prevent him from rappelling off. Then he backpedaled into the void and started down. He paused at the first overhang, perhaps 50 feet below the anchor, and could see the ends of the ropes dangling in space perhaps 20 feet off the ground. If he carried on, he'd be stuck in space with nowhere to go. His only option was to rig two prusiks and ascend the rappel ropes.

In his tired, frozen, sodden state, the task was desperate, and it took him half an hour before the prusiks were set and he could start back up. But he had the needed gear on hand, and most importantly, he'd practiced prusiking several times so he knew exactly what to do and how to do it. Half an hour later, exhausted but very much alive, Amos gained Coco and the anchors. Tired and cold as they were, they recognized the risks before them and calmly decided on the next move. Coco was able to rappel off to the left, down about 50 feet, and establish a bombproof anchor at the top of the ramp, midway up the first pitch. Amos followed, and from there the pair were able to rap directly to the ground.

While they had failed to climb their peak, their epic had been a gift of sorts, and they talked about it all the way back home. They could climb another thirty years—and indeed they would—and they'd probably never get so strung out as they had on Keller's Peak. Coming through that in one piece was an enormous boost to their confidence, and the experience removed one of the duo's last doubts: Can we manage the really tight jam? Knowing they could, they would never have to scale back their plans, nagged by the doubt that if things ever got really ugly, they might fold. Amos had said so prematurely, but it was true: The sky was their limit.

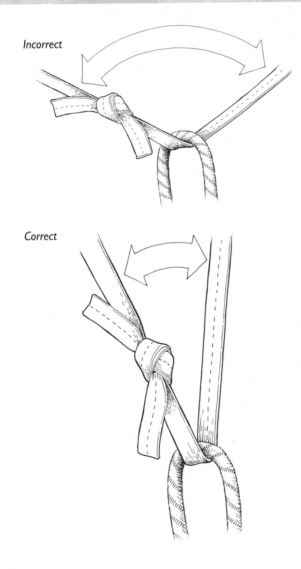

Incorrect

Correct

Anchor slings should be arranged to hang at less than a 90-degree angle (bottom) to maintain their maximum strength. The weight of the rappeller unduly loads the broadly slung configuration illustrated at top.

Fixed Anchors

Inspect fixed anchors as if your life depends on them, because it most assuredly does. Rusty pitons and bolts are particularly suspect. When in doubt, back up the existing anchor or place your own. The cost of a good nut is a small price to pay to see your children grow up, and all those who follow will benefit by your sacrifice.

At popular climbing areas bolt anchors are sometimes connected by a chain. Never simply loop your rope around the chain. If a link or bolt hanger breaks, the rope will slip right off the chain. That happened 1,000 feet up El Capitan, and three young men died. I never better understood the significance of the word grief as when I saw friends of the stricken three milling around the El Cap meadow, their faces long as doom and asking how come. There is no reason anyone should ever have to repeat their fate.

Many times, fixed anchor slings will come equipped with a heavy metal ring, like a medallion, through which you can feed the rope. These rappel rings are nice to pull a rope through and are usually quite strong—the cast aluminum ones are the best—but beware the welded steel ones. A new nylon runner threaded through the eyes or hangers of the anchor isn't given to invisible cracks or work hardening. I've heard of those rings breaking, but I've never heard of a new runner breaking on a rappel. Not once. The standard line per rappel rings is to never use just one ring. Always inspect them because they do wear out, especially if they have been toproped through. Never toprope through a rappel ring. More on this later.

Most often on fixed rappel anchors, the individual placements—be they nuts (extremely rare), pitons, or bolts—have a host of runners threaded through them from past rappels. If you're relying on fixed slings (left by previous parties), check every inch of them to make sure they haven't suffered from too much ultraviolet radiation (sun-bleached), or have been chewed by varmints. Especially check the part of the slings hidden from view, and inspect any rappel rings or links. Add a sling if there is any question about the condition of the existing slings, and add a chock or two if the other anchors don't look positively bombproof. It's your life you're dealing with here, so don't get into the fatal habit of trusting whatever fixed gear exists.

The rope is retrieved by pulling it through the slings, and the process can cause enough friction to greatly reduce the strength of the slings and occasionally even burn straight through them. Several years ago, some old slings taken from rappel anchors were tested for tensile strength, and it's reassuring to know that many of these slings were stronger than expected. Figures indicate that if there are more than four slings in place, there is little chance of all of them breaking. However, wear from the elements, cutting on sharp bolt hangers, and friction burns all factor in to greatly diminish a runner's strength. So the importance of backing up suspect slings cannot be overstated.

Wherever the anchor is, you are obliged to rappel directly below it. Gravity deems it so. A weight on the end of a string hangs directly below the string's anchor—the plumb line. After you have descended a ways, you can traverse around a bit, but a slip might set you on a dangerous, sideways tumble. So if you have to rig your own anchor, do so directly above (or as close as possible to) where you plan to descend, and don't deviate more than necessary.

Barring special circumstances, you will always rappel on a doubled rope, or ropes, which are retrieved by pulling them through the anchor slings. To facilitate this retrieval, the point where the rope runs through the slings is of vital concern. If you are on a smooth wall, it makes little difference. On a ledge, if the anchor is low, the slings should ideally extend just over the lip of the ledge so the rope is not bent over a sharp or angled edge. Even the smoothest rappeller will bounce on the rope, which will abrade over an edge, leaving a pile of sheath fiber on the rock. A sharp edge may even cut into the rope. Be keenly aware of what the rope runs over—avoiding, blunting, or even padding any hazards. Make certain the rope is not running through—or even near—any notches, cracks, flakes, or knobs. When it comes time to retrieve the ropes, they will invariably get lodged in these features. And, of course, inspect the ledge for loose or rotten rock. The action of a rappel can dislodge them, and when you are pulling the ropes down, the free end can whisk loose rocks directly onto your bean.

On a big ledge you can't extend a runner over the edge, since no one carries 20-foot slings with them. So if the anchor is located some ways back from the lip of the ledge, rig the anchor as high as you can above that ledge—say at eye level. This reduces the angle at which the rope passes over the edge, decreasing the friction on the sheath during the descent and on the whole line when you eventually pull it through the anchor. When the rope makes a sharp bend, it tends to bind on the lip, on itself, even in the slings, and retrieval is difficult, sometimes impossible. If this is unavoidable, have the first person down try to pull the ropes from below before the other climbers rappel. Ideally the ropes will have fluid action through the slings, but expect some friction. A nylon rope running over nylon slings will generate resistance no matter what the setup. If the rope won't budge, try leaving two biners through the slings. If this doesn't reduce the friction enough for retrieval, you'll have to improvise, possibly tying all your slings together so they extend farther out. And don't carry on until the ropes can be pulled from below.

Setting the Ropes

If you are making a short rappel, where one doubled rope will do, thread one end through the anchor slings, match it with the other end, and draw both strands of the rope through your hands, with one end passing through the slings until you have the middle of the rope anchored at the slings. Be careful that you accurately find the middle of the rope so you won't come up short. Some ropes have a middle mark, which is more convenient for finding the middle. Do not drag the rope over the slings as you set up the rappel. The friction will burn them. Rather, gingerly draw the rope through an arm's length at a time, or better yet, pull the rope through a carabiner that is clipped above the slings. If the rappel is longer than half a rope length, tie two ropes together. The old standard knot for doing this is the double fisherman's, or grapevine, knot (see Chapter 4), but it's rugged duty to untie after being loaded. Probably the most secure knot commonly used is a figure eight knot backed up by two grapevines. It is relatively easy to untie after weighting and works well with ropes of different diameters.

There are two other techniques that I'll mention because you are apt to see them used. The first involves tying the ropes together with a double overhand knot. You cannot use this knot for ropes of substantially different diameters, however. The double overhand creates the smallest knot profile, which decreases the chances of getting your rope stuck. A second method is to use a square knot backed up on each side by a grapevine. The square knot makes the whole thing easy to untie after loading, while the grapevines secure the square knot. I do not personally endorse either of these methods. They might have advantages in certain circumstances, but

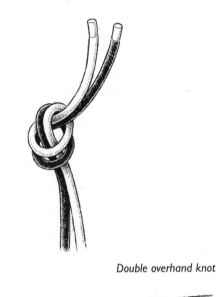

Double overhand knot

Figure eight follow-through

I prefer the safety of the figure eight backed up by two grapevines.

Whatever knot you choose, the knot will be on one side of the anchor. If you're using two ropes of different size, make sure the large-diameter rope is through the anchor and the knot is on the side of the thinner rope, especially if the rope is on slings (no metal). If you don't, differential friction on the different-sized ropes can cause the ropes to move through the anchor, sawing on the rope and making the rope ends uneven. Note the setup and remember which line you must pull to retrieve the ropes. Pulling the wrong rope entails trying to pull the knot through the slings, which is impossible 99 percent of the time, and often hopelessly binds or twists the rope in the slings. Then you're stuck and may have to climb the pitch to retrieve the line.

To toss the ropes down, both lines should be neatly piled with ends on top. Normally, you will

If there is doubt the ropes will reach, knot the ends—and for extra assurance, clip an old carabiner through that.

grab the ends and coil a 40- or 50-foot section of double rope and throw this off. This quarter-coil has some heft, and the momentum of the tossed line is usually enough to drag down the remaining line. To get a rope down a broken cliff, where danger of hang-up is real, try lap coiling, then tossing the upper half of the rope first, following with the lap-coiled ends.

Carefully inspect the rock below for anything the rope can snag. Gauge your throw to avoid these features if possible, even if you must pitch the rope some ways to the side. It should straighten out once you start down. If the ropes get bound on some feature—a bush, for instance—and you cannot pull them back up for another toss, you'll have to straighten them out during the rappel. This happens. Never rappel below a snag in your rope; you will rarely be able to untangle it from below, and in trying you could pull a rock down on yourself.

Make certain that the rope reaches the ground or the next anchor. You can normally verify this visually. If not, *always* tie a "stopper knot" in the end of each rope so you can't rappel right off the rope. This is especially important during bad weather, when it's dark, or if you're lacking experience. Most climbers do this as a matter of course, for rappelling off the end of the rope is not unheard of, and is usually fatal. The stopper knot does increase the possibility of getting the rope stuck, particularly if it's windy and the rope is blowing sideways. Some people prefer to tie the ends of the ropes together with a figure eight knot, but I've found that this prevents kinks from untwisting at the end of the rope (and every rappel produces kinks as the rope sheath binds on the core, much as clothing binds during dancing).

Rappel Brakes: Rappel Devices

Rappel devices generate friction on the rope to help control the descent. Properly rigged, rappelling is not strenuous, and the speed of your descent is easily controlled by one hand. A variety of devices are currently available. The most useful are compact and light, and they also double for belaying. Most belay/rappel devices create friction when a bight of rope is passed through a slot and clipped into a locking carabiner.

Far and away the most common rappel device is a TCU or similar unit, which doubles for belaying duties. For rappelling, the rig is set up exactly like it is when belaying, save that (normally) two strands of rope are moving through the device.

The figure eight descender was popular for about ten years, though for more than a decade it has been overshadowed by the TCU and is now an all but forgotten item. If you do buy a figure eight, make sure it's good to at least 3,000 pounds, and buy the lightest one you can.

Some of the other devices, particularly the flat plate variety (such as the Sticht plate), tend to bind and give a jerky rappel. This problem can be remedied by clipping into the rope with two carabiners rather than one, and two biners is always a better option anyway.

Figure Eight

To rig the figure eight, pull a bight of the rappel rope through the big hole and loop it around the stem, then clip the small hole into your harness with either a locking biner or two regular biners, gates opposed.

The advantages of the figure eight are ease of rigging and the relative fail-save nature of the device. The disadvantages are that they put a twist on the rope that causes kinking, they're generally heavier and more bulky than other belay rappel devices, and they allow twists to pass that could get your rope stuck. The simple solution here is to clip a sling into your harness and then to one of the rappel lines above your figure eight so no twists can pass. Figure eights do work better on icy ropes, but most rock climbers will never deal with iced ropes—yet another reason the figure eight has lost favor as a pure rock climbing tool.

The Petzl Gri Gri has come into favor over the last decade for belaying sport climbs and for guiding. However, the literature that comes with the Gri Gri states never to rappel with the device—so don't.

Figure eight descender

Remember this important point with all climbing equipment: Always strictly follow the manufacturers' instructions and recommendations. They are the ones who have thoroughly tested the gear and know best its strengths and limitations.

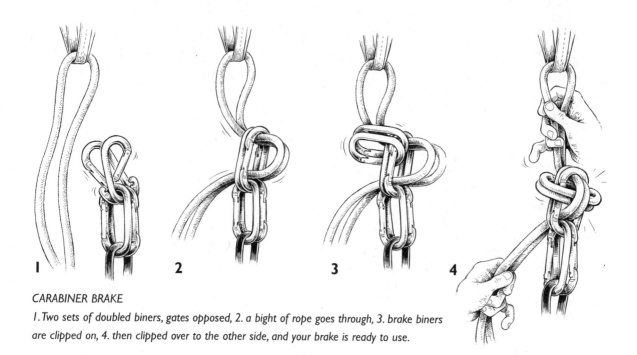

CARABINER BRAKE

1. Two sets of doubled biners, gates opposed, 2. a bight of rope goes through, 3. brake biners are clipped on, 4. then clipped over to the other side, and your brake is ready to use.

Carabiner Brake

Every climber should also know one or two alternative rappelling methods in case they forget or drop their rappel device, which happens. The age-old standard carabiner rappel is well known, but it takes a bit of time to rig.

Clip either two large-diameter locking biners or two regular biners (gates opposed) into your harness. To this, clip in two more biners, gates opposed. This second group forms the "platform" for the "braking" biners. To set up the rappel, face the anchor and, straddling the ropes, pull a bight of rope up through the platform biners. Clip the braking biners—gates down—over the platform biners and under the bight of rope.

A single brake biner usually provides enough friction when rappelling on two 11 mm ropes. On vertical or overhanging rappels, you'll want two. Rappelling on two 9 mm ropes or a single 10 or 11 mm rope, you may want three brake biners. Your weight, the rock steepness, and how much braking you do with your brake hand will determine how many braking biners work best for various rappels. Several rappels will tell you what works best for you. Two biners as the brake is the configuration to start with.

Oval carabiners are much easier to use for both the platform and the brake. Ds will work, but when the gates are opposed, the contrasting shapes reduce the space for the bight and are usually a hassle to get clipped. The carabiner brake rappel is very basic and simple, but it can be set up incorrectly. Never use only one biner for the platform and be certain to reverse the gates. The bight must pass over the back of the brake biners, not the gates, or the system is lethal.

Many of the lightweight modern carabiners are not large enough to rig a carabiner rappel. If small carabiners are all you have, a separate Munter hitch on each strand of the rappel rope works but is a major hassle. Make sure to use a locking carabiner or two carabiners with gates opposed for the Munter hitches, and extend one of the Munter hitches out from your harness with another locking carabiner or two opposed so the Munter hitches don't bind against one another. This method does put some twists in the rope because of the twisting hitches, but it serves well as a backup rappel setup for use with lightweight carabiners.

As you descend, the belay/rappel device will provide less and less friction as the weight of the rope below decreases. Sometimes even modern rappel devices don't provide as much friction as you'd like, especially if you're on steep terrain or if you're saddled with a pack or excess gear. Of course, you can wrap the rope around your hip to get extra friction, but that might wear a hole in your favorite tights—or worse—your very hide. Another option is to put a carabiner, preferably locking, on your leg loop and run the rope through this and then to your brake hand. For even more friction, wrap the rope twice around the extra carabiner.

Dulfursitz, or Body Rappel

The body rappel is the only method that uses no devices—just the rope—and, though rarely called upon, is the only viable means down a rope when other methods or gear as not available. Facing the anchors, straddle the rope. Bring the rope from behind you and across one hip, up across the chest and over the head to the opposite shoulder, and over and down the back to the opposite hand, next to where the rope passes over your hip. The rope then makes an S, and as with all rappels, the uphill hand is the guide hand, the downhill hand the brake hand. The brake hand can easily regulate speed, moving it out off the back to go faster and pulling it in around the hip to slow down. Most climbers prefer that the brake hand clasp the rope palm up.

The body rappel is a last resort. Unless you have thick clothing under every inch of passing rope, you'll feel pain—at best. Normally, a beginning climber will make a couple of body rappels and never make another in all her climbing days—but she will know how. Caught without gear and with a short, relatively low-angled route below, the climber with knowledge of the body rappel has a fairly safe means down. But aside from an old-timer showing how it's done, or a novice learning how, I've never seen someone intentionally using a body rappel in more than thirty years of climbing. The potential for rope burns and the effectiveness of other techniques have made the body rappel obsolete. Besides, by its definition, being without mechanical connection to the rope, you can fall out of the body rappel.

Rigging the Rappel

For safe rappelling, the anchors must be strong, both ends of the ropes must reach the next set of anchors or the ground, the gear must be rigged correctly, the harness must be properly fitted with the buckle double passed, and the climber must maintain absolute control during the descent. There are times when rappelling comes at the end of a hard day or in the face of poor weather, when your guard might be down a bit. Yet whenever you rappel, you must never let your guard down. Many climbers don't consider that the danger is really behind them until they're in the sack, smugly remembering their wild adventures.

Because every detail must be correct, it is critical that you double-check every aspect of the safety chain before leaning back to rappel. Double-check your harness buckle (and your partner's), the anchor and the rope's attachment to it, the rappel device and locking carabiner(s), and the rope-connecting knot. Just remember BARK—buckle, anchor, rappel device, and knot. Also, don't forget to inspect your gear often to be sure it's in good condition. Especially be sure that your harness, belay loop, slings, and rope are in good shape. Occasionally check your carabiners and belay/rappel devices for wear or notches. Retire any gear as soon as you have any doubts about its condition.

The Rappel Fundamentals

Your hands have separate jobs. The uphill, or guide, hand is used mainly for balance and should never death grip the rope. It can't stop you, and you're only instinctively trying to duplicate the friction that the carabiners or device are creating. The other hand, the brake hand, determines your speed. Most climbers keep their brake hand well below their hip, with the rope slicing over it. When they want more speed, they move the rope out and off the hip; to slow down or stop, they wrap the rope back around the hip. The prime rule of rappelling is never let go with your brake hand, lest you slide out of control down the rope. The brake hand feeds the rope through the rappel device. If you're right-handed, you'll probably want to brake with your right hand.

Once you are set up and ready to go, make certain any gear or clothing is well clear of the friction device and cannot get entangled no matter what you do. Long hair must be securely tied back. Anything loose can be drawn into the brake system, and it happens so fast that a whole shirttail or head of hair can be snatched into the brake with only one downward step. Extraction is very involved, often dangerous, and, in the case of hair, always very painful. In most cases, when something has been sucked into the braking device, it becomes locked so tight that the climber is incapable of freeing himself, and a rescue with shears is necessary.

The crux of rappelling is often getting started, particularly if you must descend over a lip. Once the rope is weighted, backpedal to the brink. Keeping your feet there, let out some rope until you are leaning well back. Don't move your feet down too soon. Stability is gained by having your weight pressing straight into the wall, requiring you to maintain a near perpendicular angle relative to the wall. Much less and your feet will skid off and you'll smack the wall—face first. After you have leaned back far enough and feel your weight driving into the wall, slowly pedal back, letting out rope and maintaining your perpendicular attitude. The moment you are established on the wall, bend your upper torso in, but keep your legs perpendicular to the cliff. Keep your feet spread apart at shoulder width for a good foundation. To see where you're going, slightly twist your upper torso toward your brake hand so you can look down.

Don't bound down the rope Rambo-style, rather "walk" down the cliff. The aim is a smooth descent, for several reasons. Heroic bounding moves or jerky action stresses the whole system unnecessarily. Too much speed heats up the friction apparatus and can singe the rope's sheath, making it brittle

and stiff to the touch. Inching down is pointless, though many beginning climbers think it is "safer." Snailing down the stone wastes everyone's time and usually means you are over-gripping with the guide hand. Small steps, fluid action, keeping your gaze below to see your way, and always keeping your legs

| **BARK** |
| Buckle |
| Anchor |
| Rappel Device |
| Knot |

perpendicular to the cliff—these are the fundamentals of a safe rappel. Steady, fluid movement—that's the goal.

A beginner's first few rappels should be accompanied with a belay from above. If there is a problem, the climber is still on belay, which can give a trembling beginner enough confidence to try again. Usually just a couple of belayed rappels is sufficient to get the knack, and you can dispense with the belay.

A technique for belaying someone after you go first is the fireman's belay, where you hold onto the bottom of the rope. If the rappeller loses control, you pull the rope tight to stop his descent. This method doesn't back up his rappel device, however, nor does it allow you to check his rappel setup.

If you need to stop while rappelling to untangle the rope or take a photo, wrap the rope around your leg three times to free your brake hand. Be sure your brake hand is ready to take the weight when you unwrap the rope to continue your rappel.

Overhanging, Free Rappels

When the rappeller is hanging in free space with nothing for her feet, the rope should run between her legs, under one leg and up to the brake hand. The added friction of the rope running under the leg is considerable, and providing your rappel apparatus is giving adequate friction, you can easily stop by folding the rope over your leg. However, try to maintain a smooth, steady descent; if you go too slowly, you'll tend to twirl on the rope. Maintain the same posture you would while sitting in a chair. A little tension from your guide hand will keep your upper torso upright.

Tying a prusik knot

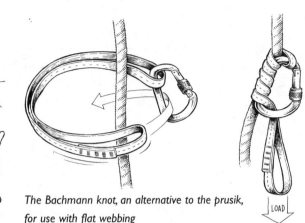

The Bachmann knot, an alternative to the prusik, for use with flat webbing

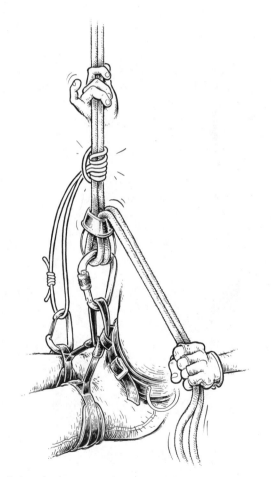

Prusik knot backup

As you come back in contact with the rock, extend your legs out like antenna, and slowly ease back onto the wall. Never race down a free rappel and suddenly stop. The quick deceleration generates enormous stress on the whole system and unnecessarily elongates the rope, which will abrade over even the smoothest lip.

Brake Hand Backups

If for some reason you are doubtful of controlling your rappel and are forced into making one—without a belay—you can rig a backup with either of two knots that bind on the rope when weighted but can be slid along the rope when not. The traditional knot is the prusik, but it must be tied with a small-diameter rope, such as 8 mm cord. Webbing will not work effectively as a prusik, but it can be combined with a carabiner to form a Bachmann knot, which serves the same purpose. Rig the Bachmann on the rope and attach it with a sling to a locking biner on your waist. When rappelling, cup the guide hand loosely over the knot, sliding it down as you go. Make sure the sling is not too long. If you do go out of control and the knot jams tight, it must be within reach to loosen, or you're stuck. And remember that unless the knot jams tight the moment you start sliding, it will never jam but will burn through.

A much better and safer system is to rig a friction knot below your belay device and clip it to your leg loop to back up your brake hand. An Autoblock works well. Simply wrap a few coils of a loop of cord around the rope, then clip it back to your leg loop. It's good to have a cord pre-tied to the right length for this safety trick, though you can use a standard sling as well. Make sure the Autoblock has enough wraps that it easily grabs the rope. To rappel, hold the Autoblock with your brake hand and slide it down the rope. Notice the greatly increased friction of the rappel setup. If you need to stop to untangle the ropes, the friction knot will hold you, freeing your hands. And if something like a falling rock causes you to let go of the rappel line, the friction knot will tighten so you don't go zipping down the rope.

Retrieving the Rope

Before the last person comes down, she must first double-check several things: Which rope needs to be pulled? Is the doubled rope crossed on itself or binding on the slings? Is it clear of all notches, grooves, loose rock, and the like? As mentioned, if there is any doubt the ropes can be pulled from below, make certain they can be before the last man descends. To facilitate easy retrieval, the last rappeller should separate any twists or kinks in the two ropes so they both run untangled to the ground or next anchor. You can most easily do this by keeping a finger of your guide hand between the two ropes as you descend. On the way down, note anything that the rope could get tangled in, or perhaps pull off, upon retrieval.

If you're on the ground, grab the end of the rope and walk away from the cliff with it before you start pulling. This gives you a better angle to pull from and decreases wear on the line. It also lessens the chance of dislodging any loose rock; though often, no matter what you do, pulling the ropes down can send rocks down as well, so be ready. Don't jerk the rope but pull smooth and steadily. As you draw in more line, the rope will often snake down and through the anchor on its own. Whatever the case, once the rope is close to coming free, warn those nearby, and once it's loose, always yell "Rope!" The end of the rope can lash like a bullwhip and people should be forewarned.

On multiple rappels, feed the free end through the new anchor slings as you pull the rope through the upper anchor. This avoids having to retie the knot at every rappel.

Stuck Line

One of the most tense moments on a multiple rappel descent is when the rope becomes stuck. Avoiding stuck rope is part experience and foresight, part luck. On steep, clean rock the ropes will usually pull nicely. As the angle kicks back and the rock becomes more featured, the chances of getting your rope stuck increase.

Because certain things are so important, and inevitable, let's go over them one more time. To avert stuck ropes, survey the terrain below, looking for cracks, bushes, trees, flakes, or other features the rope can hang up on (and sharp edges that could cut the line). The last person down needs to make sure the rope runs cleanly, with no twists. When using two ropes tied together, make a note which rope to pull before you go down, and tell your partner. If you pull on the wrong rope, the knot won't pull through the anchors. Worse, the rope could get stuck while you're trying to pull it in the wrong direction. This is fairly common.

If any doubt exists about the rope pulling, the first climber down should test the rope by pulling it for 5 or so feet before the last person goes, then resetting it with the middle at the anchors. If the rope won't pull, gradually tug harder to see if you can get it moving. Always be aware that as you pull the rope, you are also burning the slings, so be careful. If that fails, try extending the anchors with webbing, pulling or flipping the rope out of a crack or other snag, running the rope through two biners (gates opposed) rather than the nylon sling, or setting the knot below the initial lip. To set the knot below the lip, the last climber down has to downclimb or hand-over-hand down the rope to get below the knot before she can begin rappelling. (Be sure to first set the rappel device on the rope.) In this situation, it's advisable to give the last climber a fireman's belay while she gets started.

Make sure you get all knots and tangles out of

the rope before you begin to pull it down, lest the line barber poles on itself. Once you start pulling, try to keep the rope moving so it can't lodge in a constriction. Again, if you're on the ground, walking away from the cliff reduces the bending angle of the rope on the edges above, making it easier to pull.

Sometimes the rope gets hung up regardless of the best set lines. As mentioned, first be certain you are pulling the correct rope; it won't work to try to pull the knot through the anchor. Next, flip the rope side to side. If that doesn't clear it, try flipping a loop of the rope straight out, giving one end a stout jerk when the ropes are away from the wall. If all else fails, get everyone to pull on the rope with all their might. That will either free it or, more likely, jam it even worse. But since the other options are pretty grievous, try it anyway. Pulling hard on stuck ropes can damage the ropes and also pull down rocks right onto your head, so watch out.

If the rope is honest-to-God stuck fast, you have several options. If you still have both ends of the rope, tie both ends off to the new anchor and prusik up either one of the lines. If you have retrieved all or enough of one rope and the very end of the second line is mysteriously hung up (this does happen), you can lead the pitch again on the free rope. If you only have one end and not much slack, your task is pretty hateful but possible. You must tie off your end to the new anchor, fit a sturdy prusik on the rope, and lead the pitch again by moving the prusik up the rope and placing protection below it. If you fall, the rope is tied off, the prusik should hold, and you are held by any protection you have placed below the prusik. It is also a good idea to tie into the rope from time to time with a figure eight or butterfly knot to back up the prusik. If you are ever forced into this position, don't worry about style. Liberally cheat, hang on every nut, and place plenty of them. Do whatever is necessary to safely gain the snag.

If all else fails, yell for help. If somebody is nearby, certainly get their assistance before trying the prusik lead. If the ropes are stuck on top of a cliff or outcrop, there are often climbers milling about, and a jammed line can be freed in seconds. A climbing team must be self-reliant, but everybody gets a rope stuck sometime, and there's no shame in getting a hand if it's easily gotten and the other options are dangerous. Few experienced climbers have not sought help in exactly these circumstances.

Getting Back Up

If you rappel to a stance that has no place to anchor, you will have to ascend the rappel rope if you cannot climb back up. Rig two prusiks or Bachmann knots—one tied within reach of your harness and the other to a sling into which both feet may be cinched. The procedure is: Pull up legs, slide up lower knot, stand up while sliding top knot up, and repeat. Though the procedure is relatively simple, you will want to practice this before you need to use it, which is probably in an emergency, a very poor situation to be learning new techniques. (As with any form of mechanically ascending a rope, the biggest trick is knowing what length slings to use.) Because of the somewhat capricious nature of prusiks, it is important to tie into the rope periodically (below the prusik, obviously) during your ascent with a figure eight or butterfly knot. Be certain of your anchor before you simply prusik up the line. In the case of a snagged rope, prusik lead the pitch as described above. Why? Because you never want to trust that the snag will hold your weight.

Hanging Transfers

Now that you understand the basic procedure, we can look at the most exciting and frightening of all rappel situations: rappelling down a steep wall with no ledges or even stances. This procedure is most common for climbers who are retreating from big climbs, but it is also encountered by anyone who is rappelling a route with a hanging belay. The procedure is complicated and the potential for error is high, so it is essential to take every precaution.

Assume that the anchor is fixed, say three bolts. Because there is no ledge, you must tie a knot into the end of the rappel ropes to help ensure you don't rappel off the end. Total attention should always be given to this potential. The first climber down prepares the anchors for the team, then clips into and hangs from the anchors, independently of the ropes.

There are several methods for tying into the anchors. The most secure is to clip biners into all the anchors and secure yourself to them with slings girth-hitched through your harness. Only after you have done so should you unclip from the rappel rope, immediately securing the rappel rope to the anchor so it cannot get out of your reach. The next climber then comes down, clips into the anchors, and pulls the rope down, while the first person feeds the rope for the next rappel. Be extra careful, double- and triple-checking everything to make sure you've got it absolutely right.

Once you have pulled the rope through the upper anchor and fed it through the new slings at your present anchor, the first rappeller rigs his rappel before he unclips from the anchor. When the last person rappels, he must remove the biners from the bolt hangers. He might find it useful to clip slings into the rappel slings and stand in them to get enough height to remove the biners. Then he rappels down.

Trying to visualize this with little on-the-rock experience is a tall order. Most climbers bungle through the procedure several times, reread a passage like this, and then revise their strategy. Better than bungling things, have a guide show you these procedures so you are doing things safely from the start.

Coiling the Rope

Anyone who has spent time on a sailboat knows that the scoundrel who haphazardly coils a rigging line, if found out, spends the rest of his tour bailing bilge water or polishing the toilet lid—or is simply pitched overboard. The climber who haphazardly coils the rappel rope is twice a chump, for it's an easy task and usually takes but a few minutes to do properly. A poorly coiled rope is a polecat to untangle and can take several climbers fifteen minutes of steady cursing to get straight.

By far the fastest and most effective coiling method is not coiling at all, but stacking the line in a rope bag (which we've already covered). But you will not always have a rope bag on hand, especially

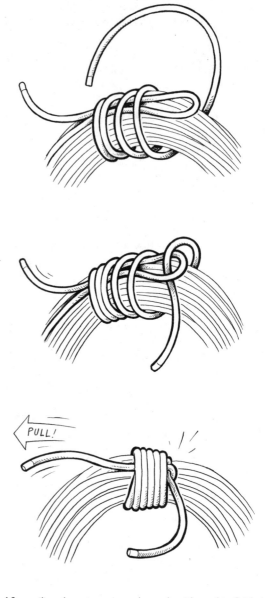

After coiling the rope, secure the ends with a whip finish: lay the short end back as a loop atop the coil; wind about 5 or 6 feet of the other end around, working toward the loop and making sure that each wrap is as snug as you can make it; and finally, finish by pulling the end through the initial loop.

on long "trad" routes, so you need to know several coiling methods.

A common technique is the standing coil. Leaving a tail of a couple feet, form successive coils about 5 feet, or two arm lengths, long. The fastest, and worst, method is to coil the rope with two free arms, where you're unintentionally twisting the rope with each successive loop. Next best is to sit and coil it around a foot and knee. My favorite method is to coil it around my neck. As you coil, shake out any kinks and twists.

With a very kinky rope, another climber should help shake out the line, leaving you to coil it. This is time consuming, and many climbers don't like the idea of a rope around their neck. But once you get past these objections, the neck coil is a viable method. If the rope is incomprehensibly twisted, you might have to walk it out and twirl it about to get it straightened. Normally this happens only to old ropes that have just been rappelled on, where the sheath has shifted around. It's best to get a new rope, though a new rope will also kink until it's broken in.

Another popular way to coil the rope is the "mountaineer's coil." This is best when you don't have a pack and you need maximum arm freedom— to do some scrambling, for example. It is difficult to say which coiling method is most popular, and foolish to claim one method is "best." Most professionals prefer the mountaineer's coil, however, since of all the quick coil methods it seems to produce fewer kinks in the rope. But since you are coiling double loops, they can entangle on themselves quite easily. The invention of the rope bag came none too soon—but you won't have one on those long climbs.

Conclusion

Because rappelling is so easy to do, climbers sometimes race through the setup, and the annual accident report is grim evidence of their haste. Like a jet pilot, the wise rappeller goes through a pre-rappel checklist that runs like this: Is the harness secure, knots and buckles tight? Is the anchor bombproof?

Coiling a rope around legs and feet Kevin Powell photo

Are the slings strong enough and tied correctly— particularly if you're using someone else's rappel slings? Are the ropes tied together properly? Do they reach the ground or next anchor? Is the braking system rigged correctly? Are loose clothes, gear, or hair far out of the way? Is the line of descent free of loose or rotten rock? Will the lines pull through okay? With a little experience, it only takes moments to check and double-check these things. Don't become a statistic; get in the habit of checking and double-checking every phase.

Heel hooked, hand latched on the bleak Enterprise *(5.12b), Owens Gorge, California, Bird Lew pauses at mid-roof to yank up slack before clipping her lead rope into the bolt just above. On strenuous, bolt-protected sport climbs, pausing to make such "clips" is oftentimes the most taxing aspect in climbing the route.* Kevin Powell photo

CHAPTER 7

Sport Climbing

Sport climbing has dominated the climbing scene for going on twenty years. Sport climbing, by common definition, is climbing on routes protected exclusively by bolts, as opposed to traditional climbing, where the protection is provided by gear placed by the leader. Of course, there is considerable overlap between the two types of climbing. For example, some routes have "mixed" protection, where the leader clips bolts and places gear. Sport climbing has also come to include climbing competitions, indoor gym climbing, and low bouldering—basically any type of climbing that is perceived to be "safe," a term that should never be applied to any form of climbing, especially bouldering. Incidentally, more broken bones arise from bouldering than roped climbing. Every time you fall you hit the ground, and even low bouldering deserves a warning to this effect.

Most sport climbing strives to remove the risk inherent in climbing, allowing the climber to focus solely on technical difficulty. It requires less commitment than traditional climbing because there is usually little penalty for error. Generally, gear consists only of shoes, a rope, a harness, and a handful of quickdraws; and if it starts raining or the "vibes" are wrong or, more likely, a finger goes, you simply lower back to the ground. The vast majority of sport climbs are 100 feet long or less, and providing the leader has a 200-foot rope (now standard gear), she simply lowers off the top anchors right back to her pack. By engineering most of the potential hazards out of the equation—meaning permanent protection bolts are spaced a body length apart—sport

climbing has become increasingly accessible to the masses, few of whom want to face the seriousness of traditional climbing.

While sport climbing is perceived as a safe endeavor, a casual attitude can still earn you a pine box. Diligent attention must be paid to every detail in the safety chain. Climbers tend to place blind faith in the bolt protection found on sport routes—and for good reason. Bolts hold tens of thousands of falls each year, with very few failures. But some failures do occur, mostly with old ¼-inch-diameter bolts—rarely found on modern sport routes—which can shoot from the stone like cloves from a holiday ham. Poorly placed larger bolts can, and do, fail. Sometimes the bolt is sound but the hanger is suspect. At any rate, inspect the bolt and the hanger before blindly trusting them. Since sport climbing is so reliant on bolts, it might be a good idea to go back and review the material on bolts in the anchors section.

Life at the Sport Crag

Here's a typical scene at the sport climbing crag. Two climbers arrive at the crag mid- to late morning. They stroll 10 feet, or ten minutes, (occasionally farther) gain the crag, then pick a route to climb. Many sport climbing crags are roadside affairs, allowing the climbers to avoid hiking and save their energy for the climbing. Interface with the natural world is often a secondary, rather than a principal, goal for many sport climbers. The emphasis is on short, gymnastic climbing in a controlled venue. If the chosen route is at a popular area, another team is probably already on it, so the arriving team either chooses another route or drops their rope tarp at the base to reserve a place in line. They will likely scope the route (or the guidebook) to determine how many quickdraws to bring and to plan the strategy for the route. They will scrutinize the other climber on the route for any tricks or secrets about the climbing sequence, learning from his mistakes. They may also seek "beta" (a detailed description, replete with lavish body language and funky crag argot) about the moves from any milling climbers who have done or attempted the route. But if the leader is going for a "best style" ascent—the celebrated "on-sight flash"—she must climb the route with no previous information and without falling or otherwise weighting the rope.

Now the route is freed up. With quickdraws racked on her harness and a shoulder-length sling for clipping into the belay, the leader sets off for the first bolt. Once there, she finds the most restful stance for clipping in. She clips the quickdraw in with the carabiner gates facing away from the anticipated direction of travel, then looks above to see which way the routes goes and to plot a sequence. Normally, she'll clip into the bolts with a standard quickdraw, but if the climbing is especially hard above, and if the result of having the rope accidentally unclip would be disastrous, she may clip in with a locking carabiner (rare). Higher on the pitch, with the rope clipped into several bolts, the last bolt is backed up by the bolts below, so a normal quickdraw will usually suffice.

Throughout, the leader strives to remain calm and relaxed, planning and executing moves as she gains the bolts, always keeping good body position, using precise footwork, gripping as lightly as possible with her hands, and resting whenever possible. Her ultimate goal is to reach the anchors at the end of the pitch without weighting the rope, in the best control possible. If she reaches a difficult section and can't decipher the moves, she may climb back down to a rest or large hold to avoid hanging on the rope and forfeiting her on-sight flash. This is often impossible, especially on overhanging routes, but it is surprising how you can often reverse one or two difficult moves if a good hold is there to return to.

The energy wasted, however, is very hard to recover unless the hold is wondrous and the leader's fitness is superb.

Reaching the top of the pitch, she uses a sling to clip into the fixed anchors, which ideally will be two bolts (⅜-inch diameter or larger) with chains or, more commonly, welded cold shut hangers. After clipping a good sewn sling into both of the bolts or shuts and then into her harness with a locking carabiner (or two carabiners with the gates opposed), she can go off belay, lean back, and rest—but only after double-checking *every* aspect of the anchor construct. Even world-class climbers have failed to do so, and have paid dearly for their oversight.

Communication

One scenario: The leader calls "off belay" because she is finished with the lead. Oftentimes after finishing a sport climbing lead (which as mentioned tends to be less than half a rope length), the leader will opt not to belay the second from atop the pitch, choosing instead to lower to the ground and belay there. But when the leader leans back to lower off, the belay is nonexistent—since she has already called "off belay"—and she whistles straight into the deck. Very poor. This is as much the belayer's fault as the leader's, but that matters little at the funeral.

Good communication between the climber and the belayer can always solve this problem. Also, an experienced belayer can and should avoid dangerous situations by *questioning the climber when her suggestions or commands are confusing, misleading, or seemingly dangerous.* If there is ever any question, the belayer should keep a stout belay on *no matter what the climber says* until the situation is absolutely clear. In the aforementioned scenario, don't call "off belay" until you've been safely lowered to the ground.

Lowering

With the advent of climbing gyms and the popularity of sport climbing routes (where a leader often cannot accomplish a lead on his or her first try and must be lowered to the ground for another go), lowering has become an integral part of the sport climbing game. The first rule of lowering is *never lower with the rope running through a nylon sling or cord*. This dangerous practice has given more than one climber an "E" ticket straight to the Golden City. As mentioned, it's a sketchy, ill-advised practice to lower or toprope through aluminum rappel rings, especially if your rope has any desert grit in it.

Every time you lean back to lower, first look down and make sure your belayer is still with you. Say "lower me" and/or give the "thumbs down" signal. Again, never say "belay off" at the end of a pitch if you intend to lower, because your partner needs to keep you on to lower you off. A few climbers have survived when their belayers took them off belay as they leaned back to lower, but more than one of them is now eating through a straw. This may sound like catastrophizing, but it's most certainly not. Belay failures are almost always enough to end someone's climbing career and are commonly fatal. Thankfully, they are very rare though by no means unheard of. And they are always avoidable. I always hold onto the belayer's side of the rope as I begin to lower— essentially lowering myself—until the belayer has me nice and tight.

The Belayer's Role

If you're lowering someone, use two hands on the brake side of the rope to control the descent and to prevent a kink from knocking a single brake hand from the rope. Make sure the rope is stacked to feed easily so you don't have to fight rope tangles while your partner is dangling. A rope bag or tarp comes in handy here. As soon as she gives you the command to lower, pull all the slack out of the rope, lock off your belay device, and lean back so she immediately has tension on the line. Don't make her lean back and "fall" onto your rope. Lower your partner at a nice steady pace, not too fast but not too slow, without jerking her like a puppet on a string. The notion that lowering a person very slowly is safer is hogwash and earmarks a scared or inexperienced belayer. Zipping a leader down the route is likewise poor form and dangerous. Slow her down as she approaches the ground and make sure she's solidly on her feet before you feed out a bunch of slack.

The biggest fears in lowering someone are that you could drop her out of control or let the end of the rope pass through your belay device so she falls to the ground. Both of these mistakes have often happened, and to very experienced climbers. The lowering anchors must be within a half rope length for your partner to reach the ground. If any uncertainty exists about the distance to the ground, tie a knot in the end of the rope so it can't whistle through your belay device if it is too short. Also, don't be too far from the touch-down zone in case the entire length of the rope may be needed.

A Gri Gri works very nicely for lowering; just squeeze the locking cam. It takes some practice to lower smoothly, however. If you're having trouble squeezing the cam, use the lever, but be extremely careful not to pull back on the lever too fast or you'll drop your partner like a ton of bricks.

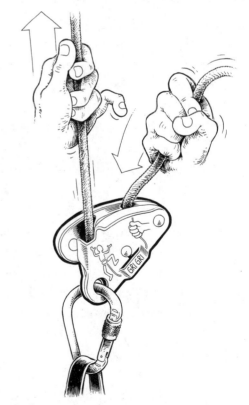

The Gri Gri in action

Amos and Coco #16:
A Family Affair

"Look!" said Danny, a young sport climber who looked like Dennis the Menace with tattoos. "It's Amos McCoy!" "Jeepers," said Thomas, who had about .007 percent body fat on his shrink-wrapped carcass. "Check out that rhino hoisting around on those little pockets."

Amos reached a good hold on the 120-degree wall, leaned off his arm and said, "Who you callin' fatty, Slim?"

Danny and Thomas barraged their good friend Amos with a torrent of trash talk, or "smack," as they walked over to Coco, belaying at the base of the 60-foot sport climb. Amos chalked up and pulled on.

"You lead this already?" asked Danny, referring to *Super Duper*, a 5.11e, the route Amos was just now completing. "Yeah," said Coco, now lowering the fireman to the base. "Amos wanted to run a lap, then we were heading over to the Wonder Wall." "We'll join you," said Thomas.

A few minutes later, after Amos had coiled up the rope, the quartet hoofed off toward the Wonder Wall. They walked a few minutes along the base of the intermittent cliffside, which like many sport climbing areas was roughly 80 feet high and comprised countless different faces, arêtes, and corners, like an accordion stretched fully open. During the day they might climb ten or twelve routes, including a few warm-ups on favorites like *Super Duper*. Then they might tackle a "project," which required multiple efforts (sometimes spread out over multiple days) before they could put all the moves together. Finally, as the day waned and the arms grew weary, they'd grope up a few last climbs to get that final "burn" before heading back.

While each climber tended to work their pet projects with their customary partner; for other more casual efforts, partners were largely interchangeable. If a rope was already strung over something that caught their immediate fancy, and they hankered for a quick toprope burn, they often tied in and had at it, even on a stranger's line. Some folks were touchy in this regard; but for the majority, once a toprope was established, folks usually asked out loud if others wanted a "go" before the line was pulled. Through this communal process, especially when Amos and Coco first started frequenting the sport cliffs, they had immediate access to routes they had no chance of leading or even climbing all the way through. But little by little—as folks on the deck screamed encouragement and instructions (that half the time were wrong)—the pair started ticking off routes that at first had "hosed" them perfectly. Shortly they were leading the same. These days it was just as likely that Amos or Coco had strung a line and asked others if they fancied a go. The students had become the teachers.

Just now they were heading for a project Coco had been working all summer. She liked her chances of getting it today.

While both Coco and Amos had gone far in embracing their opposite, undeveloped capacities, their primary strengths remained the same. Now a third-degree black belt in aikido with an influential upper body plus a heart full of contained power, Coco nevertheless shined most brightly on technical ground requiring superb flexibility and physical adroitness—and courage, which she had from the start. Similarly, Amos could nearly touch his toes with his chin these days, and through a long process that had included yoga and meditation, he had retooled his mind and linebacker's physique into the mold of a "bricked" Bruce Lee. But he still felt most comfortable where his native gusto and raw power could find play. He would never float up a desperately steep climb on small holds as Coco could, but on long and reachy endurance problems, particularly ones featuring large and sloping holds—a bane for most climbers—Amos was the business and could hold his own with most anyone in town.

Amos, Coco, Danny, and Thomas turned a corner, and before them the striking and overhanging Wonder Wall swept overhead like a breaking wave. Their eyes panned up the cobbled face to a lone figure flowing up the last moves of *Gran Kubla*, a test piece of the highest order. To Amos and Coco's eyes, there was something familiar to the leader's stylish movements; and when he finished the last moves, clipped the shuts, and yelled down "Take," they immediately recognized the voice of that magnificent mountaineer, Jules Pinkus.

Will Rogers once said that the Lord constituted everybody so that no matter what color you are, you require the same amount of nourishment. Few could hope to dine on such rich fare befitting the invincible Jules Pinkus, but here at the sport climbing cliff, he was the piteous climber who could not find nourishment to his liking.

The Climber's Job

The most common situation for being lowered is from double or triple anchors at the top of a sport route. If you can't stand on a ledge at the top of the pitch to rig the lower—and you rarely can—clip into one of the anchors with a sling (clip both anchors if you're a long ways above your last piece). If the hanger's chain links or other connecting hardware—such as the now-ubiquitous cold shuts—have a large enough opening:

1. Pass a bight (loop) of rope through the anchors and extend the bight down to your harness.
2. Tie a figure eight in the bight and clip this knot into a locking carabiner on your harness tie-in point or belay loop.
3. Double-check everything, then dismantle your original tie-in knot. You're now connected to the rope through the locking carabiner and figure eight knot. Pull the end of the rope through the anchors and give the signal to lower.

This system is quick and safe because you are never untied from the rope or off belay. If lowering requires the entire length of the rope, this trick may leave you a little short of the ground, however. Some people may complain that this technique leaves you connected to the rope with only a locking carabiner, but that's all that's holding you at the belayer's end anyway. You can certainly back up this carabiner with another, gates reversed, if you so desire.

Another alternative, especially good if a bight of rope won't fit through the anchors, or if you need the entire length of the rope to lower, is to clip into the anchors with a sling or two, then tie a figure eight in the lead line 4 or so feet from the tie-in point and clip into it with a locking carabiner. This clip-off will keep you backed up by the higher pieces in the pitch and will make it impossible for you to drop the rope, which would place you in a horribly embarrassing and potentially dangerous situation. Next, double-check everything, untie from the end of the rope, pass it through the anchors, and tie back into it. Now untie the backup knot, disconnect the slings, and lower off.

A third option that is quick but not as safe is to clip into the anchors with slings, untie the rope from your harness, pass it through the anchors, and tie back into it. The main problem here is the potential for dropping the rope and becoming stranded.

Many sport climbing areas feature open cold shuts at the top of routes for convenience. (Cold shuts are relatively soft metal rings that can be closed with a stout hammer blow; open cold shuts have not been hammered closed and allow a rope to be slipped through.) Gated, open cold shuts are now made specifically for sport climbing anchors (the others are used in industry to connect chains). It is certainly handy to flip your rope through a couple of open cold shuts at the top of a pitch and lower to the ground. While the people who set cold shuts seem to have complete confidence in them, in years past it was not a sage practice to toprope through these because their strength was unpredictable. But this was mainly in reference to smaller, thinner shuts, whereas climbers establishing new routes these days almost always go with thick and burly models that are plenty strong at the outset. However, even these will wear perilously thin over time, especially on popular routes where many dozens of climbers might lower off in a month. For this reason, shuts are often replaced every season or so. Old ones can be sketchy, even outright dangerous, so visually inspect them before using. Remember that toprope falls can reportedly put upwards of 1,000 pounds of force on the top anchors, which can further abrade the shuts.

The rope must pass through steel chain links, welded cold shut hangers, or carabiners to allow safe lowering. Conventional bolt hangers and aluminum rappel rings are unsuited for lowering or toproping directly through, so the leader may have to leave a carabiner or two to lower off such anchors, or rappel rather than lower.

When climbing, lowering, and toproping, the alert climber is always on the lookout for sharp edges that may cut the rope. If the rock is especially coarse, the leader may choose to rappel instead of lower, so the rope won't have to run under tension over the sharp rock.

If at some point, for whatever reason, you don't trust your belayer to lower you in a controlled manner, simply grab the side of the rope running back down to the belayer and lower yourself, hand over hand. This technique is standard on routes up to about seventy-five degrees. The friction of the rope running through the anchor is considerable when the line is weighted. If you're weak, or "pumped" (meaning that your arms are so pumped full of blood that they're swollen like swordfish, weak, and useless), or the rock is steep or overhanging, wrap the rope once around your leg, grab it with both hands above the wrap, and "feed" yourself down. This method is tedious and slow, and you can get wrenched onto your side. Also, you'll probably singe your clothes and perhaps your leg, but it's a lot better than decking out from on high. If you are extremely pumped and the route is severely overhanging, just rest up at the anchor for a spell, then set up a rappel and get down that way. This is likewise a useful technique if the rock is rough and the rope will run over it with some measure of drag. This is almost always the favored way if you have doubts or if things look dicey. I've mentioned the self-lowering methods because a belayer's inability to properly lower you is usually discovered only after you have descended a ways and can no longer return to the anchors to arrange a rappel. Climb long enough, and I guarantee you this will happen.

Cleaning the Route

Typically the leader will "clean" the route (remove the quickdraws) while being lowered, so the second climber can take a toprope ride without the onus of removing any of the gear, or so the team can move onto another climb. ("Team" may be a bit of a misnomer here.) Save for a warm-up climb or two, sport climbing partners may not even climb the same routes, but rather serve as belay mules for each other on their respective projects. If the route is exceptionally overhanging or if it has traversing sections, some key quickdraws should be left in place to provide a directional anchor so the toproped climber won't swing too far if he falls. Sometimes the leader will leave all the quickdraws in place. When she gets to the ground, the rope is pulled down and her partner also leads the climb.

Retreat

Sometimes a climber reaches an impasse, and even after many tries cannot continue up a route. When this happens, it's time to "bail" (retreat). The best and most convenient way to retreat is to simply leave a carabiner on the highest bolt clipped and lower to the ground. For safety's sake, also leave a biner on the next lower bolt so you'll be backed up if the high bolt fails. Before trusting your all to the top bolt, you should also thoroughly inspect it. Rather than leaving a carabiner or two (most climbers hate to leave gear), some climbers will leave a retreat sling on the high bolt and rappel from it. Unfortunately, this leaves unsightly webbing on the rock and clogs the bolt hanger. In some cases a carabiner won't fit through such a clogged hanger, leaving the next leader in a fix when she can't clip directly into the hanger and instead must clip into ratty old webbing. Also, rappelling from an open anchor is simply a bad practice.

Style

More often than not, a maxed out sport leader will hang on bolts to rest and work out the next moves. Years ago, "hangdogging" was considered shabby style, but today it's a common tool used to rehearse the sequences on especially challenging routes. As soon as the leader puts tension on the rope, however, she has lost both her on-sight flash and her free ascent, so if she wants to eventually "free" the route, she'll have to try again from the ground. On a subsequent attempt she can make a "redpoint" ascent, where she places all the quickdraws on lead and never hangs on the rope, or a "pinkpoint" ascent, where the gear has been pre-placed and she merely has to slip the rope in as she goes. In sport climbing, or any type of climbing, you haven't done a route free until you've climbed it from the bottom to the top with no rests. If you've done a route in less than perfect style, be honest reporting your accomplishments. In the climbing world, once your integrity is compromised, trying to retrieve it is like pulling someone back from the dead. It's basically impossible.

Sharpen Up

Most people who start climbing are looking for fun, exercise, and good fellowship outside the arena. A percentage of new climbers, however, develop strong performance ambitions. The following brief discussion is for that group.

The aspiring sport climbing champ is up against two main challenges: how to keep her learning curve as steep as possible and how to avoid tweaking a finger or elbow in the process. Notwithstanding sore muscles, which are part of all strenuous sports, injuries have never been a large part of traditional climbing. However, with sport climbing and its emphasis on steep to overhanging routes and concentrated difficulty, tendon and ligament sprains have become commonplace, and you must climb wisely to avoid an injury that can put you on the couch for weeks or even months. For a novice sport climber, whose muscles and tendons are not accustomed to cranking off the quick of his fingers, injury prevention is a real concern. The injury need not be grave to radically affect your fitness level—and fitness is key to sport climbing. Tweak a shoulder and skip a weekend, then the next weekend you have to go easy, and by the time you're back to where you started, a month has passed. Believe it: The only way to really advance with sport climbing is to do a lot of it, on a consistent basis, and you can't do that when you're injured.

Sport climbs tend to be hard, usually 5.9 or above, so for that first few months, the novice will be looking hard for anything he can actually climb. Given that a game novice can rapidly hone up in the climbing gym, today's sport climber usually finds himself on 5.9 terrain rather quickly. As with "trad" routes, the trick to improvement is mileage on the rock. But because your fitness dictates how many or how few sport routes you can do in a day, and because sport routes are generally pretty damn exacting, your arms are bound to give out before your ambition. Several things can help.

First, to avoid injury, always warm up on an easy route. Even experts skip this step and injuries often follow. A cold climber cranking off one-finger pockets is begging for a ruptured tendon. Because many sport climbing areas are basically roadside affairs, you can tool up to the cliff and, dead cold, start pulling down. Then cry "Uncle!" So warm up, and stay warmed up. Sport climbs tend to be very concentrated, meaning that on a given hunk of cliff, there are often a dozen or more routes, all within a stone's throw of one another. You can tick off one, move 10 feet left or right and crank another, and carry on in this fashion for a whole day. The hazards of this convenient setup are basically two: You won't get adequately warmed up and will start pulling down and get injured; or you will take too long of a break between "burns" (routes), get cold, and then jump back on the "business" and get injured that way. So warm up well, and after a break of more than a half hour, warm up again. Always.

At the outset, try to hook up with experienced climbers who like to do stacks of routes, as opposed to a world-class monster who only works impossibly difficult test pieces or a recreational group that climbs a route or two and heads for the restaurant. No harm in that, but you'll have to postpone the roast duck and crank a few more climbs if you want to soar. With an ambitious and experienced group, you won't be asked to do much leading at first, so once the toprope is strung, have at it. There's no harm in trying climbs above your limit, but this can be a trap insofar as you can't learn to climb with control and buff your technique if you're flailing like a gaffed tarpon. If a rope is strung over something you can actually do—even if you have to hang and rest here and there—climb it several times to log that footage, practicing good technique and building endurance, which are critical factors with sport climbs. If you have a local or favorite area, dial in six or seven (or more) climbs so you can work a circuit in addition to trying new projects. Also, have a project that's just out of reach, something you can aim for, work on, and knock off over time. Avoid the trap of always trying something too hard—you can't log enough footage and build endurance, and you miss the chance to climb something perfectly. Also, avoid the trap of always doing the same climbs. You don't hone your on-sight leading abilities if you know every hold on the route. Repetition also breeds boredom, so mix it up and keep it an adventure of discovery. A balance of familiar and new routes—at levels that are doable, near-limit, at your limit, and beyond your limit—is the fastest way to improve and to keep the experience fresh and exciting. The emphasis should always be on doable and near-limit climbs, preferably on routes that you have never before climbed. You might get warmed up, then first cast off on something beyond you, exhaust yourself, then rest up and go after doable and near-limit routes for the rest of the day. It is not unusual to do ten or more sport climbs on a good day, and most of those should be well below your maximum. The rub here is that the majority of routes will be near or beyond your limit when you first start out, so running laps on doable routes will probably remain your best strategy for that brief break-in period. Gym climbing during the week is a good way to rapidly improve technique and build strength.

Try to hook up with a partner who is near your own level, or perhaps a little beyond. For a novice to try to follow an ace around is frustrating for the novice and aggravating for the ace. This sometimes works out, however, and a patient ace can pull a novice up to his level in a season or two if the novice can avoid injuries.

You will have to find your own way, your own pace, and your own degree of commitment. Once you plateau, and you will many times, you'll have to make a special study of how to break through it. Since most climbers hold down a job, time is usually the limiting factor. Once you can consistently lead low to mid-range 5.11 routes (expert), you'll find that, regardless of natural ability, consistency is the key to forging into the magic realm of 5.12. To get there, and stay there, is almost impossible without climbing two or three days a week (one or two days in the gym) as well as augmenting your climbing with some cross-training. Since few folks want to devote this much time and effort, 5.12 remains a dream for the vast majority of climbers.

For a more thorough handling of the sport climbing game, refer to *Sport Climbing* in the How to Rock Climb Series.

Fred Knapp spots Shelley Presson on a hard boulder problem at Morrison, Colorado.

Stewart M. Green photo

CHAPTER 8

Training for Climbing

Few climbers, even those who take it quite seriously, are motivated enough to train regularly with climbing in mind. The great majority of climbers are only in it for fun and have lives or work schedules that preclude the necessary time for specialized workouts. But as the top climbs become increasingly more physical (sport climbing!) and leading climbers recognize themselves as world-class athletes, training attitudes trickle down into the mainstream. Over the last fifteen years, even weekend warriors have begun hitting the weight room, pull-up bar, and climbing gym hoping to increase their performance. This trend has resulted in the development and supply of training equipment specifically for climbing.

The early training apparatuses had some major drawbacks. The rope ladder, popular about twenty years ago, resulted in grievous elbow injuries from the wrenching and stress of repeated one-arm lowering. Fingertip pull-ups caused joint problems in many. Other devices, like various hand squeezers and finger-tension gadgets, were fine for recovering from injuries but did little to increase strength or endurance. Many common workouts were geared to gain the strength to do circus feats—like one-arm pull-ups—which has surprisingly little positive effect on people's climbing. As certain exercises are being eliminated because they cause injuries and new devices are introduced almost daily, it's still not clear how to attain optimum results while staying free from injuries. Likewise, it is virtually impossible to discuss various exercises and devices without taking up training philosophies. Still, there are several physiological facts that cannot be denied.

First, strong fingers and forearms are every climber's dream. Since the fingers don't have muscles, it's the sinew connections in the forearms (and the attending muscles) that must be strengthened. Second, most every climbing exercise involves some form of pull-up—duplicating the movement on the rock—and it's the latissimus dorsi, or 'lats,' which are the prime movers in this action. You simply cannot strengthen the lats alone, though. You must also train the antagonistic muscles required for the pulling movement—the chest and trapezius, as well as the abdominals for that atomic core strength—to provide balanced muscle groups and avoid injuries. Lastly, any muscle group that you train to the point of failure requires at least forty-eight hours to recover. These comments are not opinions, but incontrovertible physiological facts that should be factored into any workout. They tell us certain things that have long been overlooked by the climbing world. It is fine to concentrate on the lats and forearms, but not to the exclusion of the other muscles. To do so is to invite injury. And totally blasting those muscles every third day will bring much better results than doing so every day, or every other day.

From this we can conclude that while it is probably desirable to do specialized exercises that closely ape the climbing movement—and focus on the muscle groups most involved—it is likewise important to round out the routine and physique with an equal amount of general conditioning exercises.

Anything else results in an unbalanced machine, where weak antagonistic muscles are throwing the whole body out of kilter.

Of course, the best training for climbing is climbing itself. Nothing substitutes for mileage on the rocks for gaining strength, endurance, and fluidity of movement. For developing sheer power, and technique, bouldering has no rival. Technique, power, and endurance can also be improved in a climbing gym. If there isn't one near you, there probably will be soon. For straight power, campusing on a fingerboard has proven to be remarkably effective. And for general conditioning, weight training is second to none.

Bouldering

Bouldering is essentially climbing a sequence of moves (a "problem") where a rope is unnecessary. The world's hardest climbing—in terms of individual moves and small sequences—has always been, and always will be, done on boulders. The controlled medium, the ease of trying, trying, and trying again, and the ferocious (though mostly friendly) competition that surrounds the pastime make ideal conditions for the best climbers to try the hardest sequences imaginable. The first time I saw a world-class boulderer in action, I was thunderstruck. I'd been climbing about three months, clawing up easy climbs made difficult because—in the spirit of the great mountaineers—we bore weighty packs and climbed in hiking boots. And before me was a man in shorts, Varappe shoes, and a chalk bag, powering up overhanging rock like it was a jungle gym, ever controlled and graceful, with precision and explosive strength that was mind-boggling. The experience reoriented me in seconds. No more packs, off with the hiking boots—it was time to start bouldering.

Bouldering is such an engaging and stimulating endeavor that many climbers prefer it to roped climbing. Unquestionably, bouldering is the quickest way to gain physical climbing skill. A dedicated boulderer brings a lot of artillery to a roped climb. Strong fingers and good footwork, requisite for any difficult bouldering, are hers in abundance. But it's the experience of having done thousands of different sequences that gives her the real edge. It's doubtful that an experienced boulderer will encounter anything on a roped climb that she hasn't already done—in some fashion or another—on the boulders. Beginning climbers can master the fundamentals in several months, intermediate climbers can become experts in a year, and experts can maintain their edge with a couple of good bouldering sessions a week.

All bouldering is not low-level work, however. Highball bouldering, essentially free soloing, has long been a popular game of Russian roulette among experts. Because of their tremendous skill level, however, the chamber rarely fires on an expert soloist. As a novice or intermediate climber, you will never want to climb any higher than a point where you feel comfortable jumping off. If you must assume an upside-down or awkward position, have a friend spot you. Make sure your spotter is alert and ready, with his hands up to prevent your head and shoulders from hitting the ground if you fall. And remember, if you fall off, you do hit the ground. Always clear the landing zone of problem stones or other detritus that could cause twisted or broken ankles—the most common injuries in bouldering. If you think bouldering is for you, invest in a crash pad. There are many models to keep you from bruising an ankle. If there is any doubt about the seriousness of a bouldering problem—that it's too high or the fall is ugly—rig a toprope.

Toproping

Toproping involves rigging an anchor above the desired climb. The rope runs up from the base of the climb, through the anchor, and back down—one end for the climber, the other for the belayer who is anchored on the ground. Toproping lets a climber ascend with protection from above. For many beginners, toproping will be the only climbing done at the outset. As such, it stands out as a method of climbing all its own.

Though toproping should be a fairly straightforward procedure, much depends on the circumstances. The actual setup, the rigging of the anchor itself, is of crucial importance. Unless you want to be

Toproping
Remember to use doubled biners on the anchor!

First on the agenda is selecting a toproping site. Many climbing areas have routes that have become designated toproping climbs. These are easily accessed from below via trail or third class scrambling and oftentimes are fitted with bolt anchors. Just as often, however, you must rig your own anchor or extend the anchor via slings, et al., to the anchor point below the lip of the wall you are climbing on (to avoid rope drag and wear).

To set a toprope anchor, you'll have to get close to the lip of the cliff. Use caution! Every year climbers are killed when they slip off a ledge while preparing their climb. If the ledge is sloping or wet and you feel uncomfortable, choose another site or get belayed into position to rig things up. Find a way to anchor yourself so you can concentrate on the task at hand. And be careful of loose rocks that can bean people below. Have your partner(s) stand away from the base. When those below are at a safe distance, they're better able to make sure and verbally confirm that you're lining the rope directly over the climb.

Hopefully the route you've selected to toprope has a stout tree at the top. This makes for a quick and easy anchor. I generally carry two pieces of 1-inch tubular webbing (one 20 feet and one 30 feet in length), a couple of shoulder-length slings, and, of course, locking biners. Again, hulking trees are usually the best natural anchors, but boulders can work well too. Just make sure they are stationary and there is no possible way for the slings to slip off the boulders. You can use nuts and cams to this end, but then you're getting into advanced territory. Know what you're doing.

The anchor slings must extend from the anchor to just over the lip of the climb, allowing the rope to run freely through the biners. Because anchors are sometimes well back from the lip, equalizing the anchor and extending it to hang in exactly the right place can involve some engineering, mainly in arranging slings of exactly the right length. Because you are probably not yet a good judge of what is bombproof and what is not, make sure that both your anchor and any extensions are ten times more secure than you think they need to be.

carried out in a body bag, a basic knowledge of anchor systems is required. (See *Anchors and More Climbing Anchors,* part of the How to Climb Series.)

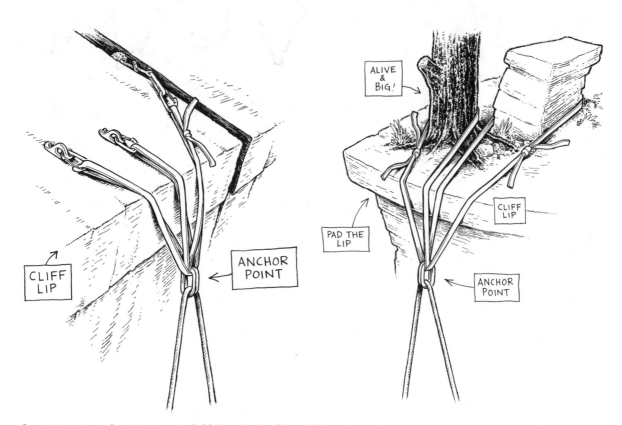

Be certain your anchor point is extended below the lip of the cliff. Your belay rope must not run over any sharp edges. Any slings that do should be well padded.

Whenever you must extend the anchor with slings, check for loose rock or other choss that may be knocked loose. Toproping involves continuous climbing and lowering on the system, meaning the anchors and any extensions will be under pressure and will no doubt move or shift around a little. This movement and pressure can send off anything loose directly onto those below.

At the top anchor point (through which the climbing rope runs), clip the rope off with two locking carabiners. They should be opposite and opposed. And always make sure the top anchor point is draped over and below the lip, if only 6 or 8 inches. Otherwise the rope will be running over the lip. What with all the weighted lowering, even a rounded, polished lip will abrade the rope. If the lip

is pronounced, a single lowering can wear right through the sheath—if the anchor point is not below the lip. It is common to find big balls of sheath fuzz on top of popular toprope setups. Can I say it enough? Extend the anchor point below the lip.

The combination of stretch in the rope, friction on the top anchor, and a discrepancy in weights between belayer and climber often necessitates a ground anchor. Sometimes it is difficult to find one. If the angle of the rock is less than vertical, it is less critical that the belayer be anchored, though it's always desirable. If the angle is steep or the belayer is much lighter than the climber, an anchor is essential. It's no fun for a climber on toprope to hit the deck from 15 feet up. For that matter, it's no fun for a belayer to be yanked off her feet and slapped into the rock. Both happen.

When climbing with a toprope, try to climb in line with the anchor as much as you can. Anytime you traverse out of the plumb line—to either side of the top anchor point—gravity will swing you back into the plumb line if you fall. The closer you get to the top anchor point, the more pronounced the swing. This means that as you near the top, try to climb directly up to the anchor point. If you're near the top anchor point and are climbing off to the side, your swing will be hard and fast if you fall. If the route wanders and the person who sets the top anchor is experienced, she can place directionals on rappel. Directionals are cams or nuts that keep the rope more in line with the direction of the route and help control the amount of swing a falling climber takes. As the climber ascends, he unclips the directional and then reclips it while being lowered. Like everything else, directionals need to be bomber, lest you want to pendulum more dramatically than you would have without the directional in the first place.

Most beginning toprope climbs are on slabs or moderately angled face climbs, or follow lower-angled cracks. However, there are occasionally overhanging toprope climbs that follow huge bucket holds and are technically quite easy—like working up a ladder or a giant jungle gym. The potential problem here is that if you fall off, you'll swing out into space. Unless the angle is quite overhanging—which is almost unheard of on a beginning toprope climb—you can usually get reestablished on the rock by simply kicking your legs, which will get you swinging, hopefully toward the rock. If you can't get back onto the wall, lower off and try again. Whenever it's possible that a toprope fall can swing the climber out into space, the ground belay must have a sound anchor. Otherwise the weight of the dangling climber can lift the belayer off the ground (particularly when the climber outweighs the belayer by more than twenty pounds). Also, in those rare instances when the beginning toprope climb is quite overhanging—a proper jug haul—the climber will swing way out away from the wall if she pings. It is crucial that you know what you might smack if you come off. Climbers routinely bang into tree limbs and even high boulders at the base, which can result in bad injuries. So scope any possible obstacles and rig the toprope somewhere else if necessary.

Lastly, a toprope fall should be no longer than the stretch in the rope. Remember that the more rope that is out, the more stretch, so belayers should be extremely vigilant when a climber is just starting out on a toprope ascent. If the toproped climb is a long one—say 50 feet—that means that there's more than 100 feet of rope in use. With just a little slack in the line, a falling climber can easily stretch the rope and fall 5 feet, or more. Again, on a long toprope climb (anything over 40 feet), the most dangerous time is at the outset, when the rope will stretch the most and when the chances of hitting the ground are the greatest. If there is any doubt or if the climber feels a little "iffy," consider keeping a little tension on the line as the climber starts the route. Even ten pounds of tension on a toprope can reduce the fall to mere inches.

Beginners and experienced climbers alike benefit from toproping. It's a relatively safe way to hone technique, as you can concentrate solely on the choreography of ascent rather than finding and placing sound gear. Many experts climb on toprope, often to wire a difficult and dangerous climb in preparation for the redpoint.

Perhaps the best teacher of all is the firsthand experience you will get from frequenting popular toprope areas. Watch and learn. Pick out an experienced climber and ask her questions per the rigging and so forth till you understand every aspect backwards and forwards. Once you understand several basic principles (spelled out in Chapter 4: Ropes, Anchors, and Belays), you can globalize those basics to fit most any circumstance. But there's nothing like seeing these principles carried out in real life. Most experienced climbers will gladly give you a quick breakdown regarding how and why they do things. Seek and ye shall know.

Climbing Gyms

Climbing gyms are springing up all over the country—a testament that indoor climbing is one of the

Watch and weep. Tiffany Levine cranking off one-finger holds on a finger board. Bill Hatcher photo

fastest growing sports today. Originally indoor climbing took place in a dank basement or cluttered garage. Home walls were a last resort to keep in shape during the winter or a stretch of bad weather. Soon climbers realized the benefits—training at any time, user friendly holds (for the most part), customized problems, predictable weather, gorgeous hard-bodied women and lecherous men with no jobs, rapid skill gains, and lots of fun.

Modern climbing gyms are state-of-the-art. They feature giant overhanging walls, slabs, roofs, arêtes, crack systems, toprope and lead climbing, air ventilation systems, and gymnastics mats to cushion a fall. Many feature specialized training areas—bouldering walls and system or campus boards. The safe and controlled environment of rock gyms makes them a great place to learn the basics and meet future partners. And the sheer number of routes and drop-dead convenience mean you can get in much more climbing than you would in a normal outdoor setting.

Cast out of epoxy or resin and sand, climbing holds have evolved to simulate pulling on actual rock quite well. The wide variety and availability of modular holds give gym route setters almost limitless creativity in the setting of masterpiece routes. In fact, route setting is an art in itself.

Climbing walls are great places to hone footwork and general technique. Most gyms hold local climbing competitions, as well as a number of clinics throughout the year, which are usually small theme-based classes taught by established climbers who often compete on the sport climbing circuit. Get involved and you'll get better: A little friendly competition can push a climber to excel.

Tendon-nagging injuries happen most often indoors, so take heed. While the shape and texture of holds is generally finger friendly, watch out for tweaky "crimp fests" (a series of crimps on micro holds) on vertical and less than vertical walls. Such routes can be difficult, and it is essential to warm up sufficiently before launching off onto the wall. If you're just getting started with indoor climbing, or if you haven't done it lately, start off slow and be sure to take rest days; finger tendons are quite delicate, and you're likely to end up on the sidelines with a strained tendon if you crank too hard, too fast.

You can quickly get strong climbing in an indoor gym. And this leads to another climbing gym problem: The transition from indoor to outdoor climbing. People who have climbed exclusively indoors and then try to climb at the same level outside are in for a rude and possibly dangerous awakening. Climbing outdoors is serious. You have to deal with weather, rockfall, holds breaking, and route finding; and most importantly, you must demonstrate a sound knowledge of protection, gear, anchor systems, and self-rescue techniques (see Chapter 4: Ropes, Anchors, and Belays). I recommend going with an experienced friend, or better yet a certified guide, for your first few times out of the gym. They will instill in you a proper respect for the serious nature of outdoor climbing.

All told, climbing gyms are a great place to learn technique and develop strength quickly. Perhaps best of all, they have become a positive social hangout for climbers.

Specialized Apparatus

Hangboards, first introduced in late 1986, are wooden or molded-resin boards (usually about a foot high by 2½ feet long) that are mounted up high like a pull-up bar. The board features various holds resembling those on a climb, from good jugs to rounded nothings, and the usual routine involves pulling up on the holds, as well as free hanging for timed intervals. There are half a dozen commercially available, and each comes with a suggested workout. There is no doubt that they can increase finger, hand, and forearm strength, and that the carryover value to climbing is high; but the verdict is mixed on whether they cause more injuries than benefits. It is probably a matter of the routine. Increasing stress beyond normal climbing levels, especially free hanging for long periods on the board's punier holds, virtually assures injuries. One danger is that the tendon connections at your shoulders—if you are hanging fully extended—have less strength than you can develop with your fingers. This means that as you hang to exhaustion on your fingertips, your body weight naturally sags to the tendon connectors at your shoulders; it is these connectors that risk separating. Adding weights (around your waist or ankles) will reduce the time spent on your fingers, and that will tend to keep you off your shoulders. Whatever routines you decide on, remember that if you push yourself to muscle failure, you need forty-eight hours to fully recover. So to optimize your results on any board, heavy workouts every third day are far superior to those every day, or every other day. And again, be sure to start off slow and gradually increase the intensity of your workouts.

A campus board is basically a sheet of plywood with foot-long, horizontal wooden edges screwed into the plywood every 4 to 8 inches, in a ladder formation running from eye level to about 10 feet. The plywood is mounted on a wall at an angle of about fifteen to twenty degrees overhanging, and the object is to "campus" up the holds without your feet. The normal campus board has a vertical line of holds at three different widths—decent (about an inch), bad (half an inch), and pathetic (smaller still). Many climbers train only on the larger edges to avoid injuries. You need to get thoroughly warmed up before yarding up these units, and it usually takes a few weeks to get used to the strain, if you ever can. A beginner basically has no chance of doing much campus board work, but a fit athlete can work up to it quickly. To be sure, you will see your strength skyrocket if you can work consistently at this exercise and remain injury free. Training on a campus board every three or four days is plenty to see big strength dividends. Six to ten laps, with five-minute rest intervals between "burns," is a standard workout at my gym. This is not endurance training but strength training, so the accent is on how hard you make it (by skipping holds, using smaller holds, et al.), not on how many laps you can do at one go. Hence the long rest period. Of course you could train finger endurance on a campus board if you had that in mind. There are a lot of instructions and recommended workout routines that come with these boards (and are posted in responsible gyms). Read up on them if you plan to include campus boards in your workout routine (this is specialized knowledge not germane to a general book like this).

Cross-Training

The practice of training for a sport by doing exercises outside the sport itself is nothing new. Called crossover training, or simply cross-training, it is used by all professional athletes: Skiers run stairs and lift weights; football players run, lift weights, and do stretching exercises to reduce the chance of injury; divers jump on a trampoline and lift weights; and swimmers lift weights, jump rope, and ride a stationary bike, as do basketball players. All of these athletes count on their routines to give them a sharp conditioning edge that will cross over to their keynote sport.

Weight Training

For years climbers scorned weight training, usually for the wrong reasons. Strength-to-weight ratio has long been deemed the aim of all climbing workouts, and most climbers are loath to add any size to their whippet-thin physiques—not knowing that a mere five pounds of brawn might increase their strength upwards of 10 percent. (Also, many people think you can throw on five or ten pounds of muscle with a couple of workouts. In fact, a rabid lifter is lucky to add one pound of muscle every two to three months.) Correct weight training is tough duty, certainly more toil than joy, which makes it all the more unpopular.

Other misconceptions have also kept many climbers off the iron. The first is the notion of excess bulk. As absurd as it is, people think that lifting weights automatically makes you huge. It's food, rather than iron, that increases body size. Controlling your diet controls size, and you can't eat a dumbbell. Second is the notion of the muscle-bound oaf who can't comb his hair for all the huge deltoids. If anything, correct weight training—which entails full-range-of-motion exercises and a lot of stretching between sets—increases flexibility. But you have to do things right.

This is not the venue to spell out specific workout routines. A comprehensive iron routine can be easily designed to focus on a climber's needs. There are hundreds of books and videos to show you what's what. The best routines take into account a person's physique and mentality and are so personal that little applies across the board. For the climber new to weights, it's best to start a normal, conservative routine and customize it as your knowledge increases. Perhaps the best thing about weight training is that it is very difficult to incur serious injuries. Soreness and tweaked muscles are part of any training, but in more than twenty years of being an "iron rat," I've never once gotten an injury lifting weights that has kept me out of the gym for longer than a week.

Freehand Exercises

Essentially calisthenics, freehand exercises involve all the Jack LaLanne-type routines (save towing the boats): push-ups, pull-ups, sit-ups, dips. It's pretty hard to get a well-rounded workout doing just freehand exercises, but they require little in the way of specialized gear and are certainly better than doing nothing. As with weight training, it is hard to injure yourself doing them.

Step aerobics, jazz dancing, swimming, Nautilus machines, yoga (excellent for sport climbing), and untold other routines are also possible and popular. Anything that promotes overall fitness and flexibility can only help your climbing.

Cardiovascular Exercises

A strong heart and good wind are vital for strenuous climbs. Increased circulation helps in another respect as well: It brings more oxygen to your muscles, which mean faster recovery and tissue repair. Any action sport, such as basketball or mountain biking, is good. Pure running or cycling are also good—just watch those knees. The king of all cardiovascular activities, however, is the jump rope. Its popularity in the climbing world can probably be attributed to the fact that it requires a lot of skill to be good. Single revolutions (skipping) on a rope marks beginning level; double revolutions between jumps, intermediate; and triple revolutions, advanced. The person who can consistently do triple revolutions on a jump rope has the heart of a lion and lungs strong enough to fill the sails of a good-sized bark. Make sure to get a leather rope.

Stretching

With today's gymnastically difficult routes, flexibility is becoming increasingly important. Being flexible will help you with side stems and high steps, and you will be able to keep your hips closer to the rock on steep terrain, allowing you to get more weight onto your feet. Good flexibility will also help to prevent injuries. Traditional stretching exercises are good, and a few sport-specific stretches have also been developed. Many rock gyms offer stretching and yoga classes to help improve your flexibility, as well as contact your inner magician. Yoga is also excellent in connecting your movement with your breath, a crucial aspect of hard climbing and graceful living.

Injuries

As the technical envelope is pushed further, debilitating injuries are becoming more commonplace. Aside from the normal muscle tweaks and strains inherent in any physical endeavor, climbers are particularly prone to elbow and finger injuries, most of which involve some form of tendonitis. Having suffered these impairments on numerous occasions, I can assure you that ignoring the injury can result in pain so intense that straightening the arm or closing the fingers is virtually impossible, and climbing is out of the question. Concerning treatment for these conditions, I defer to climber/orthopedist Dr. Mark Robinson, who has conducted several studies involving climbing injuries and is in an experienced position to give advice. Here are some self-cures for tendonitis from Dr. Robinson.

1. Decrease activity until pain is gone and all swelling and tenderness disappear.
2. Wait two weeks more.
3. Start with easy strength exercises—putty, gum, rubber squeezers (two to three weeks).
4. Low-angle climbing on big holds (1 month).
5. High-angle climbing on big holds (1 month).
6. Back to full bore.

Dr. Robinson adds: "Anti-inflammatory medicines (aspirin, ibuprofen, etc.) can be used to control symptoms and speed the recovery process. They should not be used to suppress pain to allow even more overuse, since this will eventually lead to worse problems and a longer recovery period. Various mystical and pseudo-scientific remedies, such as copper bracelets, dietary modifications, herbal cataplasms, horse liniments, ethnic balms, etc. are at best unproven. Very few, if any, of them bear any conceivable relation to what is known to be the basis of the problem."

What the doctor is telling us is that he doesn't fancy homeopathic remedies, and that time and patience are key ingredients to a full recovery. There are certainly people with different opinions—and case histories to support a more holistic approach to recovery. But, in fact, the key to healing is probably common sense: If it hurts, lay off it till it doesn't hurt, and in the meantime do whatever works to reduce the pain. Whatever your healing method, returning prematurely to high-stress climbing with an injury is as foolish as ignoring an injury in the first place. "The tissues of the musculoskeletal system are capable of remarkable feats of repair and restoration," Dr. Robinson assures us, "but these processes are slow." Furthermore, there is nothing scientifically

proven to accelerate these processes, except the use of anti-inflammatory drugs, which simply eliminate the restrictions and allow the healing to proceed. Many swear by herbs and other alternative therapies ("alternative" is generally a term referring to everything but prescription drugs), such as Epsom salts. (*How to Climb 5.12* and *Better Bouldering* in the How to Rock Climb Series provide in-depth information on injury and injury prevention.) But it's my opinion that all the fancy pills and gadgets have very limited effects on tendon injuries—though any sports medicine clinic will gladly assure you the opposite, and bankrupt you in the process.

The tendency to race back onto the cliffside and crank our brains out the second the pain is gone must be curbed. Experts and horse sense assure us this can only exacerbate the injury. Do what you want, but it's my feeling that Dr. Robinson's advice is probably the sagest course to full recovery (providing you augment his routine with the effective supplements, especially glucosamine and chrondroitin).

Injury Prevention

We know the medical experts and countless wounded sport climbers have told us that certain exercises virtually assure injuries, and we should avoid these if we're in for the long haul. But aside from that, what can we do? Some support of critical tendons can be achieved by taping. Tape the trouble spots around the fingers on either side of the main (second) joint, around the wrist, and around the forearm just shy of the elbow. (For more on taping, see Chapter 3: Crack Climbing Skills.) But professional athletes are more and more relying on two things to avoid injuries, stretching and warming up. Aerobics and yoga might not make you stronger, but they may keep you from getting injured. And a very important practice is to do a little stretching and some easy climbing before jumping onto a hard climb. Warming up is part of any sport, and is essential for climbers whose movements so stress the elbows and fingers. This is particularly true for bouldering and sport climbing. Get limbered up with a running sweat, then max yourself. And if you tweak something, stop before you make it worse.

Amos and Coco #17:
On the Big Stone

Amos bent down, shimmied up against the haul bag, slipped his arms through the shoulder straps, and struggled to his feet. Eighty pounds never felt so heavy. Most of the weight was water, six gallons of it. Coco's face looked as if framed by a gigantic Christmas wreath, with two bandoleer slings over her shoulders that were heaped with seventy biners, fifty-five pitons, and as many nuts, and over which rested two green ropes.

The two climbers looked at each other and smiled slightly. Yes, they were really going for it. Amos couldn't figure out if he felt like he was heading for the firing squad or El Dorado. "Lead the way, Tarzan," said Coco. Amos turned and lumbered toward the trail. Now was when all their training would finally pay off—in a big way.

After a few minutes they picked up the thin path winding through the ponderosa pines. The excitement and apprehension before this, their first big wall, had kept Amos tossing half the night, and now his feet were moving as though he were walking on hot coals. Amos had the enthusiasm and power and Coco had the courage and skill. And after three years of climbing together, they felt they were ready for the "Big Stone." It seemed remarkable that they had gotten here more or less on their own. Hands-on instruction and coaching had been such an integral part of Amos's sports background, and there had been a seer or teacher almost every step of the way for Coco's yoga and meditation. But now it was just the two of them.

The pair had taken only a two-day beginning seminar and a three-day inter-mediate class, and then they had spent two days building anchors under the tutelage of that intrepid mountaineer, Jules Pinkus. Aside from a couple more days of guided climbing and a brief seminar on big wall techniques, also from the poised, polished, and plucky Pinkus, Amos and Coco had by and large been self-taught. They'd gleaned enormous insight from books, maga-zines, and fellow climbers, for in fact the climbing community itself is the "teacher at large." But it still seemed as though they were getting away with something, sneaking under the wire and thieving their way toward majesty. But there were no review boards or certificates or credentials or bonds needed to pick a route, even a colossal route like The Nose on El Capitan, and to pack a bag and give it a go.

Soon the trees opened up and the pair stumbled up a rocky trail, wind-ing through boulders and talus blocks. As the path steepened, they slowed, quickly understanding that the ritual of walking to the base of your first big wall has no equal. No words can describe it, no feeling can surround it, and neither climber could appreciate it till they were following the footsteps of the hundreds of others who'd made the same march, every last one of whom battled the urge to dump the loads and dash for the beach or a bar or any-where far, far away from the High Lonesome. More than a few could never complete the hike in; others tromped to the base, took one long look up and marched away, never to climb again. Others still could gear up, but couldn't drive the first piton. One chink in your resolve and fear would flow into you like a tidal drift, washing away the best-laid plans. Only the dream and the whispers of the High Lonesome itself could keep the drive alive.

Not till Amos got to the base and dumped the haul bag could he look up, and when he did his heart jumped into his throat. The great white wall rose steep as a skyscraper, reaching three-quarters of a mile into the clouds. He went over and put his hands against the rock and a calm came over him. He belonged here. They both did.

"I got the feeling this is going to be the start of something big," said Amos, putting Coco on belay. Coco checked her knot for the tenth time, drew a big breath, and said, "Here goes everything."

And they were off. . . .

CHAPTER 9

Getting Started and Staying Alive

Thirty years ago, finding professional climbing instruction was a difficult task. Today, there is nearly always a guide service/climbing school operating around every popular crag, and good instruction is easy to find. For the complete neophyte, I advise taking at least a beginning seminar. It allows you to get a good grip on the fundamentals and is the single most valuable investment a beginner can make. The appendix following this chapter lists sources of information on both instruction and equipment.

For an outlay of about $250, a beginner can buy a pair of rock shoes and two days of professional instruction. If you choose to carry on, you will need to purchase some climbing gear. Richard Leversee of Black Diamond Equipment has plotted the following course for the beginner looking to make climbing his or her sport.

After mastering basic techniques for safety and movement on rock, the novice should seek the company of more experienced partners to advance his skill. After buying a pair of rock shoes, his investment can be minimal, since the new climber can limit his purchases to personal, rather than community, necessities. The gear listed below will allow the beginner to climb with anyone who has a rope and rack (and, of course, the knowledge to use them).

Harness	$74.75
Locking carabiner	$20.70
Belay/rappel device	$18.40
Oval carabiners (four @ $6.90 each)	$27.60
Gear sling	$13.80
Chalk bag with chalk	$20.70
Total	$175.95

Climbing with others is a crucial learning time, as a novice needs mileage before jumping out on the lead. The opportunity for adventure really opens up once a climber buys a rope and rack. There are many options available in selecting a rope, but the beginner can't go wrong buying either a 10.5 mm or 11 mm UIAA-approved 50-meter kernmantle rope from any of the manufacturers listed in the appendix.

A "foundation" rack should include a variety of passive (nonmechanical) nuts—tapers and hexentrics and the like—because they are lightweight, simple, secure, and inexpensive. At this stage it is important to become adept at placing passive nuts. Even spring-loaded camming devices require this knowledge for sound placements. The following foundation rack will allow the climber to set up topropes.

Rope	$150.00
Carabiners (seven @ $6.90 each)	$48.30
Locking carabiners (two @ $20.70 each)	$41.40
Taper nuts (five @ $8.65 each)	$43.25
Hexentrics (five @ $8.65 each)	$43.25
Nut extraction tool with keeper sling	$11.50
Shoulder-length sewn slings (six @ $3.45)	$20.70
Extra webbing (twenty feet @ 35 cents per foot)	$7.00
Local guidebook	$17.25
Total	$382.65

As the climber builds a solid base of experience, he will naturally want to begin leading. So he must upgrade the foundation rack, allowing for more versatility and safety. SLCDs, three-cam units, sliding nuts, micro nuts, and other sophisticated forms of protection will complete the rack for leading. A standard lead rack might consist of the following gear.

Rope	$150.00
Micro wedge nuts (five @ $11.50 each)	$57.50
Wedge nuts (ten @ $8.65 each)	$86.50
Small passive camming devices (three @ $17.25 each)	$51.75
Spring-loaded camming devices from ½ inch to 3 inch (nine @ $69.00 each)	$621.00
Carabiners (thirty-six @ $6.90 each)	$248.40
Locking carabiners (four @ $20.70 each)	$82.80
Quickdraws (eight @ $3.45 each)	$27.60
Shoulder-length slings (six @ $4.00 each)	$24.00
Double-length sling	$5.75
Nut extraction tool with keeper sling	$11.50
Gear sling	$13.80
Total	$1,380.60

Add and subtract gear as required for the chosen route, or add gear if you protect a lot. If you plan to climb only at bolt-protected sport climbing areas, you can pare this whole list down to just a rope, sixteen quickdraws with carabiners, a couple of shoulder-length slings, and a couple of locking carabiners, for a total cost of roughly $480. At the rare sport climbing area that features routes with more than sixteen protection bolts, add a couple more quickdraws to the list. A standard quickdraw can be bought as a composite unit (two biners and a sewn quickdraw) for $18 to $21 (a few bucks less when on sale). Top end units featuring wire gates combine high functionality with the suave look of pricey jewelry, and can run as high as $32.

For about $1,400 an advanced leader can have a world-class rack for traditional routes of all lengths, which makes rock climbing the cheapest of all adventure sports. Moreover, after the initial investment, there are no additional expenses save gas to get to the cliff and minimal fees to climb inside state or national parks. Rock climbing is essentially free: no lift tickets, no referees, nothing but you, your friends, and the challenge at hand. By far the biggest cost of climbing is that once you get hooked you don't want to work anymore.

Responsibilities

Throughout rock climbing's evolution, the simple joy of being the master of your fate, of seeing success or failure as a result of your efforts has—as in any great sport—remained the heart of the experience. Self-reliance and the ability to account for your actions are among the virtues (at least to the Western mind) that climbing encourages.

But there are many more climbers out on the cliffs than ever before. The community of climbers—once a small, counterculture, "outcast" society comprised chiefly of young men from dysfunctional families—now impacts the outdoors in profoundly visible ways. Trails and trash are found at the base of wilderness cliffs. The responsibility for this lies with all of us, of course. Part of the allure of rock climbing is that it is more than just a physical exercise; we are intrinsically bound to features that nature has provided us. The environment is fragile, and the promise to maintain it is an integral part of our outdoor experience. The following suggestions address some of these issues.

Serve yourself and others by picking up trash when you find it, whether or not you brought it to the cliffs yourself. Relieve yourself away from the bottom of the route. Make a practice of carrying a small plastic bag to carry out all toilet paper, and mindful that uncovered feces decompose faster, keep such deposits well clear of established trails and paths. On longer routes, urinate away from where others must climb. Anything else is gauche and unacceptable.

Stick to established trails whenever possible. Although competent to travel over the roughest country in pursuit of the most direct line to a selected route, climbers should more often demonstrate their sensitivity to the effects of rampant erosion that are the result of zealous proliferation of access trails. Nesting birds should be respected and left as you find them. Remember that you are a guest of the crags and its inhabitants.

Codes of proper cliffside etiquette are, of course, no different than those most people try and practice in the greater world. There are, however, situations that are unique. Usually, the first party to the base of a route gets the route first. You might offer the route to a clearly faster party, but once on a route, you should feel under no obligation to let a party pass if for any reason you are not comfortable with them above you. Again, if they are obviously a quicker team, it is probably a nice thing to offer, but if, for instance, loose rock is an issue, don't feel compelled to let anybody by; they made their choice at the beginning of the route. Another frequent problem is that certain climbs are particularly popular as end-of-the-day trade routes or are simply local classics and, as such, often have folks queuing up despite there usually being fifty similar routes to either side. Camping on a local favorite is questionable form, but so is breathing down a party's neck to hurry up and clear out. If a climb is taken, move on to something else—there's always something else. And if parties are waiting, do your "bidness" and move on.

As climbing moves well into this new century, one of the biggest problems confronting all climbers is access to the cliffs. The loss of access to climbing or bouldering areas is an issue that affects every climber, regardless of technical ability or stylistic preference. The responsibility for solving or preventing access problems likewise rests with each and every climber. Minimizing environmental impact, being sensitive to behavior which could affect access, and taking responsibility for your own actions by not suing landowners, climbing gyms, or belayers if you get hurt will help prevent problems. Climbing is inherently dangerous, and if something goes wrong, trying to blame someone else rarely reverses the damage. A climber is owed nothing. When access problems do arise, the Access Fund can help negotiate, organize, and even litigate closures of climbing areas. In some situations they actually finance the purchase or preservation of climbing and bouldering areas. Your tax-deductible contribution to the Access Fund is a concrete way of giving something back to climbing and making a real difference in the effort to save the rich diversity of climbing resources in the United States. Send your donation (of any amount) to the Access Fund, P.O. Box 17010, Boulder, CO 80308; (303) 545–6772; www.accessfund.org.

Staying Alive

Rock climbing is potentially hazardous, and it is the task of the individual to learn and understand the proper techniques to ensure the safest possible participation. Though no substitute for professional instruction or years of climbing experience, this manual has hopefully helped both the novice and the expert to a greater knowledge of rock climbing's fundamentals and nuances. In summary, I offer part of a longer essay on safety that appeared under the same name in the introduction of the *Yosemite Climber's Guide*. Prepared by the head rescue ranger, John Dill, the essay contains wisdom distilled from more than three decades of seeing every kind of accident in every kind of situation by every kind of climber—from rank beginner to world-class hero. To one and all, says John, "State of mind is the key to safety. It's impossible to know how many climbers were killed by haste or overconfidence. Many accident survivors will tell you that, somehow, they lost their better judgment just long enough to get hurt. It's a murky subject. Nevertheless, these mental lapses generally fall under three categories: ignorance, casualness, and distraction."

Ignorance

Even the most conscientious climber can get into trouble if he's unaware of the danger ("I thought it never rained. . . ."). There is always something more to learn, regardless of experience. There are two basic steps to fighting ignorance.

- Continue to read, and listen to climbers who have survived. Back issues of climbing magazines are full of pertinent articles. Case histories in the American Alpine Club's *Accidents in North American Mountaineering*, a yearly compilation of accident reports, will show you how subtle factors may conspire to catch you unaware. Such accounts are the next best thing to being there.
- Practice. Reading may make you aware but not competent. Regardless of the written word, which is sometimes wrong, you must ultimately think and act for yourself. Several climbers have

waited to learn how to prusik until it was dark and raining, the route was overhanging, and they were actually in trouble. They had read about it, but they still had to be rescued despite having the gear to improvise their own escape. Book-learning alone gave them a complacency that could have proved fatal.

Casualness

"I just didn't take it seriously." It's a common refrain. It's often correct, though it's more a symptom than a disease—there may be deeper reasons for underestimating your risk. Ignorance is one. Here are some more.

- Habit reinforcement occurs when nothing goes wrong. The more often you get away with risky business, the more entrenched your lazier habits become. Have you unconsciously dropped items from your safety checklist since you were a beginner?
- Your attitudes and habits can be reinforced by the experiences (and states of mind) of others. The sense of awe and commitment of the 1960s is gone from the big wall "trade routes," and young aspirants with no grade VIs or even Vs to their credit speak casually about them. Yet most of the accidents on El Capitan occur on easy pitches.
- Memory Decay. "I'm not going up again without rain gear—I thought I would die!" A week later this climber has forgotten how scared he had been in that thunderstorm. Rain gear was now too heavy, and besides, he'd rap off the next time. Many of us tend to forget the bad points. We have to be hit again.
- Civilization. With fixed anchors marking the way and generous amounts of chalk telling of hundreds of previous ascents, it may be hard to realize how high the potential danger actually is. Some say the idea of a fast rescue adds to their casualness. Maybe, but who wants a broken leg, or worse, in the first place?

- Overconfidence. "It'll never happen to me. I'm a safe, cautious climber." Many of those killed were described by friends as very cautious.

Distraction

It is caused by whatever takes your mind off your work: fear, thirst, sore feet, skinny-dippers below—the list is endless. Being in a hurry is one of the most common causes. Here are two examples in which being distracted has caused problems (often fatal).

- Experienced climbers have often been hurt after making "beginner errors" (their words) to get somewhere quickly. There was no emergency or panic, but their minds were elsewhere—on a cold beer or a good bivouac, or they were just sick of being on that route for a week (often called summit fever). Their mistakes were usually shortcuts in protecting easy pitches, on both walls and day climbs. As one climber put it, "We were climbing as though we were on top."
- Darkness once caught two day climbers for the first time. Unprepared, upset, and off route, they rushed to get down, arguing with each other about what to do. After several errors, which they knew to avoid, one climber was killed rappelling off the end of his rope.
- Learn to recognize when you or your partner are becoming distracted. Stop, get your act together, then proceed.

Despite the macabre sound of ranger Dill's observations, the percentage of accident victims is minuscule compared to the hundreds of thousands of active rock climbers. But the dangers are real, and should you or a ropemate be so unfortunate as to suffer an injury, Dill has put forth the following concerning rescues.

Despite the best of preparations, an accident can happen to anyone. Self-rescue is often the fastest and safest way out, but whether it's the wise course of action depends on the injury and how well prepared you are. Combining with a nearby party may often give you the margin of safety you need, but do not risk aggravating an injury or getting yourself into a more serious predicament—ask for help if you need it. Sometimes a bit of advice, delivered through a loudspeaker, is all that's required.

If you don't have formal first-aid training (which is highly recommended), at least know how to keep an unconscious patient's airway open, how to protect a possible broken neck or back, and how to recognize and deal with external bleeding and serious blood loss (shock). These procedures are lifesaving, do not require fancy gear, and are easy to learn and perform.

Note that head injury victims are apt to be irrational and very strong. Even if he's unconscious, if you have to leave him, make it impossible for him to untie himself.

The Other Sides of the Game

Climbing is a broad game of which rock climbing is only a part—a fundamental, popular part, but by no means even half the game. Big walls will always provide the most awesome form of pure rock climbing, because the venues—towering monoliths like El Capitan in Yosemite Valley and Hidden Tower in Pakistan—are peerless for grandeur and intimidation. Huge sixth class routes are steep, often unnerving trials that terrify and amaze even twenty-year veterans. They are sometimes three-quarters of a mile high, and a hanging bivouac at that altitude is an ordeal no climber is fully prepared for—or ever gets completely accustomed to. It's always a game of "keeping the lid on" when most everything around you, as well as your own instincts, tells you to clear the hell off and fast. But the climber who paws over the lip of a big wall, still whole in body and soul, has experiences and memories that no other sport can hope to match.

Mountaineering, in its extreme form, is the riskiest of all the climbing games. Sudden storms, avalanches that sweep entire mountains, horrific rockfalls, hidden crevasses, and physiological disorders from altitude and cold are all out of a climber's hands and have drawn the curtain on hundreds of veterans. The old method of sieging the mountain, using armies of climbers, bottled oxygen, and countless other helpful strategies, has slowly given way to "alpine" ascents, where a handful of climbers go for broke with little or no backup, are irreversibly committed, and survive only through personal prowess, iron will, and the grace of God. Successful parties invariably return with tales fantastic and astounding; and the ill-fated, by no count the minority, have stories none the less remarkable, though often with a tragic twist.

There are a hundred different games that fall somewhere in the middle, somewhere between the ace poised on a boulder in the British Virgin Islands and the ironman who has just soloed Mt. Everest. Some make a specialty of ice climbing, clawing up overhanging icicles or up gleaming arctic gullies. There are peak baggers who have never seen a rope, solo climbers who rarely use a rope, sea cliff climbers, limestone climbers, desert climbers, gym climbers, sport climbers, snow climbers, ski mountaineers, and people who own thousands of dollars of gear and only talk a good game. Chances are that the modern climber, whatever his specialty, has mastered the fundamentals while rock climbing. It remains the basic form in acquiring the knowledge of rope management, physical movement, and the mental conditioning required and applicable to any mode of ascent. The competent rock climber can readily cross over onto big walls or big mountains and is qualified to make the transition quickly and safely. Happy climbing.

Amos and Coco #18:
Last Vista

Hip to hip, Amos and Coco sat in the tall grass in the El Cap meadow as after-noon shadows crept up the titanic bulk of El Capitan itself, rearing bold and proud half a mile in the distance. Amos lowered the binoculars from his eyes and set them in his lap, nodded, and said, "Well, her life will never be the same now." "That first time we were up there . . . ," Coco said, rolling back the years. "I never saw this coming."

Amos chuckled at the rare and unfore-seen path they'd traveled since first tying into a rope some thirty-five years before, years that had worn the burrs off his personality but enriched his soul manyfold. They had just watched their daughter, Amy, not yet twenty, top out on The Nose on El Capitan, her first, but not her last, time up the Captain, the crown jewel of world rock climbing. Amy hadn't been alive six months when she began accompany-ing Amos and Coco on their weekend excursions to the mountains. She'd started climb-ing shortly after learning to walk. Her older sister and kid brother hadn't taken to the work—climbing is not for everyone. But like her folks, Amy had found a channel for her en-ergy—a vehicle to new worlds and, most im-portantly, new friends. Her folks knew from experience that her greatest adventures were still before her, wending into the horizon like switchbacks to the stars.

A stream of memories flowed through Amos's mind, some beyond words, others perilous and hateful, but all of them vital and real. His long fellowship on the High Lonesome had been the axis around which his life had turned, and from the very beginning he'd known there was something divine in the process. He had always felt a strange blend of honor and nostalgia when climbing an old classic route like The Nose, first established by icons now lost to the ages. When moving out on the "sharp end," he felt like a warrior of an immortal tradition, a tradition he'd been baptized into by his mentor, the incomparable Jules Pinkus. And when he had coiled his rope for the last time, a few years before, how superb that Amy had pushed on and would carry the torch till she too could pass it on to the next soul fired by the idea of discovering the miracle of their own being. Amos knew this heritage of ascent was what gave all climbers a kinship with something greater than themselves, the sum and substance of which sent their souls soaring when they climbed. And Amos knew there was no greater accomplishment in life than to find a felicitous home for the soul.

Amos looked up at El Capitan, which towered like a dauntless flame over all he had pondered for the last few moments. It made him feel sad and amazed to think that someday he would die and would no longer be able to gaze up at El Capitan and dream the everlasting dream of every climber who ever booted up and said, "Watch me, I'm going for it!" But Amy, and others not yet born, would keep the dream alive and that's when he understood, in a brand-new way, the rush he used to feel when climbing the old classics—that, in a sense, anyone who climbed such a route, or any route, was climbing for everyone who ever made good on the dream. And Amos knew that was good enough for him.

Coco pulled a small flat rock from her day pack and held it in her open hand. On the rock she had hand-painted a short poem by Clark Schurman, the charismatic chief guide on Rainier during the 1930s and 1940s. Amos read the words he knew so well but had never fully appreciated till now:

"Last campfires never die,
And you and I on separate trails to life's December,
Will always dream by this last fire,
And have this mountain to remember."

Amos reached over and put his hand over the rock and around his wife's hand. Smiling at each other, they both set the rock in the tall grass.

Appendix

Sources

One of the happier consequences of a wider participation in rock climbing is easy access to good information. What follows is a listing of many of these sources.

Magazines, Books, and Videos

Climbing magazines are colorful and well-produced, and besides offering accounts of climbs and cliffs, they are a wealth of information on the latest gear. Current guidebooks to just about every crag in America are published every few years and can be found in most local specialty mountain equipment shops. Climbing and mountaineering has perhaps the most active literary heritage of all sports, and many books and videos, from expedition accounts to full-color documentary pictorials, are constantly being published.

Rock & Ice
Post Office Box 3595
Boulder, CO 80303
(303) 499–8410

Climbing
Post Office Box 339
Carbondale, CO 81623
(303) 963–9449

Falcon Publishing/The Globe Pequot Press
Post Office Box 480
Guilford, CT 06437
(800) 243-0495
www.GlobePequot.com

The American Alpine Club
710 Tenth Street
Golden, CO 80401
(303) 384–0110
www.americanalpineclub.org

The Mountaineers
1011 S.W. Klickitat Way
Seattle, WA 98134

Chessler Books
Post Office Box 4359
Evergreen, CO 80437
(303) 670–0093
(800) 654–8502

Guides and Instruction

There are many schools competent in the instruction and guiding of modern rock climbing. Most are members of the American Mountain Guides Association (reached at 710 Tenth Street #101, Golden, CO 80401; 303–271–0984; www.AMGS.com). In addition, many of the specialty outdoor shops offer seasonal classes in rock climbing.

Equipment

Current issues of climbing magazines are a good source of manufacturers and distributors of climbing gear. The magazines will also give an indication of the diversity of equipment available. If your local outdoor shop only handles a few carabiners, nuts, and ropes, chances are good they are not knowledgeable about what is happening in the sport.

Glossary

The following is a compilation of technical terms and jargon used throughout this book. This is a strictly American glossary; Brits, French, Italian, Spanish, or Japanese undoubtedly use somewhat different terminology.

aid: using means other than the action of hands, feet, and body English to get up a climb

anchor: a means by which climbers are secured to a cliff

arête: an outside corner of rock, like the outer spine of a book

arm bar or arm lock: a means of holding onto a wide crack

bashie: a piece of malleable metal that has been hammered into a rock seam as an anchor; used in extreme aid climbing

belay: procedure of securing a climber by the use of a rope

bight: a loop (as in a bight of rope)

biners: see carabiners

bolt: an artificial anchor placed in a hole drilled for that purpose

bomber or bombproof: absolutely fail-safe (as in a very solid anchor or combination of anchors)

bucket: a handhold large enough to fully latch onto, like the handle of a bucket

cam: to lodge in a crack by counterpressure; that which lodges

carabiners: aluminum alloy rings equipped with a spring-loaded snap gate; called biners

ceiling: an overhang of sufficient size to loom overhead

chock: a wedge or mechanical device that provides an anchor in a crack

chockstone: a rock lodged in a crack

clean: routes that are variously free of vegetation or loose rock, or where you don't need to place pitons; also the act of removing chocks and other gear from a pitch

cold shut: a relatively soft metal ring that can be closed with a hammer blow; notoriously unreliable for withstanding high loads; commonly found as anchors atop short sport climbs

crimper: a small but positive sharp edge

crux: the most difficult section of a climb or pitch

dihedral: an inside corner of rock, like the oblique angle formed by the pages in an opened book

drag: usually used in reference to the resistance of rope running through carabiners

dynamic or dyno: lunge move

edge: a small rock ledge, or the act of standing on an edge

exposure: that relative situation where a climb has particularly noticeable sheerness

free, free climb, or free ascent: to climb using hands and feet only; the rope is only used to safeguard against injury, not for upward progress or resting

gobies: hand abrasions

hangdog: when a leader hangs from a piece of protection to rest, then continues on without lowering back to the ground; not a free ascent

jam: wedging feet, hands, fingers, or other body parts to gain purchase in a crack

jugs: like a jug handle

lead: to be first on a climb, placing protection to safeguard a fall

lieback: the climbing maneuver that entails pulling with the hands while pushing with the feet

line: the path of weakness in the rock which is the route

mantle: the climbing maneuver used to gain a single feature above your head

move: movement; one of a series of motions necessary to gain climbing distance

nut: same as a chock; a mechanical device that, by various means, provides a secure anchor to the rock

on-sight: to climb a route without prior knowledge or experience of the moves, without falling or otherwise weighting the rope (also on-sight flash)

opposition: nuts, anchors, or climbing maneuvers that are held in place by the simultaneous stress of two forces working against each other

pinkpoint: to lead (without falling) a climb that has been pre-protected with anchors rigged with carabiners

pins: pitons

pitch: the section of rock between belays

pitons: metal spikes of various shapes that are hammered into the rock to provide anchors in cracks (also pins or pegs)

placement: the position of a nut or anchor

protection or pro: the anchors used to safeguard the leader

prusik: both the knot and any means by which you mechanically ascend a rope

quickdraws: short slings with biners at both ends that help provide drag-free rope management for the leader

rappel: to descend a rope by means of mechanical brake devices

redpoint: to lead a route, clipping protection as you go, without falling or resting on pro

runout: the distance between two points of protection; often referring to a long stretch of climbing without protection

second: the second person on a rope team, usually also the leader's belayer

sling or runner: a webbing loop used for a variety of purposes to anchor to the rock; used to sling gear on

smear: to stand on the front of the foot and gain friction against the rock across the breadth of the sole in order to adhere to the rock

stance: a standing rest spot, often the site of the belay

stem: to bridge between two widely spaced holds

thin: a climb or hold of relatively featureless character

toprope: a belay from an anchor point above; protects the climber from falling even a short distance

traverse: to move sideways, without altitude gain

wall or big wall: a long climb traditionally done over multiple days, but which may take just a few hours for ace climbers

Twenty-five hundred feet above the treetops, Luther Burr clips his aid sling into the next placement on the Shield Route, El Capitan, Yosemite, one of the world's most spectacular rock climbs. Here, in the rarified cosmos of "big air," a climber becomes a granite astronaut, belonging to neither heaven nor earth, living breath by breath and an inch at a time in a vertical world that has no name in any language.

Beth Wald photo

Index

ACCESS: IT'S EVERYONE'S CONCERN

The Access Fund is a national nonprofit climbers' organization working to keep climbing areas open and conserve the climbing environment. Need help with a climbing related issue? Call us and please consider these principles when climbing.

- **ASPIRE TO CLIMB WITHOUT LEAVING A TRACE:** Especially in environmentally sensitive areas like caves. Chalk can be a significant impact. Pick up litter and leave trees and plants intact.
- **MAINTAIN A LOW PROFILE:** Minimize noise and yelling at the crag.
- **DISPOSE OF HUMAN WASTE PROPERLY:** Use toilets whenever possible. If toilets are not available, dig a "cat hole" at least six inches deep and 200 feet from any water, trails, campsites or the base of climbs. Always pack out toilet paper. Use a "poop tube" on big wall routes.
- **USE EXISTING TRAILS:** Cutting switchbacks causes erosion. When walking off-trail, tread lightly, especially in the desert on cryptogamic soils.
- **BE DISCRETE WITH FIXED ANCHORS:** Bolts are controversial and are not a convenience. Avoid placing unless they are absolutely necessary. Camouflage all anchors and remove unsightly slings from rappel stations.
- **RESPECT THE RULES:** Speak up when other climbers do not. Expect restrictions in designated wilderness areas, rock art sites and caves. Power drills are illegal in wilderness and all national parks.
- **PARK AND CAMP IN DESIGNATED AREAS:** Some climbing areas require a permit for overnight camping.
- **RESPECT PRIVATE PROPERTY:** Be courteous to landowners.
- **JOIN THE ACCESS FUND:** To become a member, make a tax-deductible donation of $35.

P.O. Box 17010
Boulder, CO 80308
303.545.6772

your climbing future
www.accessfund.org